FIRESIDE

*Album Quilt: pink and navy sun is focal point of
many-patterned design; patchwork motifs include Dutch star, log cabin,
wild goose chase, pineapple, and basket; one block is appliquéd.
New York State. For directions, see pages 24 and 25.*

Billie Ann Bybee

The McCall's Book of Quilts

by The Editors of McCall's Needlework & Crafts Publications

A Fireside Book Published by
Simon and Schuster / The McCall Pattern Company

A Fireside Book
Published by Simon and Schuster
A Division of Gulf & Western Corporation
Simon & Schuster Building
Rockefeller Center
1230 Avenue of the Americas
New York, New York 10020

Manufactured in the United States of America

1 2 3 4 5 6 7 8 9 10

Library of Congress Cataloging in Publication Data

The McCall's book of quilts.

    Includes index.
    1. Quilting.   2. Patchwork.   3. Appliqué.
I. McCall's needlework & crafts.
TT835.M23   746.4'6   75-11933
ISBN 0-671-22134-5
ISBN 0-671-22787-4 pbk.

Contents

General Directions

MAKING THE QUILT TOP

Patterns and Patches: Following individual directions for each quilt, make patterns for patches or appliqués. If making patterns that will be used repeatedly, as for a patchwork quilt, trace master pattern on thin cardboard and cut out with sharp scissors. Because pattern edges become frayed from marking, cut several of each piece. Discard frayed patterns as necessary.

Press all fabric smooth. To determine the straight of the fabric, pull a thread. Place each pattern piece on wrong side of fabric, making sure each piece is placed in correct relationship to the straight of fabric.

Squares and oblongs must be placed with the weave of the fabric parallel to edges. Diamond-shaped patches need two sides on straight of the fabric. Right-angle triangles may be cut with two sides on the straight of the goods. For tumbler shapes, the half-pattern should be cut with the fold on the straight of the fabric.

Using light-colored pencil on dark fabric and dark-colored pencil on a light fabric, trace around each pattern. When tracing a number of pieces on one fabric, leave space between patterns for seam allowances. For patches and appliqué pieces, you will need ¼" seam allowance all around. **Note:** Yardage requirements in this book are based on careful placement of pattern on fabric. Unless otherwise indicated, patterns should be placed leaving ½" between two — this will give you the full ¼" seam allowance that is necessary for each.

After cutting a large number of varied patches, separate pieces according to shape and color. String each group together by running a single thread, knotted at one end, through the centers. This will keep pieces easily available; simply lift off each as needed.

Piecing: Hold patches firmly in place, right sides facing. Using sewing thread, carefully make tiny running stitches along marked outlines to join. Begin with making a small knot; end with a few back stitches.

To avoid bunching of fabric, excess thickness at seams may be trimmed as pieces are assembled. If two bias edges come together, keep thread just taut enough to prevent seams from stretching.

Unless otherwise indicated, press pieced sections with seams to one side; open seams weaken construction. Compare finished units to make sure all are the same size.

When sewing blocks together, make sure all strips are even with one another.

The size of an allover geometric quilt is easily controlled, for piecing may stop anywhere without the danger of throwing the design out of balance. Quilts with a definite central design, however, such as a large star, can be adjusted in size only by changing the size of the component pieces.

PREPARING TO QUILT

The quilting design is usually marked on the quilt top after the top is completed but before it is joined to the batting and lining. Select your quilting design carefully to suit the quilt. The designs shown here are some of the more popular and some of the easiest to do. They should be enlarged to three or four times the size shown. Border designs are to be traced around the outside, with all-over quilting in the center.

There are two simple methods for transferring the quilting design. The first is to mark the fabric using dressmaker's carbon and a dressmaker's tracing wheel. The second method is to make perforated patterns. Trace the pattern on wrapping paper and, with needle unthreaded, machine-stitch along lines of the design. The design is marked by laying the perforated pattern on the quilt top, rough side down, and rubbing stamping powder or paste through the perforations. Straight lines can be marked with a ruler and tailor's chalk. For very simple quilting that follows the lines of the patchwork, appliqué, or print of fabric, it is not necessary to mark the fabric.

After quilting design has been marked on the quilt top, assemble top, batting, and lining. Cut or piece lining fabric to equal size of quilt top. Place lining, wrong side up, on large flat surface. Place one layer of cotton or Dacron batting on top of lining, smoothing out any bumps or wrinkles. If quilt is planned for warmth, interlining may be thicker. Remember, the thinner the layer of padding, the easier and finer the quilting will be. Before adding quilt top, baste batting to backing by taking two long stitches in a cross.

Place quilt top on top of batting, right side up. Pin all layers together to hold temporarily. Baste generously through all thicknesses. To prevent shifting, first baste on the lengthwise and crosswise grain of the fabric. Then baste diagonally across in two directions and around sides, top, and bottom. **Note:** If quilting is to be done using a quilting hoop, extra care must be taken to keep basting stitches close, so they will hold in place as you change the position of the hoop.

QUILTING

Quilting may be done by hand or on the sewing machine.

When quilting by hand, the quilt may be stretched on a frame or in a quilting hoop (more easily handled and movable). If neither frame nor hoop is used, quilting may be done in the lap over small areas at a time. The first method for making quilting stitches (see below) is best in lap quilting.

Quilting on a Frame: If a frame is used, sew top and bottom edges of lining to the fabric strips which are attached to the long parallel bars of your quilting frame. Using strong thread so that quilt will not pull away from frame when stretched taut, sew securely with several rows of stitches. After quilt is secured in frame, start quilting midway between the long parallel bars of frame and sew toward you.

Quilting with a Quilting Hoop: The quilting is started at the center of the quilt, then worked toward outer edges.

Pull quilt taut in hoop and move any extra fullness toward the edges. If necessary, cut basting thread as work progresses. As your quilting comes closer to the edge, smaller embroidery hoops may be substituted for the larger quilting hoop, thereby assuring that fabric will remain taut.

The quilting stitch is a short, even running stitch. There are two methods of making this stitch. One is done in two separate motions — first pushing the needle down through the three thicknesses, then pushing it up again close to the first stitch. One hand is always under the quilt to guide the stitch; stitches should be of equal length on both sides of the quilt.

The second method is to take two or three little stitches before pulling the needle through, holding quilt down at quilting line with the thumb of one hand. (Tape this thumb to prevent soreness.) Make from five to nine stitches per inch, depending on thickness of the fabrics.

If you are a beginner, practice quilting a small piece in an embroidery hoop to find the easiest and best way for you to work.

The usual quilting needle is a short, sharp needle — No. 8 or 9 — although some experienced quilters may prefer a longer one. Strong white sewing thread between Nos. 30 and 50 is best. To begin, knot end of thread. Bring needle up through quilt and pull knot through lining so it is imbedded in interlining. To end off, make a simple backstitch and run thread through interlining.

Quilting on a machine can be done with or without a quilting foot. When working on a sewing machine, the best quilting patterns to use are sewn on the diagonal or on the bias. Fabric gives a little when on the bias, making it easier to keep the area you are working on flat. Cotton batting should be quilted closely (quilting lines running no more than 2″ apart); Dacron lining may be quilted with the lines no more than 3″ apart.

As a rule, machine quilting is done with a straight stitch. Stitch length control should be set from 6 to 12 per inch. Pressure should be adjusted so that it is slightly heavier than for medium-weight fabrics.

If you are using a scroll or floral design, it is best to use the short open toe of the quilting foot. This allows you to follow the curved lines with accuracy and ease.

TUFTING

If you wish to tuft rather than quilt, use several layers of padding between the top and the lining. Mark evenly spaced points on the top surface with tailor tacks or pins. Thread a candlewick needle with candlewick yarn, or use a large-eyed needle with heavy Germantown yarn or knitting worsted. Using thread double, push needle from top through layers to back, leaving thread end on top. Push needle back up again to surface, about ¼″ away. Tie yarn in firm double knot. Clip ends to desired length (at least ½″).

QUILT CARE

Dry clean all fine quilts. If a quilt is washable, you may put it in the automatic washer on a short-wash cycle. Be sure to use only a mild soap or detergent. Do not wring or spin dry. Let quilt drip dry, and do not iron.

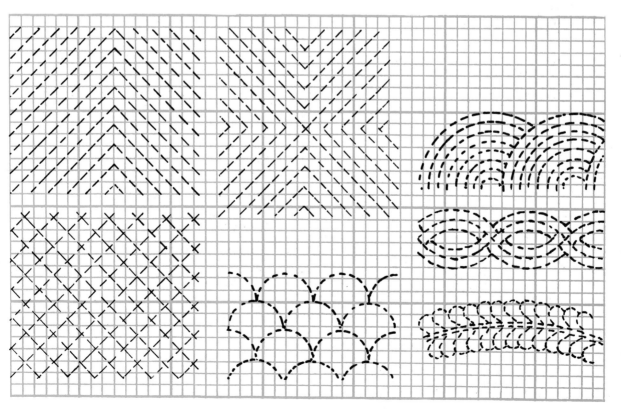

Patchwork Quilts

A series of borders surrounding a central star
creates a magnificent design called Framed Medallion.
Pieced borders alternate with plain borders; star is appliquéd.
Quilt, from Pennsylvania, is undated, but some
patches are printed with bits of political sloganry
from the 1820's—"Success to Adams" and "Forever Jackson;"
other fabrics seem to be even earlier.

FRAMED MEDALLION QUILT

SIZE: About 110½" square.

EQUIPMENT: Ruler. Scissors. Thin, stiff cardboard. Light and dark-colored pencils. Tracing paper. Tailor's chalk. Sewing and quilting needles. Quilting frame (optional).

MATERIALS: Quilt top: scraps of closely woven cotton print fabrics in shades of dark red, brown, tan, beige, light blue, pink, and green, plus plain white (see Note and directions). Lining: white fabric 60" wide, 6¼ yds. White and matching sewing thread. Dacron polyester or cotton batting (Stearns & Foster).

Note: Description of colors has been simplified in directions below. In each border of quilt, we have specified the colors that seem most prominent. Study illustration for variations in colors and in their relation to each other. In original quilt all colored fabrics are prints.

DIRECTIONS: Read General Directions on pages 6 and 7. Quilt is made up of an appliquéd center square surrounded by ten borders, five pieced and five plain. Mark all patterns on wrong side of fabric and add ¼" seam allowance around all pieces, i.e., center square, patch pieces, and plain border strips. Sew pieces together with right sides facing, making ¼" seams. Dimensions given are finished size of each piece after quilt is assembled and do not include outside seam allowances.

Center Square: Trace pattern for Large Diamond; complete quarter-pattern indicated by dash lines. For quarter-star pattern mark diamond pattern on cardboard, then mark another diamond adjacent to first; cut along outer lines. Cut four quarter-stars from large-print brown fabric. Sew quarter-stars together to make two half-stars, then sew half-stars together for star. For background, cut piece 15" square from white fabric. Indicate horizontal and vertical center lines on white square (fold and crease or mark lines with ruler and tailor's chalk). Appliqué pieced star to center of white square, using center lines as guides (see How to appliqué on page 90).

First Border: Cut 12 strips ¾" wide: from green fabric cut two strips 15" long, two 16½" long, two 18" long, and two 19½" long; from red fabric, cut two strips 16½" long and two 18" long. Sew 15" green strips to sides of white center square, then 16½" green strips to top and bottom, then sew on red strips in same manner, then remaining green strips. Quilt piece should measure 19½" square.

Second Border: Mark a rectangle on cardboard 2-7/16" x 3½"; mark midpoint on one short side of rectangle; draw lines diagonally from midpoint to two opposite corners. Cut on marked lines for triangle pattern with 2-7/16" base. Cut 32 triangles from white fabric and 36 from dark red (or pink) fabric. Assemble triangles into four strips, each strip with eight white triangles and nine red triangles, alternating colors and sewing triangles together on long sides. For corners, make another triangle pattern in same manner as first, using a rectangle 3-3/16" x 3⅜" to make a triangle with 3-3/16" base. Cut four triangles from white fabric. Mark a 2¼" square on cardboard; draw a diagonal line connecting two opposite corners; cut on marked lines for right-angle triangle pattern. Cut four right-angle triangles from red fabric. Sew each red triangle on long side to base of a white triangle, for corner piece. Place each pieced strip horizontally with white triangles on upper side; sew a corner piece to right end of strip. Sew the four strips to sides of quilt piece, matching white-triangle side of strip to green borders. Sew ends of strips together. Quilt piece should measure 26½" square.

Third Border: Cut four strips 3¼" wide from white fabric, two 26½" long and two 33" long. Sew shorter strips to sides of quilt piece and longer strips to top and bottom. Cut four strips 1" wide from light blue fabric, two 33" long and two 35" long. Sew on in same manner as first strips. Quilt piece should measure 35" square.

Fourth Border: Draw a 3½" and a 2½" square on cardboard; draw a diagonal line on each square between two opposite corners; cut on marked lines to make patterns for large and small triangles. Cut 64 large triangles from white fabric, 64 small triangles from pink fabric, 32 small triangles from navy fabric, and 32 small triangles from brown-and-yellow fabric. Sew six triangles together as shown in Piecing Diagram to make a block 5" square, combining navy, pink, and white triangles for one half-block and brown, pink, and white triangles for other half. Make 31 more blocks in same manner. Sew blocks into two strips of nine blocks each and two strips of seven blocks each; in each strip, place blocks so that colored-triangle sides are adjacent, but with colors in alternate positions. Sew shorter strips to sides of quilt piece and longer strips to top and bottom. Quilt piece should measure 45" square.

Fifth Border: Cut four strips 2½" x 50" from blue fabric with a flowered band. Sew strips to quilt piece, with an equal margin extending at end of each strip. Miter corners. Quilt piece should measure 50" square.

Sixth Border: Trace pattern for Small Diamond; complete quarter-pattern indicated by dash lines. Make cardboard pattern for diamond patch. To make a star block, cut four diamonds from light fabric (blue, tan, or pink) and four from dark fabrics (brown or dark red). See page 10 for Joining Diamonds. Sew diamonds into two half-stars, then the half-stars into a whole star, alternating light and dark colors. For background of star block, cut cardboard pattern 2-1/16" square. Cut four squares from white fabric. Cut square pattern in half diagonally for triangle pattern and cut four triangles from white fabric. Sew white squares and triangles alternately between points of stars to make block 7" square. Make 23 more star blocks in same manner. Draw a 7" square on cardboard; draw a diagonal line between two opposite corners; cut on marked lines for large tri-

continued on page 12

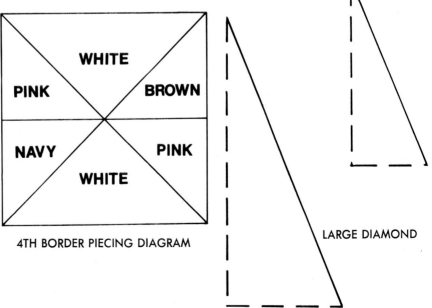

WHITE

PINK   BROWN

NAVY   PINK

WHITE

4TH BORDER PIECING DIAGRAM

SMALL DIAMOND

LARGE DIAMOND

FOUR STARS QUILT

SIZE: About 81″ square.

EQUIPMENT: Thin, stiff cardboard. Ruler. Scissors. Light and dark-colored pencils. Tailor's chalk. Tracing paper. Paper for pattern. Tracing wheel. Dressmaker's carbon (tracing) paper. Sewing and quilting needles. Quilting frame (optional).

MATERIALS: Closely woven cotton fabric 36″ wide: orange, 2¼″ yds.; red (or pink), 2 yds.; tannish green, 3⅔ yds. (**Note:** Fabrics may be solid color or in very small prints.) White fabric, 45″ wide, 7 yds. (includes lining). Matching sewing threads. Dacron polyester or cotton batting (Taylor Bedding).

DIRECTIONS: Read the General Directions on pages 6 and 7. Quilt is constructed of four pieced stars, set in a white background with a striped border. To make stars, trace actual-size pattern for diamond patch. Cut several diamond patterns from cardboard; replace patterns as edges become worn and points rounded from repeated use. Marking pattern on wrong side of fabric and adding ¼″ seam allowance all around, cut diamond patches as follows: cut 224 from orange fabric, 192 from red fabric, and 384 from green fabric.

Joining Diamonds: When joining diamonds to form a straight row, stitch all pieces together along sides cut on straight of goods. If the rows of diamonds are then joined together, you will be stitching along the bias edges; keep thread just taut enough to prevent seams from stretching. When diamonds are joined to form shapes other than straight rows, it is preferable to sew an edge cut on the straight of goods to one that is cut on the bias; two bias edges sewn together tend to stretch, and the slightest deviation can distort the final result. Stitch from the wide-angled corner towards the pointed ends.

After joining diamonds, whether in rows or other shapes, press pieced sections with seams to one side; open seams tend to weaken construction. Trim seams at points, as you piece. There are two methods for joining the diamonds. **First method:** Hold patches together, right sides facing; seam together with small running stitches on pencil lines. If the problem of sharp points and true meeting of seams proves difficult with this method, prepare each patch as follows: **Second method:** Cut firm paper patterns the exact size and shape of cardboard patterns. Fit paper pattern within pencil outline on wrong side of patch, hold patch with paper pattern uppermost. Fold seam allowance over each side, and tack to the paper with one stitch on each side, allowing the thread to cross the corners. Finish by taking an extra stitch into the first side; cut the thread, leaving about ¼″. To make removal of tacking easier, do not knot thread or make any backstitches. Hold prepared patches right sides together, matching the edges to be seamed exactly. Whip together with fine, even stitches (about 16 to the inch), avoiding the paper as much as possible. The paper patterns may remain in place until the octagon shape is completed. To remove the papers, snip tacking thread once on each patch and withdraw thread; lift papers out.

Each star is made up of eight identical diamond-shaped sections meeting at a center point, and each section is made up of five rows of five diamond patches each. See Piecing Diagram for one section. Following Diagram for color placement, make a section as follows: piece together five rows, starting first, third, and fifth rows with a green patch and second and fourth rows with an orange patch. Matching corners carefully, join the five rows together to make diamond-shaped section. Make 31 more sections in same manner. For star, join four sections for each half, with orange points meeting

in center, then join halves for complete star. Make three more stars in same manner. Each star point should measure about 9″ along side edges. (Check measurements before cutting white background pieces.)

For white background of quilt top, make cardboard pattern 9″ square. Marking on wrong side of fabric and adding ¼″ seam allowance, cut eight squares from white fabric. Cut cardboard in half diagonally for triangle pattern. Cut eight triangles from white fabric, in same manner as for squares. Make cardboard pattern 18″ square and cut one square from white fabric. Cut square pattern in half laterally for rectangle pattern and cut four rectangles from white fabric.

For center (star area) of quilt top, place all pieces together, following color illustration. Join white pieces to stars, right sides together, starting with corner pieces, then side pieces, and, finally, the large center square. Center of quilt top should measure about 61½″ square.

For first border, cut four strips from green fabric 2″ x 65″ (measurements include ¼″ seam allowance all around). Sew a strip to each side of quilt top, right sides together and with an equal amount extending at each end; miter corners. For each remaining border, cut and sew on four strips as follows, mitering corners: Second border: white, 1½″ x 67″. Third border: red, 1½″ x 69″. Fourth border: green, 2″ x 72″. Fifth border: white, 2″ x 75″. Sixth border: red, 2¼″ x 78½″. Seventh border: white, 1¾″ x 81″. Quilt top should measure 81″ square.

continued on page 12

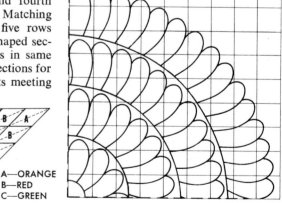

LARGE MEDALLION QUILTING PATTERN

SMALL MEDALLION QUILTING PATTERN

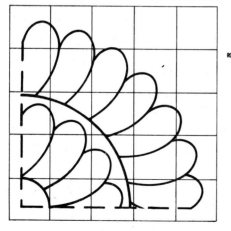

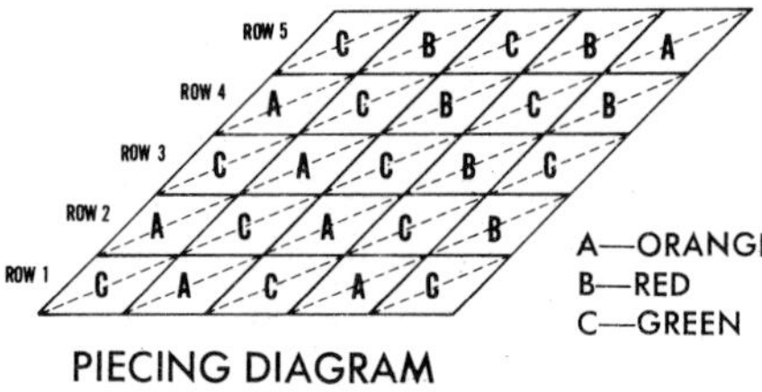

PIECING DIAGRAM

A—ORANGE
B—RED
C—GREEN

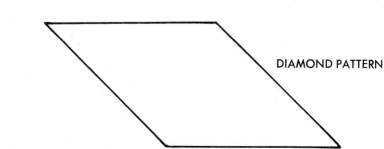

DIAMOND PATTERN

Khaki, orange, and pink—three colors in unusual combination work together in a four-star design! Graceful feather-wreath quilting complements the pieced stars and striped border. Made by Nancy Stephens, born 1842, in Malaga, Ohio.

FOUR STARS QUILT
continued from page 10

For lining, cut two pieces from white fabric 42″ x 81″. Sew together on long sides to make piece 81″ square. Cut batting same size as lining and quilt top.

Quilting: Enlarge medallion quilting patterns on paper ruled in 1″ squares; complete quarter-patterns indicated by dash lines. Using dressmaker's carbon and tracing wheel, transfer large pattern to large center white square of quilt top. Transfer half of pattern to each white rectangle at sides, with straight line of the semi-circle on outer side of rectangle.

Transfer small pattern to each small white square of quilt top; transfer half of small pattern to triangles.

With ruler and tailor's chalk, mark diagonal quilting lines ¼″ apart in corners of all white pieces. Mark same diagonal pattern on borders. On stars, mark nine straight parallel lines on each diamond-shaped section; draw lines in lengthwise rows through points of diamond patches.

Pin and baste lining, batting, and quilt top together, following General Directions. Quilt on all marked lines.

To bind edges of quilt, cut four 1″-wide strips from green fabric 81½″ long (or piece to get these lengths). Right sides together and with ¼″ seams, sew strips to top of quilt. Turn to back of quilt and slip-stitch to lining, turning in edges of strips ¼″.

FRAMED MEDALLION QUILT
continued from page 8

angle pattern. Cut 20 large triangles from tan fabric and 24 from brown fabric. Cut triangle pattern in half for small triangle pattern; cut four small triangles from tan fabric and four from brown fabric. Sew one shorter side of a large brown triangle to one side of each of the 24 star blocks, keeping a four-sided shape. On 20 of the star blocks, sew a large tan triangle to side opposite brown triangle, making a parallelogram. Sew parallelograms into four horizontal rows of five pieces each, with tan triangles on upper edge and brown triangles on lower edge. Sew a small tan triangle to upper left side of each row, sewing long side of triangle to side of star block. Sew remaining star blocks with brown triangles to right end of each row, keeping to pattern. Finish each row by adding a small brown triangle to star block at lower right end. Sew rows to each side of quilt piece, with small tan triangle at upper left flush with left edge of quilt piece and half of large tan triangle at upper right extending beyond right edge of quilt piece. Sew ends of rows together. Quilt piece should measure 69¼″ square.

Seventh Border: Cut four strips 2½″ x 74¼″ from tan and white fabric with a flower-print stripe. Sew strips to quilt piece as for Fifth Border, mitering corners. Quilt piece should measure 74¼″ square.

Eighth Border: Draw 3¾″ square on cardboard; draw a diagonal line between two opposite corners; cut on marked lines for small triangle pattern. Cut 64 small triangles each from white, tan, dark red, and brown fabrics (use as many different fabrics as desired, as long as the number of triangles cut from each is divisible by four and the total number of triangles includes 128 light and 128 dark). Sew red and white triangles together on long sides to make 64 patches 3¾″ square. Sew two patches together, alternating colors; then sew two more patches together in same manner. Sew the two pieces together, alternating colors, for a block 7½″ square. Make 15 more red/white blocks in same manner. Make 16 tan/brown blocks in same manner. Draw a 7½″ square on cardboard; draw a diagonal line between two opposite corners; cut on marked lines for large triangle pattern. Cut 28 large triangles from red fabric and 32 from tan fabric. Cut large triangle pattern in half for medium triangle pattern. Cut four medium triangles from red fabric and four from tan fabric. Assemble pieced blocks and large and medium triangles into strips and sew to quilt piece, in same manner as for Sixth Border; alternate red/white and brown/tan blocks all around border. Quilt piece should measure 95½″ square.

Ninth Border: Use same fabric as for Seventh Border and sew on in same manner. Cut strips 2¼″ x 100″. Quilt piece should measure 100″ square.

Tenth Border: Draw a 5″ square on cardboard; draw a diagonal line between two opposite corners; cut on marked lines for triangle pattern. Cut 42 triangles each from red, tan, brown, and beige fabrics. Join red and tan triangles on their long sides to make 42 patches 5″ square. Make 42 brown/beige patches in same manner. Sew patches into four strips with 21 patches each, alternating red/tan with brown/beige in each strip; keep dark colors on one long edge and light colors on the other. Sew on strips, one end flush with quilt piece, the other end extending one patch beyond. Sew ends of strips together. Quilt top should measure 110½″ square.

Lining: Cut two pieces 55¾″ x 100½″. Sew together on long edges with ½″ seams; press seam open. Cut batting same size as lining and quilt top.

Quilting: Using ruler and tailor's chalk, mark quilting lines over quilt top, one section at a time.

Center Square: On star, mark horizontal and vertical center lines, falling on center seams and making four right angles. On each quarter-star, mark four right-angle lines ½″ apart, parallel to center right angles. On white background, mark diagonal lines ½″ apart in both directions, skipping over star.

First Border: Mark pattern of parallel triangles over entire border, making lines ¼″ apart.

Second Border: On each triangle, mark three lines ¼″ apart, parallel to long sides of triangle.

Third Border: Mark diagonal lines ½″ apart in both directions.

Fourth Border: Divide each block into four equal sections, and mark a pattern of concentric squares in each section, making lines ¼″ apart.

Fifth Border: Same as Third Border.

Sixth Border: On stars, mark three lines ½″ apart on each diamond, parallel to two opposite sides. On white squares, mark horizontal and vertical lines ½″ apart. On white triangles, mark lines ¼″ apart parallel to long sides. On triangles outside star blocks, divide each triangle into two equal parts meeting at right angles in center; mark a pattern of right angles in each half, making lines ¼″ apart and parallel to center right angle.

Seventh Border: Same as Third Border.

Eighth Border: On square blocks, mark horizontal and vertical lines ½″ apart over entire block. On large triangles, mark same pattern as for large triangles in Sixth Border.

Ninth Border: Same as Third Border.

Tenth Border: On each square patch, mark diagonal lines ½″ apart in one direction only; mark lines parallel to center seam on red/tan patches and in opposite direction on brown/beige patches; match lines carefully at seams joining patches, thus creating a pattern of parallel triangles over border.

Following General Directions, pin and baste lining, batting and quilt top together. Starting in center and working around and outward, quilt on all marked lines with white thread.

To finish edges, cut four strips 1″ x 111″ from brown fabric. Sew strips to front of quilt, right sides together and with ¼″ seams. Fold strips to back of quilt, turning in edges ¼″, and slip-stitch to lining. Press edges of quilt.

BLUE FANS QUILT

shown on page 15

SIZE: About 66¾" x 77¾".

EQUIPMENT: Tracing paper. Pencil. Scissors. Paper for patterns. Thin, stiff cardboard. Ruler. Compass. Tailor's chalk. Straight pins. Sewing and quilting needles. Sewing machine (optional).

MATERIALS: Closely woven cotton fabric, 44"-45" wide: blue, 2⅔ yds.; white, 6⅔ yds. (includes lining). White sewing thread. Dacron polyester or cotton batting.

DIRECTIONS: Read General Directions on pages 6 and 7. Quilt is made up of 42 identical 11"-square blocks. See Piecing Diagram for one block. Trace actual-size pattern for B piece. To make patterns for A and C pieces, draw main outlines of block on paper, following heavy lines and dimensions of Piecing Diagram: draw an 11" square; on two adjacent sides of square, mark points 5½", then 9" from corner. With compass set at 5½", then 9", draw arcs to connect points.

Make cardboard patterns for A, B, and C pieces. Marking patterns on wrong side of fabric and adding ¼" seam allowance all around, cut patch pieces as follows: from blue fabric, cut 42 A pieces and 378 B* pieces; from white fabric, cut 42 C pieces and 336 B* pieces. *(**Note:** When cutting B pieces, place left straight edge of pattern on straight of goods.)

To make one block, sew nine blue B pieces and eight white B pieces together on long sides, alternating colors and beginning and ending with a blue B piece; see Piecing Diagram. Sew inner curve of pieced B section to curve of an A piece. Sew outer curve of B section to curve of a C piece, to complete block. Make 41 more blocks in same manner. Sew blocks into seven vertical rows of six blocks each; in each row, place first block with fan in upper right corner, second block with fan in upper left corner; continue alternating placement of fans to end of row. Sew rows together to make quilt top, reversing direction of fans in alternate rows; see color illustration. Quilt top measures 66½" x 77½", including outside seam allowance.

For lining, cut two pieces 34" x 77¾". Sew together on long edges, with ½" seams. Press seam open. Lining will be ¼" larger than quilt top all around. Cut batting same size as lining.

Quilting: Using tailor's chalk and compass, mark curving quilting lines ⅜" apart on all A and C pieces, starting at curved edge of each piece and following contour of the fan; on A pieces, mark lines only up to 1¾" from corner.

Pin and baste quilt top, batting, and lining together, following General Directions. Starting in center and working around and outward, quilt on all marked lines; on each blue B piece, quilt close to straight seam lines, omitting lines on outer edge of block. Use white thread for all quilting.

To bind edges of quilt, cut 1¼"-wide strips from white fabric, two 67¼" long and two 78¼" long, piecing to get lengths. Right sides together, sew a strip to each edge on front of quilt, with ¼" seams. Turn strips to back of quilt, turning in raw edges ¼", and slip-stitch to lining, to make edging ⅜" wide. Press all edges of quilt.

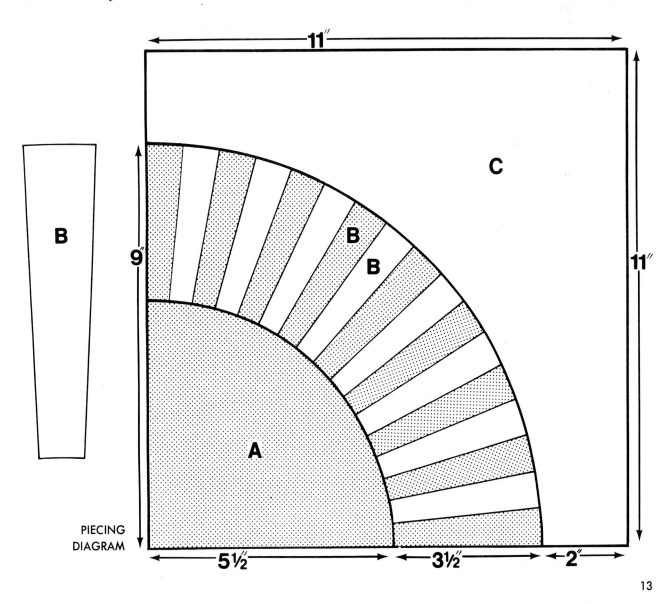

PIECING DIAGRAM

Red pineapples (or "wild goose chase," whichever you see first)
pattern a square quilt made of 49 identical blocks. No border is needed.
Each block is pieced with triangles, strips, and a square. Quilting
follows the patchwork pattern. Directions for Pineapple Quilt, page 18.

A bold red star features five little stars within and
a feathered edge. Patch pieces are relatively few; star points
are joined to the nine-patch center block. Coverlet is
splendidly quilted with wreaths and a serpentine border.
Made in Ohio, about 1870. Feathered Star Quilt, page 16.

Little stars against jagged peaks: this rugged design, called
"delectable mountains," is one of the few that can be traced back to
colonial days. Set with "flying geese" borders, quilt is
pieced entirely with squares and triangles. Ca. 1910. See page 19.

Fans—big, bold, and blue—are a 1930's "modern" departure
from the many-colored pattern called grandma's fan. Coverlet
is all machine-stitched, including the contour quilting
in each block. Directions for Blue Fans Quilt on page 13.

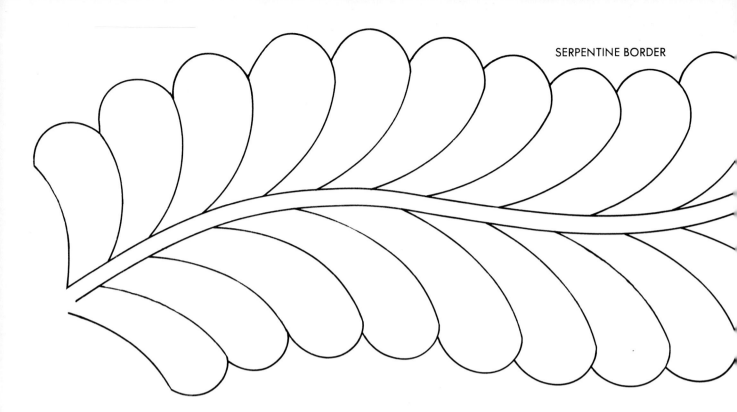

FEATHERED STAR QUILT
shown on page 14

SIZE: About 74½" square.

EQUIPMENT: Ruler. Scissors. Thin, stiff cardboard. Tracing paper. Dressmaker's (carbon) tracing paper. Tracing wheel. Tailor's chalk. Sewing and quilting needles. Pencil. Quilting frame (optional).

MATERIALS: Closely woven cotton fabric, 44"-45" wide: 2½ yds. red, 8¼ yds. white (including lining). Dacron polyester or cotton batting (Taylor Bedding). White sewing thread.

DIRECTIONS: Read General Directions on pages 6 and 7. Large star is constructed with eight pieced star points joined to a nine-patch center block. Center block has five pieced small-star blocks joined to four plain blocks. To make the small-star blocks, cut a cardboard pattern 2¾" square. Marking pattern on wrong side of fabric and adding ¼" seam allowance all around, cut 20 square patches from white fabric and five square patches from red. Draw two corner-to-corner lines on cardboard pattern, crossing in center, to divide square into four equal triangles. Cut out a triangle for pattern and cut 260 triangles from red fabric and 272 from white, in same manner as for squares. Only 40 of each are used for small-star blocks; remainder are for rest of quilt. Right sides together, sew a red triangle to a white triangle on short sides to form a larger triangle; sew two larger triangles together on long sides to form a square (see star points of small-star blocks in color illustration for design of squares).

Make 19 more pieced squares in same manner. To assemble small-star block, join four white squares, one red square, and four red-and-white pieced squares into one block of three rows of three squares each (see color illustration). Make four more small-star blocks in same manner. Blocks should measure 8¼" square, plus outside seam allowance. Make a cardboard pattern 8¼" square and cut four red blocks, adding ¼" seam allowance. Join the small-star blocks and the red blocks into three rows of three blocks each to form center block of large star (see color illustration for arrangement). Center block should measure 24¾" square, plus outside seam allowance.

To make star-point blocks for large star, cut cardboard rectangle 9" x 10"; cut in half diagonally to make pattern for large triangle. Cut eight large triangles from red fabric, adding seam allowance. Trace actual-size diamond pattern; complete quarter-pattern indicated by dash lines. Cut eight diamonds from red fabric. Putting aside 16 small white triangles and four small red triangles, join remaining small triangles into 2" squares by sewing the long side of a white triangle to the long side of a red triangle. Join squares into strips, placing squares so that all red triangles are on one side of strip: make eight five-square strips, eight seven-square strips, and four 30-square strips.

To assemble a star point, place a large red triangle with 10" side vertical at left and long side diagonally at right. Join a five-square strip to 10" side of triangle and a seven-square strip to

long side. Complete tip of star where the two strips meet by adding two white triangles and a red diamond; see color illustration for placement of pieces. Make another star point in same manner, but with the 10" side of large triangle at right and long side at left. Join the two star points into a double-pointed block by sewing a red triangle between. Sew the double-pointed block to one side of center block. Make three more double-pointed blocks in same manner and sew to remaining three sides of center block to complete large star.

For white background of star, cut cardboard pattern 14¾" square. Marking on wrong side of fabric and adding ¼" seam allowance, cut four squares from white fabric. Cut pattern in half diagonally to make a triangle pattern and cut four triangles from white fabric in same manner. Sew the squares and triangles alternately between the points of large star, to make piece 54¼" square, plus outside seam allowance. Sew a 30-square strip to each side of piece, with red triangles inside and starting first strip flush with edge of pieced center. For white borders, cut four 8¼"-wide strips, two 58¾" long and two 74¼" long (measurements include ¼" seam allowance). Sew a shorter strip to each side of quilt top; then sew longer strips to top and bottom of quilt top. Quilt top should measure 74¼" square.

For lining, cut two pieces 37⅝" x 75¼". Sew together on long sides, to make lining ½" larger all around than quilt top. Cut batting same size as *continued on page 18*

continued on page 18

SMALL WREATH

FLOWER

LARGE WREATH

DIAMOND
PATTERN

FEATHERED STAR QUILT
continued from page 16

quilt top.

Quilting: Trace actual-size quilting patterns; complete quarter-patterns indicated by dash lines. Using dressmaker's carbon and tracing wheel, transfer patterns to quilt top as follows: Place a small wreath in each large red square of large star, in center of each triangle of white background (with a flower in each outer corner), and in each corner of white border, 1″ from outer edge. Place a large wreath in each corner square of white background. Repeat serpentine border design along center of each white border. With ruler and tailor's chalk, mark straight quilting lines as follows: On small-star blocks, mark diagonal lines ¾″ apart in both directions, going through corners; mark same pattern on all blocks with a small or large wreath design, skipping over wreath itself. On points of large star, mark large triangles with diagonal lines ½″ apart in one direction parallel to long side of triangle; mark same pattern on small triangles and diamonds, changing direction of lines so they are parallel to long sides of small triangles; mark same pattern on borders, making lines parallel to triangles of pieced border strips and extending lines across white border; skip over serpentine design.

Pin and baste quilt top, lining, and batting together, centering two top layers so that lining extends ½″ all around. Quilt on all marked lines. To finish quilt turn lining to front, turn in raw edges ¼″, and slip-stitch to quilt top. Press edges of quilt.

PINEAPPLE QUILT
shown on page 14

SIZE: About 70½″ square.
EQUIPMENT: Scissors. Ruler. Pencil. Thin, stiff cardboard. Paper for patterns. Glue. Straight pins. Sewing and quilting needles. Quilting frame (optional).

MATERIALS: Closely woven cotton fabric 44″-45″ wide: red, 5 yds.; white*, 2⅔ yds.; fabric for lining, 4⅔ yds. Dacron polyester or cotton batting. Matching sewing thread. *(In original quilt, the white fabric has a small blue dot, not visible in illustration.)
DIRECTIONS: Read General Directions on pages 6 and 7. Quilt is constructed of 49 identical square blocks. To make patterns for patch pieces, first draw an actual-size pattern for a complete 10″-square block, following design and dimensions of Piecing Diagram. Draw all horizontal and vertical lines of block first, 1″ apart, extending lines to edges of square; intersections will then act as guide points for drawing the triangles. Glue pattern to thin cardboard. Cut along lines of pattern to make an individual pattern for patch pieces A, B, C, D, E, F. Marking patterns on wrong side of fabric and adding ¼″ seam allowance all around, cut patches for entire quilt: from white fabric, cut 49 of patch A, 784 of B; from red fabric, cut 196 each of C, D, E, F.

To join patches for one block, start in the center and work outward, sewing four C triangles to an A square, then four B triangles to the C triangles, then four D strips, then four B triangles, etc., until completing block; piece should measure 10″ square, plus outside seam allowance. Make 48 more blocks in same manner. Join blocks in seven rows of seven blocks each; then sew rows together for quilt top. Piece should measure 70½″ square.

For lining, cut two pieces 35¾″ x 70½″. Sew together on long sides with ½″ seams. Press seam open. Cut batting same size as lining and quilt top.

Quilting: Quilt near all seam lines, starting in center of quilt and working around and outward.

To bind edges, cut four 1″-wide strips from red fabric, 70¾″ long (piece to get these lengths). Stitch to top of quilt, right sides together and with ¼″ seams. Turn strips to back of quilt and slip-stitch to lining, turning in raw edges of strips ¼″.

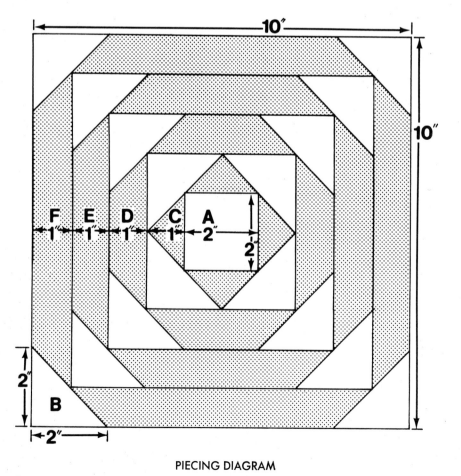

PIECING DIAGRAM

18

DELECTABLE MOUNTAINS QUILT

shown on page 14

SIZE: About 68¾" x 90¾".

EQUIPMENT: Scissors. Ruler. Thin, stiff cardboard. Tailor's chalk. Light and dark pencils. Sewing and quilting needles. Quilting frame (optional).

MATERIALS: Closely woven cotton fabric 44"- 45" wide: white, 11¼ yds. (includes lining); navy*, 4¾ yds. Cotton or dacron polyester batting. White sewing thread. *(In original quilt, navy fabric has a small white dot, not visible in illustration.)

DIRECTIONS: Read General Directions on pages 6 and 7. Quilt is made up of twelve 19½"-square blocks set with pieced borders. See Piecing Diagram for one quilt block; smaller blocks within are indicated by heavy lines; dotted lines indicate quilting patterns. Cut cardboard patterns for patch pieces as follows, labeling each pattern: Pattern A — cut a 1½" square. Pattern B — draw a 1½" square; draw two corner-to-corner lines, crossing in the center, to divide square into four equal triangles; cut a triangle for pattern. Pattern C — draw a 3-3/16" square cut in half diagonally for a triangle pattern. Pattern D — draw a 1½" square; cut in half diagonally for a triangle pattern. Pattern E — cut a 1-1/16" square. Pattern F — draw a 6" square; cut in half diagonally for a triangle pattern. Pattern G — draw a 5-5/16" square; cut in half diagonally for triangle pattern. Cut patch pieces for all quilt blocks as follows, marking patterns on wrong side of fabric and adding ¼" seam allowance all around: from blue fabric, cut 12 A, 1056 B, and 144 C; from white fabric, cut 48 A, 768 B, 96 D, 144 E, 96 F, and 48 G.

To join pieces for one complete quilt block, begin with the star block in center. Right sides together, sew a blue B triangle to a white B triangle on short sides to form a larger triangle; repeat and sew two larger triangles together on long sides to form a square. Make three more pieced squares in same manner. To assemble star block, join four white A squares, one blue A square, and four blue-and-white pieced squares into a block of three rows of three squares each (see Piecing Diagram). Star block should measure 4½" square, plus outside seam allowance.

For center block (surrounding star block), join a C triangle to each side of star block. Join a blue B triangle and a white B triangle on long sides to make a square. Make 55 more blue-and-white squares in same manner. Lay 16 blue-and-white squares, four E squares, four D triangles, and eight separate blue B triangles around C triangles of center block as shown in Piecing Diagram, making sure pieced squares are placed as shown; sew pieces into four strips. Sew strips to C triangles to complete center block; piece should measure 8½", plus outside seam allowance.

For side blocks, sew two C triangles to an F triangle, with C triangles meeting at right angle of F triangle. Lay 10 blue-and-white squares, four blue B triangles, two E squares, and one D triangle around C-F pieced section, following Piecing Diagram and making sure pieced squares are placed as shown. Sew pieces into three strips; sew strips to C-F section to complete side block. Block should measure about 5-5/16" x 8½", plus outside seam allowance. Make three more side blocks in same manner.

Sew a side block to each side of center block. To complete quilt block, sew four G triangles to sides and four F triangles to corners of piece, making a block about 19½" square, plus outside seam allowance. Make 11 more quilt blocks in same manner. **(Note:**

If blocks do not measure exactly 19½" square, adjust dimensions given in following paragraph so that pieced strips will fit blocks.)

For borders and joining strips, cut cardboard pattern 1-7/32" square (between 1-3/16" and 1¼" on your ruler); cut square in half diagonally to make triangle pattern. Marking pattern on wrong side of fabric and adding ¼" seam allowance all around, cut 1072 triangles from blue fabric. Cut another cardboard pattern 1-11/16" square, cut square in half diagonally to make triangle pattern. Cut 536 triangles from white fabric. Join two blue triangles to one white triangle to make a rectangular piece by sewing long side of each blue triangle to each short side of white triangle. Make 535 more rectangular pieces in same manner. Join pieces into strips by sewing long sides together, with white triangles all pointing in the same direction: make nine strips of 16 pieces each, two strips of 52 pieces each, two strips of 70 pieces each, and two strips of 74 pieces each.

continued on page 25

PIECING DIAGRAM

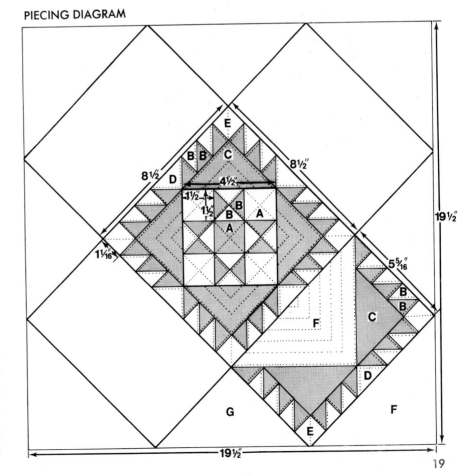

HOUSES QUILT

SIZE: About 75" x 81".

EQUIPMENT: Scissors. Ruler. Pencil. Thin, stiff cardboard. Tailor's chalk. Paper for patterns. Compass. Sewing and quilting needles. Quilting frame (optional).

MATERIALS: Closely woven cotton fabric, 36" wide: several prints in soft reds, blues, grays, and beiges, totaling about 2⅔ yds.; red and white print, 1⅛ yds. Cotton fabric 45" wide: white, 2⅛ yds.; fabric for lining, 4½ yds. (blue and white gingham was used in original quilt). Matching sewing thread. Dacron polyester or cotton batting. White bias binding tape, 8⅔ yds.

DIRECTIONS: Read General Directions on pages 6 and 7. Quilt is constructed of 36 pieced blocks, set with white joining strips and a pieced border. To make house block, enlarge pattern by copying on paper ruled in 1" squares. Make a cardboard pattern for each size patch piece (each window can be one piece, if desired, with the sash appliquéd on). Marking patterns on wrong side of fabric and adding ¼" seam allowance all around, cut 14 patch pieces (shaded areas on pattern) from one print fabric and nine from white fabric. Assemble pieces for house block measuring 9" x 10", plus outside seam allowance. Make 35 more house

blocks in same manner, using one print for each house.

For joining strips, cut 30 pieces from white fabric 2¼" x 9", adding ¼" seam allowance all around. Sew house blocks into six horizontal rows of six blocks each, with a joining strip between every two blocks. Cut five strips from white fabric 2¼" x 71¼", adding ¼" seam allowance all around. Join pieced rows for main body of quilt top, with white strips between rows; note that three rows face in one direction and three rows face in the opposite direction. Piece should measure 65¼" x 71¼", plus outside seam allowance.

For white border, cut four strips 1¾" wide, two 65¾" long and two 74¼" long (measurements include ¼" seam allowance). Sew shorter strips to sides of quilt top, then longer strips to top and bottom. For pieced border, mark 1½" square on cardboard and cut square in half diagonally for triangle pattern. Cut 136 triangles from red-print fabric and 132 from white fabric, adding ¼" seam allowance. Cut triangle pattern in half and cut eight small triangles from white fabric. Join triangles into long strips by sewing short sides of red-print triangles to short sides of white triangles; make two strips, each with 32 red triangles and 31 white triangles; add a small white triangle to beginning and end of each strip. Sew a pieced strip to each side of quilt top, with the red-triangles side inward. Join remaining triangles into two

strips, each with 36 red triangles and 35 white triangles; add a small white triangle to both ends of each strip. Sew strips to top and bottom of quilt top.

For outer border, cut four 2¾"-wide strips from red-print fabric, two 70½" long and two 81" long (measurements include ¼" seam allowance). Sew shorter strips to sides, then longer strips to top and bottom. Quilt top should measure about 75" x 81".

For lining, cut two pieces from lining fabric 38" x 81". Sew together on long sides with ½" seams. Cut batting same size as lining and quilt top.

Quilting: With ruler and tailor's chalk, mark diagonal quilting lines 1" apart in both directions over white background of quilt top, excluding white border; continue lines in one direction only onto red-print border. On white border, mark a zigzag pattern, making points about 1" apart on each edge. On front of houses, mark a circle 1¼" in diameter centered between door and roof peak.

Pin and baste quilt top, batting, and lining together, following General Directions. Starting in center and working around and outward, quilt on all marked lines. On houses, quilt on each colored patch, omitting window sashes, ⅛" in from seam lines. On roofs, quilt an extra horizontal line across center of piece. On pieced border, quilt on red patches, ⅛" in from seam lines.

Insert edges of quilt into fold of bias tape and stitch in place.

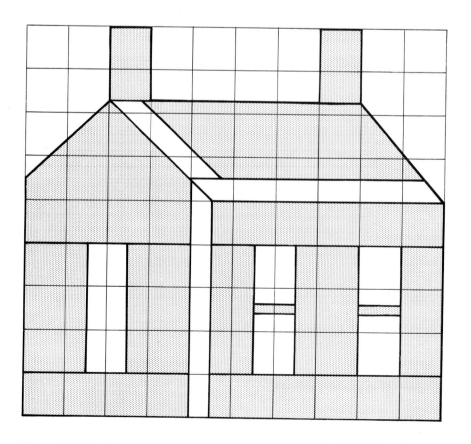

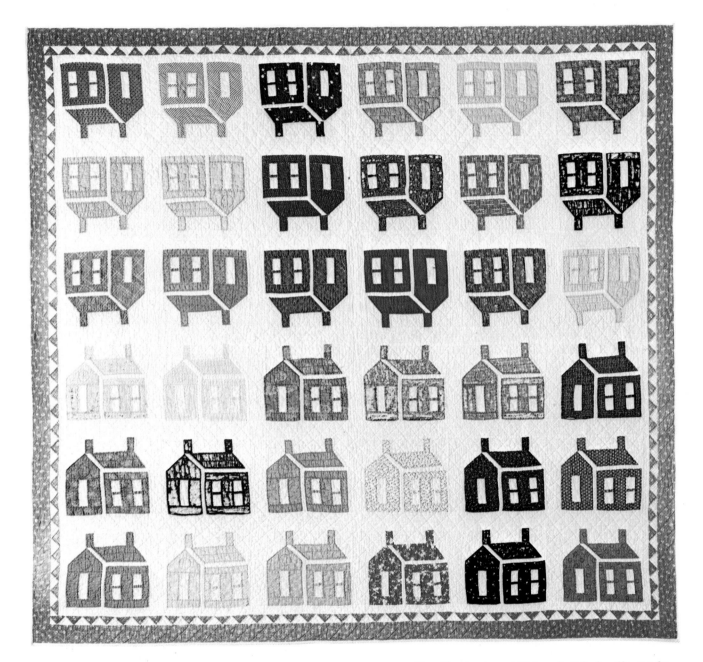

Mrs. Harrington of Ohio, a builder's wife, made this delightful quilt for her husband around 1860. Although many of the fabrics are faded and worn, the combination of soft reds, blues, beiges, and grays is still appealing. Each house is a pieced block, set into the quilt with white background strips.

COLLECTION OF PHYLLIS HADERS, AMERICAN QUILTS

MARINER'S COMPASS QUILT

SIZE: About 78¾″ square.

EQUIPMENT: Compass. Thin, stiff cardboard. Light and dark-colored pencils. Scissors. Ruler. Tailor's chalk. Tracing wheel. Dressmaker's (carbon) tracing paper. Sewing and quilting needles. Quilting frame (optional).

MATERIALS: Closely woven cotton fabric 36″ wide: dark blue, 5⅜ yds.; red, 1 yd.; green, 1 yd.; gold, 1 yd.; red and white print, 1⅛ yds. White fabric 45″ wide, 6¼ yds. (includes lining). White sewing thread. Dacron polyester or cotton batting (Taylor Bedding).

DIRECTIONS: Read General Directions on pages 6 and 7. Quilt is constructed of nine pieced blocks, set with pieced joining strips and borders. To make block, trace actual-size patch patterns; complete half- and quarter-patterns indicated by dash lines. Patterns for Nos. 2, 3 and 4 are superimposed on No. 1. Make six separate cardboard patterns. Marking patterns on wrong side of fabric and adding ¼″ seam allowance all around, cut patch pieces as follows: cut 36 of No. 1 from green fabric; 36 of No. 2 from gold; 72 of No. 3 and nine of No. 5 from red; 144 of No. 4 from red-and-white print; 288 of No. 6 and 36 of No. 7 from white.

To piece circle (or "compass") in each block, begin at the center and work outward: sew four No. 7 patches around a No. 5, to form a small circle; sew four No. 1 patches around circle, matching corners to the No. 5 piece; continue with four No. 2 pieces between the No. 1 pieces, eight No. 3 pieces, 16 No. 4 pieces, and 32 No. 6 pieces, to form circle 19″ in diameter, plus outside seam allowance. For quilt block, make a cardboard pattern 21″ square. Draw a circle 19″ in diameter in center of square; cut out and discard, leaving pattern for square "frame." Marking pattern on wrong side of fabric and adding ¼″ seam allowance all around inner and outer edges, cut frame from blue fabric. Right sides together, sew pieced circle to frame, for quilt block.

(Note: Another method is to appliqué circle to a solid square. However, this is not the way original quilt was made.) Make eight more blocks in same manner.

continued on page 25

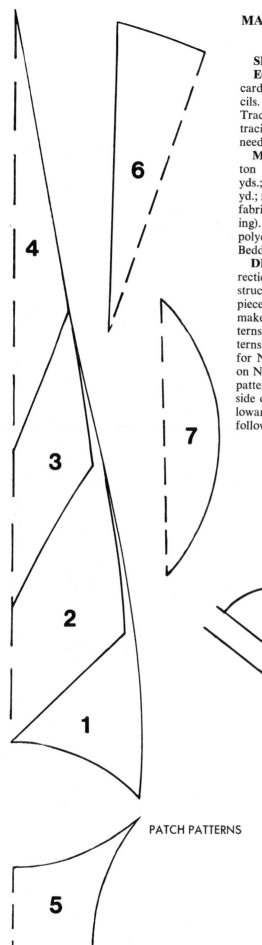

PATCH PATTERNS

CLAMSHELL QUILTING PATTERN

Each brilliant "compass" is set off by a blue frame, appropriately quilted in the clamshell pattern. Quilts of this type were often appliquéd, but ours was made entirely in patchwork, with stunning results. Connecticut, around 1870.

COLLECTION OF PHYLLIS HADERS, AMERICAN QUILTS

ALBUM QUILT

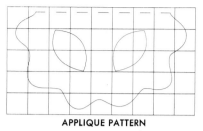

APPLIQUE PATTERN

EACH SQUARE = ¾″

EACH SQUARE = ¾″ OR 1″

EACH SQUARE = ½″

BORDER BLOCKS

EACH SQUARE = ½″

EACH SQUARE = ½″

EACH SQUARE = ½″

EACH SQUARE = 1″

EACH SQUARE = ½″ OR ¾″

EACH SQUARE = ½″

EACH SQUARE = ½″

EACH SQUARE = ½″ OR ¾″

EACH SQUARE = ½″

EACH SQUARE = ½″

EACH SQUARE = ½″

EACH SQUARE = ½″

EACH SQUARE = ½″

EACH SQUARE = ½″

EACH SQUARE = ½″

EACH SQUARE = ½″

EACH SQUARE = ½″

EACH SQUARE = ½″

EACH SQUARE = ½″

EACH SQUARE = ½″

EACH SQUARE = ½″

ALBUM QUILT
shown on page 2

SIZE: 71" x 88".

EQUIPMENT: Ruler. Pencil. Paper for patterns. Stiff cardboard. Scissors. Straight pins. Quilting needle. Quilting frame (optional).

MATERIALS: Cotton percale fabric in various colors and prints. Unbleached muslin for plain patches. Unbleached muslin for lining 45" wide, 4 yards. Cotton batting. Sewing and quilting thread.

DIRECTIONS: Read General Directions on pages 6 and 7. Quilt may be assembled using all the different patterns or by repeating a few patterns for the whole quilt. Some patterns are repeated with different colors. Plan colors of each block of patch pieces. Patterns are given on squares on page 24, shaded areas on patterns indicate darker colors, plain areas are muslin or light colors. To enlarge the squared patterns, rule paper into ½", ⅜", or ¼" squares as indicated under each pattern. A few of the patterns indicate two sizes of squares, which may be used to make the block large or small. Rule the same number of squares as given on the graph, and copy the heavy outlines of pattern on the larger squares. Make a separate cardboard pattern for each different size patch piece. Cut out patches as directed in General Directions. To piece together star-pattern blocks, read directions for Joining Diamonds on page 10. Following graph patterns, assemble blocks. For appliqué block, enlarge pattern on 1" squares, completing half-pattern indicated by dash lines. Cut muslin for block 10" square. Cut appliqué from print fabric, adding ⅛" seam allowance all around. Cut out oval shapes ⅛" in from their out lines; clip into ⅛" seam allowances around curves; turn allowance in and press. Pin appliqué to center of muslin square and slip-stitch around outside and around edges of ovals to secure muslin. (For more about appliqués, see page 90).

To plan quilt, lay out all pieced blocks on a large flat surface, using large star block as center. Add strips of dark color fabric between and around blocks, in width required to make them fit together (remember to add ¼" seam allowance around each strip). Use the small blocks as borders, repeating them in various colors. Quilt shown has wide borders along sides and narrower borders across top and bottom. Join strips and blocks in same manner as for joining patches. Sew small blocks together for borders, and add the borders to sides, top, and bottom.

Quilting: The quilting is done in a long zigzag pattern down length of quilt. Make zigzag lines about 1¼" apart, using edges of patch pieces as guides to keep lines straight.

Pin and baste quilt top, batting, and muslin lining together, and quilt as directed in General Directions. To finish quilt, trim away edges of cotton batting ½" all around edge. Turn edges of quilt top over edge of batting to inside. Turn in edges of quilt lining; fold edges of lining over top and stitch all around for finished edge.

MARINER'S COMPASS QUILT
continued from page 22

To make joining strips and borders, cut cardboard pattern 2" square. Cut 190 squares from blue fabric. Cut cardboard pattern in half diagonally for triangle pattern. Cut 380 triangles from white fabric and 12 from blue fabric. Cut triangle pattern in half to make pattern for small triangle. Cut 24 small triangles from white fabric. Join pieces as shown in illustration into long strips. First, make six strips, each with seven blue squares and 14 white triangles; add one blue triangle at one end and two small white triangles at other end. Join quilt blocks into three horizontal rows of three blocks each, with a strip between every two blocks. Make four more strips as for shorter strips, each with 24 blue squares, 48 white triangles, one blue triangle, and two small white triangles. Join the three rows of blocks together with a horizontal strip between rows; add a strip across top and bottom. Make two strips, each with 26 blue squares, 52 white triangles, one blue triangle, and two small white triangles. Join strips to sides of piece. Piece should measure 74¼" square, plus outside seam allowance. Cut four 2½"-wide strips from blue fabric, two 74¾" long and two 78¾" long. Right sides together and with ¼" seams, sew shorter strips to top and bottom of quilt top, then longer strips to sides. Quilt top should measure 78¾" square.

For lining, cut two pieces from white fabric 40⅜" x 79¾". Sew together on long sides with ½" seams, to make lining 79¾" square. Cut batting same size as quilt top.

Quilting: With ruler and tailor's chalk, mark straight lines on blue frames of quilt blocks, ¼" in from outer edges. Mark a circular line on inner edge of frame, ¼" from edge of pieced circle. Trace actual-size clamshell quilting pattern. Using dressmaker's carbon and tracing wheel to transfer pattern, mark a row of clamshells in corner areas of blue frame, keeping within outer marked line and diminishing number of shells in each row to one clamshell in corner.

On joining strips and borders, mark lines on blue squares and triangles, ¼" in from edge. Mark two corner-to-corner lines within each marked square, to form an X. On solid blue borders, mark diagonal lines ¼" apart to form pairs; make pairs ¾" apart.

Center batting and quilt top over lining, so that lining extends ½" all around beyond edge of top layers; pin and baste, following General Directions. Starting in center and working around and outward, quilt on all marked lines with white thread. Quilt also on patch pieces of circles and white triangles of strips, ¼" in from edges. Make extra quilting lines ¼" inside first quilting lines on red No. 5 pieces, green No. 1 pieces, and gold No. 2 pieces.

To finish edges of quilt, fold excess lining over front of quilt; turn in edges ¼" and slip-stitch to front. Press edges.

DELECTABLE MOUNTAINS QUILT
continued from page 19

To assemble quilt top, join quilt blocks into three horizontal rows of four blocks each, with a 16-piece joining strip between each block; white triangles in joining strips should all point in the same direction. Join the three horizontal rows by sewing a 70-piece strip between rows, with white triangles pointing in same direction. Sew 52-piece strips to the sides, with triangles on left side pointing up and triangles on right side pointing down. Sew a 74-piece strip across top, white triangles pointing to the right, and a 74-piece strip across the bottom, white triangles pointing to the left. Quilt top should measure about 68¾" x 90¾", including outside seam allowance.

For lining, cut two pieces from white fabric 35⅜" x 91¾". Join on long sides, right sides together and with ½" seams; press seam open. Lining will be ½" larger all around than quilt top. Cut batting same size as quilt top.

Quilting: With ruler and tailor's chalk, mark straight lines on quilt top, following dotted lines on Piecing Diagram. Make parallel lines on F and C triangles about ½" apart; repeat same quilting pattern on all the C, F, and G triangles of block. Pin and baste quilt top, batting, and lining together, centering top two layers so that lining extends ½" all around. Starting in center and working around and outward, quilt on all marked lines. On borders and joining strips, quilt on each long side, close to seam line; quilt also on each white triangle, close to all three seam lines.

To bind edges of quilt, turn excess lining to front, turn under raw edge of lining ¼", and slip-stitch to quilt top.

RADIANT STARS QUILT

SIZE: Approximately 76" x 78".

EQUIPMENT: Ruler. Scissors. Thin, stiff cardboard. Light and dark-colored pencils. Tracing paper. Dressmaker's (carbon) tracing paper. Tracing wheel. Tailor's chalk. Sewing and quilting needles. Quilting frame (optional).

MATERIALS: Closely woven cotton fabric: small prints 36" wide: red, ⅓ yd.; blue, 5 yds. White 45" wide, 7 yds. (includes lining). White sewing thread. Dacron polyester or cotton batting (Taylor Bedding).

DIRECTIONS: Read General Directions on pages 6 and 7. Quilt is constructed of 12 pieced star blocks, set with pieced panels. To make star block, see Piecing Diagram. Make cardboard patterns for star-block patches as follows. Pattern A: cut a 5" square. Pattern B: cut a ⅞" square. Pattern C: draw a ⅞" square; draw a diagonal line between two opposite corners; cut on marked lines for triangle. Pattern D: draw a rectangle ⅞" x 1"; draw a diagonal line between two opposite corners; cut on marked lines for triangle. Pattern E: make triangle from 1⅞" square in same manner as for C. Pattern F: trace actual-size diamond pattern. Pattern G: cut a 3⅛" square. Pattern H: make triangle from 4¾" square. Make several patterns for smaller pieces and replace when edges begin to fray.

Marking patterns on wrong side of fabric and adding ¼" seam allowance all around, cut patch pieces as follows: from red fabric, cut 96 of E; from blue fabric, cut 12 of A, 48 of B, 336 of C, 96 of D, 96 of F; from white fabric, cut 480 of C, 96 of D, 48 of G, and 48 of H. Assemble patch pieces as follows for one star block, following Piecing Diagram. Make 24 pieced squares by sewing 24 blue C triangles to 24 white C triangles on their long sides. Make eight pieced squares by sewing eight blue D triangles to eight white D triangles. To make one star point, join small patches as shown in diagram and sew to two sides of a red E triangle. Make eight star points in all and sew to sides of a blue A square, matching corners of A square and E triangles carefully, with a blue C patch between points on each side. To complete star block, set four white G squares and four white H triangles alternately between star points as shown in diagram. Block should measure 13" square, plus outside seam allowance. Make 11 more star blocks in same manner.

To frame blocks, cut 48 strips 2½" wide from blue fabric, 24 13½" long and 24 17½" long (measurements include ¼" seam allowance). Sew two shorter strips to opposite sides of each

block and two longer strips to remaining sides of block. Framed blocks should measure 15" square, plus outside seam allowance.

To make pattern for six-sided white panels, draw rectangle 5" x 17⅛" on cardboard. Mark midpoint on each short side; on each long side, mark a point 2½" from corner. Draw four diagonal lines connecting midpoints to nearest side points. Cut on marked lines for a six-sided shape. Marking pattern on wrong side of fabric and adding ¼" seam allowance all around, cut 31 panels from white fabric.

To begin assembling quilt top, make three vertical rows as follows, alternating five white panels with four star blocks in each row. Place star blocks

with their shorter blue framing strips at top and bottom. Sew a white panel between blocks and at top and bottom of row, centering long edge of panel on blue edge of block; to aid in centering, mark points on blue edges 1⁷⁄₁₆" from corners.

Join the three vertical rows by sewing four white panels between rows, centering on blue edges as before. Add a row of four white panels to left and to right of piece made.

To fill in spaces, cut 40 strips from blue fabric 2½" x 9⅝" (measurements include ¼" seam allowance). Sew ends of strips across corners of blocks, matching corners of each strip with angle of white panels where they join

continued on page 30

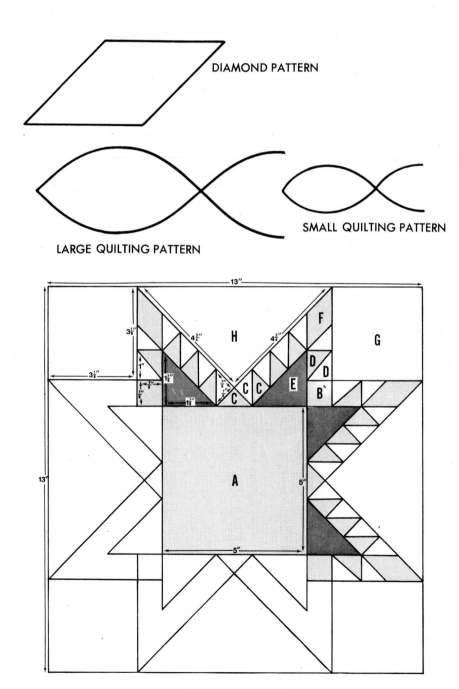

DIAMOND PATTERN

LARGE QUILTING PATTERN

SMALL QUILTING PATTERN

PIECING DIAGRAM

Radiant Stars Quilt *is entirely pieced, including the "garden maze" framing (compare with appliquéd Oak Leaf Quilt on page 93). New York State, 1860-1870.*

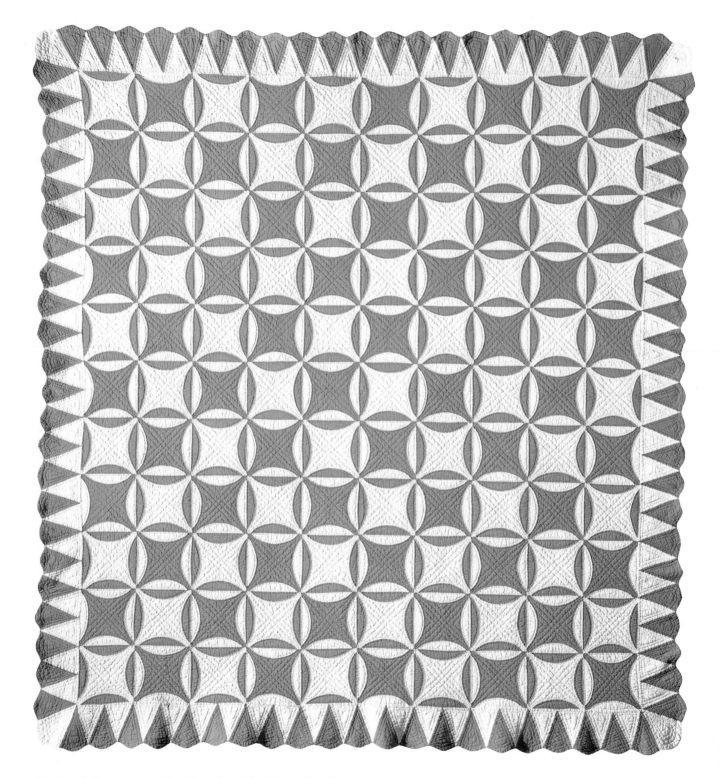

*The lovely "orange peel" pattern is not for the novice; it
takes careful cutting and stitching to fit the curved patches together.
This one won a prize at the Indiana State Fair, around 1930.
Directions for Orange Peel Quilt are on page 31.*

QUILT FROM MARGARET PENNINGTON

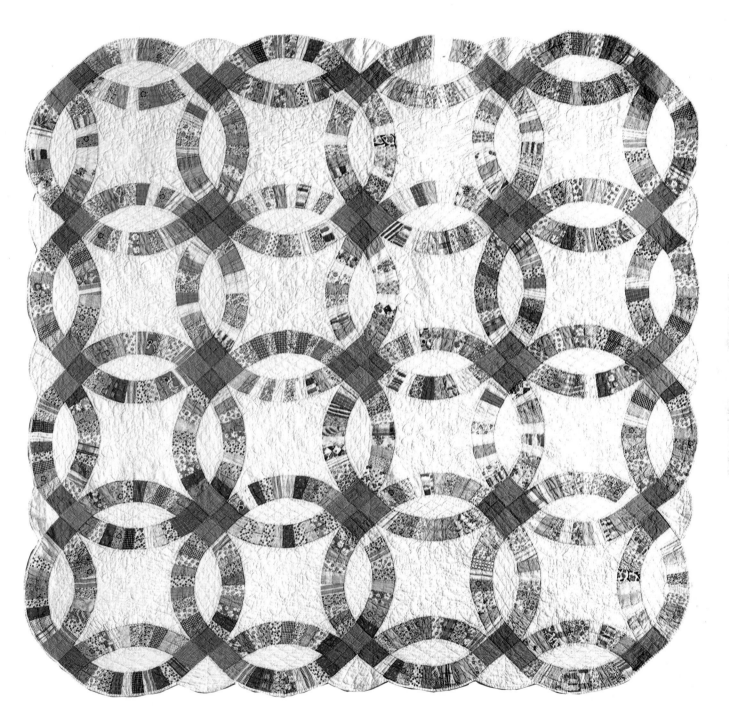

The "double wedding ring" seemed to be a favorite design in the 1920's, when this quilt was made. Little multi-colored wedges are pieced together to make oval segments, which are joined for an effect of overlapping rings. Wedding Ring Quilt on page 31.

RADIANT STARS QUILT

continued from page 26

blocks. Pin strips to short sides of white panels and across corners of diagonally opposite blocks, overlapping strips where they meet. Trim overlapped corners of blocks and overlapped strips to ¼″ from seams; sew seams.

To fill in edges, make triangle pattern by marking a 1½″ square on cardboard, drawing a diagonal line between opposite corners, and cutting on marked lines. Marking pattern on wrong side and adding ¼″ seam allowance all around, cut 18 triangles from white fabric. Sew triangles in place along edges. Trim outer ends of blue strips to match seam allowance of white triangles. Piece should measure 71″ x 93″, plus outside seam allowance.

For border, cut four strips 3″ wide from blue fabric, two 93½″ long and two 76″ long (measurements include ¼″ seam allowance). Sew longer strips to sides of quilt top and shorter strips to top and bottom. Quilt top should measure 76″ x 98″.

For lining, cut two pieces 38½″ x 98″. Join on long sides with ½″ seams; press seam open. Cut batting same size as lining and quilt top.

Quilting: With ruler and tailor's chalk, mark quilting lines on star blocks as follows. On each large white triangle (H), mark lines ¼″ in from two shorter sides of triangles; continue to mark lines ¼″ away until entire triangle is covered. Divide large blue square (A) into four right-angle triangles by marking corner-to-corner diagonal lines in both directions; mark each triangle section with same pattern as for H triangles. On smaller white squares (G), mark same pattern as for A. On red triangles (E), mark lines ¼″ in from seam lines, then mark another set of lines ¼″ inside first set.

Trace large and small quilting patterns. Using dressmaker's carbon and tracing wheel, transfer large pattern to all blue strips, continuing pattern to cover length of each strip. Transfer small pattern to white panels in diagonal rows ¼″ apart, parallel to a short side. With ruler and tailor's chalk, mark three parallel lines between rows.

Following General Directions, pin and baste lining, batting, and quilt top together. Starting in center and working around and outward, quilt on all marked lines; quilt on both sides of seams joining blue strips with panels and blocks. Quilt ⅛″ in from seams of each small patch.

To bind edges of quilt, cut four strips 1″ wide from blue fabric, two 76½″ long and two 98½″ long. Right sides together, sew strips to front of quilt along edges, with ¼″ seams. Fold strips to back of quilt; turn in edges ¼″, and slip-stitch to lining.

ORANGE PEEL QUILT

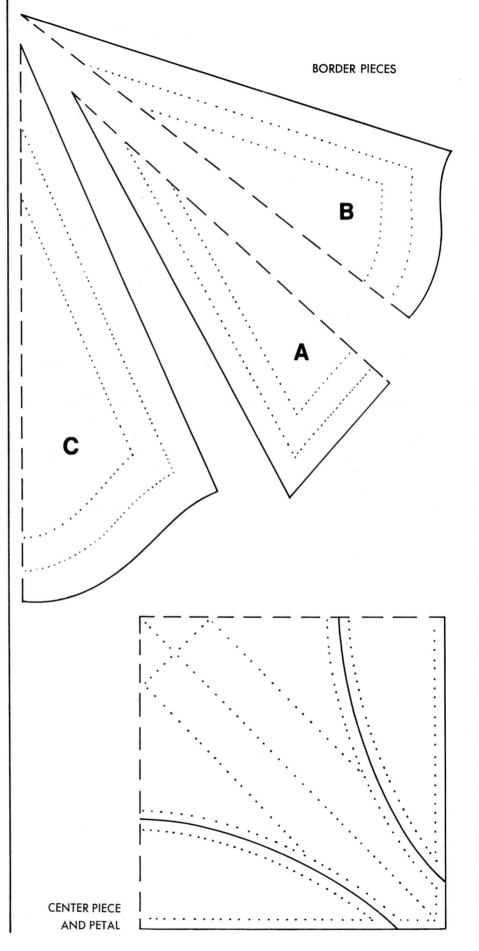

BORDER PIECES

B

A

C

CENTER PIECE
AND PETAL

ORANGE PEEL QUILT
shown on page 28

SIZE: About 76″ x 82½″.

EQUIPMENT: Tracing paper. Thin, stiff cardboard. Pencil. Ruler. Scissors. Straight pins. Sewing and quilting needles. Dressmaker's (carbon) tracing paper in a light color. Tracing wheel. Quilting frame (optional).

MATERIALS: Quilt top: Closely woven cotton fabric 44″-45″ wide: 4⅔ yds. each white and blue. Lining: White fabric 44″-45″ wide, 4¼ yds. Matching sewing thread. Dacron polyester or cotton batting (Stearns & Foster). White bias tape, 11 yds.

DIRECTIONS: Read General Directions on pages 6 and 7. Trace actual-size patterns; complete half and quarter-patterns indicated by long dash lines. Dotted lines indicate quilting. Make a cardboard pattern for the four-pointed center piece, the petal, and for each of the three border pieces. To cut patches, place patterns on wrong side of fabric with sides of points on the grain; mark and cut, adding ¼″ seam allowance all around. From blue fabric, cut 55 four-pointed center pieces, 220 petals, and 88 of border piece B (place left straight side on grain of fabric). From white fabric, cut 55 center pieces, 220 petals, 84 of border piece A (place right straight side on grain of fabric), and 4 of border piece C.

To make a square block, stitch four blue petals in place around a white center piece, right sides together. Block should measure 6½″ square, plus outside seam allowance. Make 54 more blocks in same manner. Make 55 blocks of four white petals stitched in place around a blue center piece. Clip into seams at curves; press to one side.

Beginning and ending with blue-centered blocks, make a vertical strip, alternating six blue-centered blocks with five white-centered blocks. Make four more vertical strips in this manner. Beginning and ending with white-centered blocks, make a vertical strip, alternating six white-centered blocks with five blue-centered blocks. Make four more vertical strips in same manner. Alternating color combinations, sew vertical strips together to form center of quilt top. Piece should measure 65″ x 71½″, plus outside seam allowance.

Beginning and ending with border piece B, make a border strip, alternating 21 border pieces B with 20 border pieces A. Make another border strip in same manner. Beginning and ending with border piece B, make a border strip, alternating 23 border pieces B with 22 border pieces A. Make another strip in same manner. Place border strips with scallops of border piece B toward you and sew a border piece C to the left end of each strip.

Matching longer strips to longer edges of quilt top and shorter strips to shorter edges, sew border strips to quilt edges. Sew remaining straight edge of border piece C to edge of adjacent strip at each corner. Quilt top should measure about 76″ x 82½″.

For lining, cut two pieces from white fabric 41¾″ x 76″. Sew together along long edges, right sides together and with ½″ seam allowance. Press seam open.

Quilting: Using dressmakers' carbon and tracing wheel, transfer dotted lines of patterns to appropriate fabric pieces. Following General Directions, pin and baste lining, batting, and quilt top together. Using matching thread, quilt on marked lines, beginning at center and working around and outward. Trim edges of lining and batting even with top layer. Insert quilt edges into fold of bias tape and stitch in place.

WEDDING RING QUILT
shown on page 29

SIZE: About 68″ square.

EQUIPMENT: Thin, stiff cardboard. Tracing paper. Pencil. Scissors. Ruler. Tailor's chalk. Tracing wheel. Dressmaker's (carbon) tracing paper. Sewing and quilting needles. Quilting frame (optional).

MATERIALS: Closely woven cotton fabric, 36″ wide: white, 7 yds. (includes lining); blue and red gingham, ⅓ yd. each; assorted prints totaling about 4 yds. Dacron polyester or cotton batting (Taylor Bedding). White thread. White bias tape, 7¾ yds.

DIRECTIONS: Read General Directions on pages 6 and 7. Quilt is constructed of 948 patches to make a design of 16 overlapping rings; there is no border. Trace actual-size patterns for patch pieces No. 1, 2a, 2b, 4, 5 on page 36; complete half and quarter-patterns indicated by dash lines. (Dotted lines indicate quilting patterns.) Cut a cardboard pattern for each piece. For patch piece No. 3, cut a cardboard pattern 2⅜″ square. Marking patterns on wrong side of fabric and adding ¼″ seam allowance all around, cut patches as follows: From white fabric, cut 40 of No. 1, 16 of No. 4, and 12 of No. 5. From print fabrics, cut 640 2a and 160 2b; cut one side of each patch on straight of fabric. From red and blue gingham, cut 40 each of No. 3.

Sew No. 2 pieces into curving strips by joining on long edges, right sides together and stitching on marked seam line. Make 80 strips of 10 pieces each, beginning and ending each strip with a No. 2b; all others in strip are No. 2a. On 40 of these strips, sew a blue gingham No. 3 piece to one end of strip and a red gingham No. 3 to other end. Assemble a shorter and a longer strip around a No. 1 piece to make a pointed oval shape; see Piecing Diagram A (page 36). Make 39 more ovals in same manner; clip into curves and press seams to one side. Assemble four ovals around one No. 4 piece, matching curves and placing ovals so that red gingham squares are adjacent to blue gingham squares; sew the five pieces together to make a circle. Make seven more circles in same manner.

To construct quilt top, see Piecing Diagram B (page 36); completed circles are indicated by shading. Place circles in rows as indicated and fill in with remaining ovals and No. 4 pieces, always placing a red gingham square against a blue gingham square (see color illustration). Sew pieces together; clip into seams and press to one side. On each side of quilt top, sew three No. 5 pieces in indentations. Quilt top should measure about 68″ square.

For lining, cut two pieces 34½″ x 68″. Join pieces on long sides, right sides together and with ½″ seam allowance. Press seam open. Cut batting same size as lining and quilt top.

Quilting: Using dressmaker's carbon and tracing wheel, transfer dotted-line quilting patterns from patch patterns to quilt top; straight-line patterns can be marked with a ruler and tailor's chalk. The dash line of piece No. 5 is also a quilting line.

Pin and baste lining, batting, and quilt top together, following General Directions. Starting in center and working around and outward, quilt on all marked lines.

Trim batting and lining to match contours of quilt top. Insert edges of quilt into folds of bias tape and sew edges of tape to quilt top and lining.

CAROLINA LILY QUILT

SIZE: 58" x 73¼".

EQUIPMENT: Scissors. Ruler. Thin, stiff cardboard. Hard, sharp pencils. Dressmaker's (carbon) tracing paper. Paper for pattern. Tracing paper. Tracing wheel. Tailor's chalk. Sewing and quilting needles. Straight pins.

MATERIALS: Closely woven cotton fabric 44"-45" wide: 6½ yds. white (includes fabric for lining), 1 yd. each red and apple green. Dacron polyester or cotton batting. Matching sewing thread.

DIRECTIONS: Read General Directions on pages 6 and 7 and How To Appliqué on page 90. Quilt is constructed of 20 pieced-and-appliquéd flower blocks set with plain blocks of squares and triangles; appliquéd borders are added and quilt is bound around edge.

To make flower blocks, see Piecing Diagram. A block is made with seven main patch pieces, indicated on diagram by heavy outlines and capital letters. Patch pieces A, B, and C are each made up of eight small patches, indicated on A by small letters. Stems and buds (indicated by dash lines) are appliquéd on after block is pieced together. Draw a pattern for 8¾"-square block, following dimensions given on Piecing Diagram; omit appliqués. Mark off main patch pieces (A, B, C, D, E, F) and small patch pieces in A. Be sure that all angles are accurate. When drawing piece A, begin by marking points along sides of square where angles touch, following given dimensions; then, as temporary guidelines, draw two corner-to-corner lines intersecting at center of square. All pattern lines will connect with marked points or guidelines. Make a separate cardboard pattern for small patch pieces a, b, c, d and for large patch pieces D, E, F. Cut patch pieces for entire quilt at once as follows, marking pattern on wrong side of fabric and adding ¼" seam allowance all around: From white fabric, cut 60 of a, 180 of b, 40 of D, 20 of E, and 20 of F; from red fabric, cut 240 of c; from green fabric, cut 60 of d. Following General Directions, piece patch A together with a, two b's, 4 c's, and d, then piece B and C (B and C are the same as A, except for two pieces transposed in each). Then piece together A, B, C, E, F and two D's, to make a complete block.

For appliqués, cut ½" strips from green fabric: 20 for main stem 7¼" long, 40 for curving stems 5½" long, and 40 for bud stems 1¾" long. Turn in raw edges ⅛" to make ¼"-wide stems. Trace actual-size pattern of bud; make a cardboard pattern and cut 40 buds from red fabric, adding ⅛" seam allowance all around. Draw guidelines on pieced block with tailor's chalk for placement of appliqués; make bud stems ½" from sides of Piece F and curving stems ½" below seam joining pieces E and F. Appliqué pieces in place. Make 19 more pieced-and-appliquéd blocks in same manner.

For plain white quilt blocks, make cardboard pattern 8¾" square. Cut 12 squares from white fabric, adding ¼" seam allowance all around. Cut cardboard pattern in half diagonally and cut 14 large white triangles in same manner. Cut cardboard triangle in half and cut four small white triangles.

To assemble quilt top, place flower blocks alternating with white blocks in diagonal rows, starting and ending each

continued on page 37

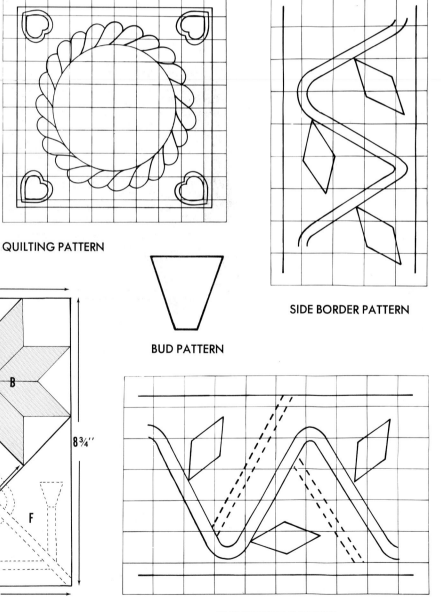

QUILTING PATTERN

SIDE BORDER PATTERN

BUD PATTERN

PIECING DIAGRAM

END BORDER PATTERN

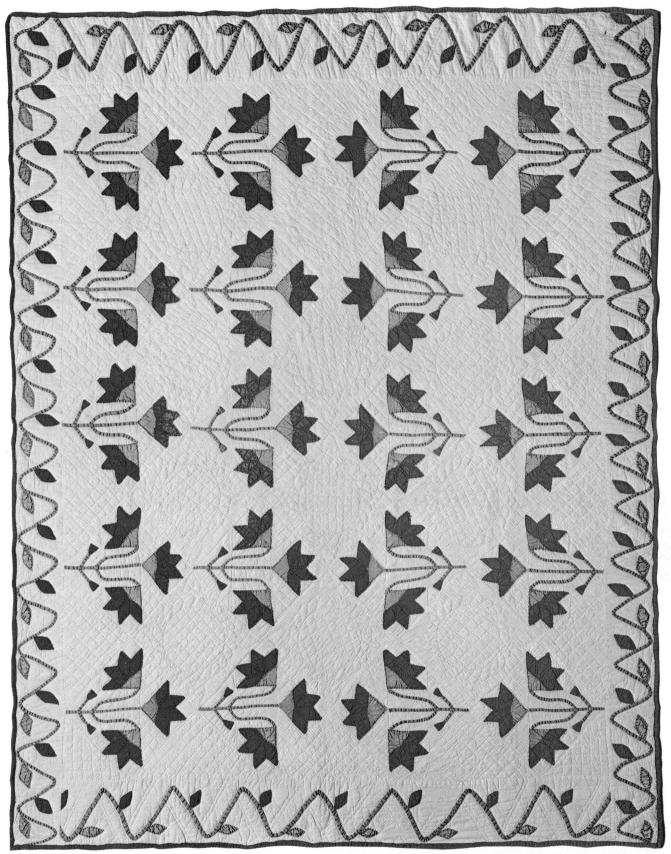

Red lilies bloom on a field of white in one of the most charming of the old patchwork patterns. Plain white blocks, alternating with flower blocks, are quilted in wreath design. Coverlet was made in Indiana but we call it by its most common name, Carolina Lily. COLLECTION OF MARY LAMB HARDING

SUNBURST QUILT

SIZE: About 82″ square.

EQUIPMENT: Tracing paper. Thin, stiff cardboard. Ruler. Light and dark-colored pencils. Tailor's chalk. Scissors. Sewing and quilting needles. Straight pins. Brown wrapping paper for pattern. Square. Quilting frame (optional).

MATERIALS: Quilt top: Closely woven cotton fabric 36″ wide: navy (A), 1¾ yds.; white-dotted navy (B), 1¾ yds.; light brown (C), 1½ yds.; yellow print (D), 1½ yds.; light orange print (E), 1⅜ yds.; pale green (F), 1¼ yds.; yellow-green print (G), 1⅛ yds.; medium green print (H), 1 yd.; pink print (I), 1 yd.; medium red print (J), ¾ yd.; dark red print (K), ½ yd.; light blue print (L), 5½ yds.; very dark red print (M), ⅛ yd. Lining: Print or plain fabric 44″ wide, 4⅝ yds. White and matching sewing threads. Dacron or cotton batting (Taylor Bedding).

DIRECTIONS: Read General Directions on pages 6 and 7. Trace diamond pattern. Cut several diamond patterns from cardboard; replace patterns as edges become worn and points rounded from repeated use. Cut diamond patches from fabric, following General Directions; mark on wrong side of fabric and leave space for ¼″ seam allowance. Cut 288 diamonds from fabric A, 272 B, 256 C, 240 D, 224 E, 208 F, 192 G, 176 H, 160 I, 144 J, 128 K, 104 L, 8 M. Make a triangular pattern by cutting a diamond pattern in half, crosswise. Cut 200 triangles from fabric L, in same manner as for diamonds.

Joining Diamonds: When joining diamonds to form a straight row, stitch all pieces together along sides cut on straight of goods. If the rows of diamonds are then joined together, you will be stitching along the bias edges; keep thread just taut enough to prevent seams from stretching. When diamonds are joined to form shapes other than straight rows, it is preferable to sew an edge cut on the straight of goods to one that is cut on the bias;

two bias edges sewn together tend to stretch, and the slightest deviation can distort the final result. Stitch from the wide-angled corner towards the pointed ends.

After joining diamonds, whether in rows or other shapes, press pieced sections with seams to one side; open seams tend to weaken construction. Trim seams at points, as you piece. There are two methods for joining the diamonds. **First method:** Hold patches together, right sides facing; seam together with small running stitches on pencil lines. If the problem of sharp points and true meeting of seams proves difficult with this method, prepare each patch as follows: **Second method:** Cut firm paper patterns the exact size and shape of cardboard patterns. Fit paper pattern within pencil outline on wrong side of patch, hold patch with paper pattern uppermost. Fold seam allowance over each side, and tack to the paper with one stitch on each side, allowing the thread to cross the corners. Finish by taking an extra stitch into the first side; cut the thread, leaving about ¼″. To make removal of tacking easier, do not knot thread or make any backstitches. Hold prepared patches right sides together, matching the edges to be seamed exactly. Whip together with fine, even stitches (about 16 to the inch), avoiding the paper as much as possible. The paper patterns may remain in place until the octagon shape is completed. To remove the papers, snip tacking thread once on each patch and withdraw thread; lift papers out.

The octagonal sunburst design is made up of eight identical triangular sections. Each section is made up of 25 rows; see Piecing Diagram (page 37). Make each section as follows: Starting with Row 1, piece together a light blue (L) triangle and a navy (A) diamond; then piece a white-dotted navy (B) triangle to the opposite side of the navy diamond, making a straight row. Continue piecing diamonds, following Piecing Diagram, until Row 1 is completed, ending with a very dark red (M) diamond. Piece Row 2 in same

manner, starting with a light blue triangle, but ending with a dark red print (K) diamond; Row 2 is one diamond shorter than Row 1. Continue piecing rows according to Piecing Diagram 1, with each row one diamond shorter than previous row, until reaching Row 25, which consists of one light blue triangle. Sew the 25 rows together in order, matching corners carefully, to form a triangular section. Make seven more sections in same way. Join four sections for each half of octagon, then join the halves for complete octagonal sunburst.

Measure octagon from point A to point B (see Piecing Diagram No. 2), disregarding outside seam allowance. Using this measurement for the sides, make a square from brown wrapping paper; the paper square is represented by heavy lines on Piecing Diagram No. 2. Draw a line on paper square from point A to point C. Place one-quarter of octagon face down on square as shown in diagram, first pinning back outside seam allowances along lines E-D and D-B. Draw lines on brown paper along octagon from point E to D and D to B. Remove octagon and cut out piece C-D-E and C-D-B from brown paper; use paper patterns to make cardboard patterns. Using cardboard pattern, cut eight corner pieces from light blue fabric, marking on wrong side of fabric and adding ¼″ seam allowance all around. Sew corner pieces together and to octagon, as shown in diagram. (**Note:** An alternate method of finishing quilt top: Sew two strips together (see next paragraph) to make a square of appropriate size for octagon. Appliqué octagon to square. However, this is not the way original quilt was made.)

Completed quilt top should measure about 82″ square. Cut two pieces from lining fabric, each 41½″ x 82″. Sew the two pieces together along long edges, with right sides together and making ½″ seams. Press seam open. Cut batting same size as lining and quilt top. Pin and baste lining, batting, and quilt top together, following General Directions.

Quilting: Using ruler and tailor's chalk, mark quilting lines parallel to seam lines of octagon, extending lines onto blue border to cover quilt top; mark lines ¼″ from seam lines on each side. Quilt along marked lines with white thread. (Original quilt was quilted on the machine.)

To bind edges of quilt, cut four 1″-wide strips of dark red fabric, each 82½″ long (or piece to get these lengths). With right sides together and making ¼″ seams, sew strips to top of quilt, ¼″ from edges. Turn to back of quilt, turn edges under ¼″, and slip-stitch to lining. Press edges.

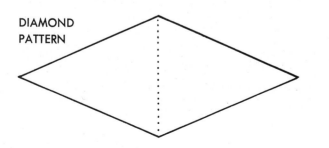

DIAMOND PATTERN

Radiant sunburst design is composed of 2500 small diamond patches sewn into eight triangular sections, which are joined for the octagon shape. A challenge for the expert seamstress only! Directions include special hints for joining diamonds. Circa 1870.

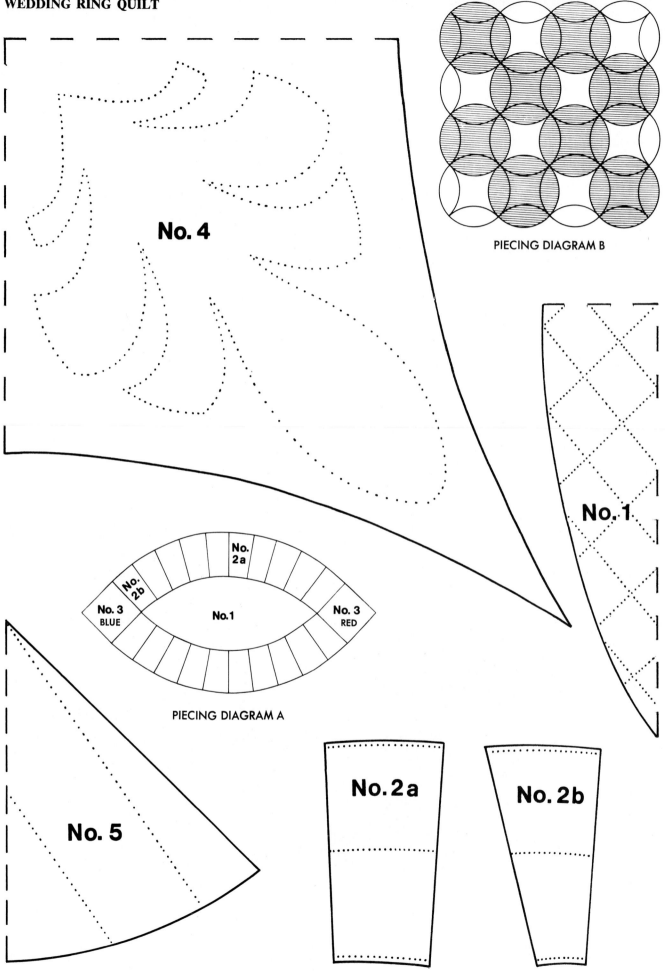

No. 4

PIECING DIAGRAM B

No. 1

No.
2a

No.
2b

No. 3
BLUE

No. 1

No. 3
RED

PIECING DIAGRAM A

No. 5

No. 2a

No. 2b

CAROLINA LILY QUILT
continued from page 32

row with a flower block. Row 1: 1 block. Row 2: 3 blocks. Row 3: 5 blocks. Row 4: 7 blocks. Row 5: 7 blocks. Row 6: 5 blocks. Row 7: 3 blocks. Row 8: 1 block. As quilt top is assembled, position flower motifs so that those on the left half of quilt face right and those on the right face left; see illustration. Place four large triangles on each long side of quilt top and three at each end; place a small triangle in each corner. Pin pieces together on seam allowances with right sides facing; stitch. Finished piece will measure 49½″ x 61¾″, including outside seam allowance.

For end borders, cut two strips from white fabric 6¼″ x 49½″. Sew a strip to top and bottom of quilt top, making ¼″ seam allowance. Enlarge the two Border Patterns by copying on paper ruled in 1″ squares. Using dressmaker's carbon and tracing wheel, transfer appliqué pattern (solid line) of End Bord-er to strips, ½″ from long edge of each strip but starting directly on side edge; repeat pattern all across strip to other side edge. Cut strips of green fabric ⅝″ wide for vine; turn in raw edges ⅛″ to make vine ⅜″ wide. Make cardboard pattern for leaves; cut outer leaves of green and inner leaves of red, adding ⅛″ all around for seam allowance. Appliqué vines and leaves to end borders.

For side borders, cut two strips of white fabric, each 4¾″ x 73¼″. Sew to sides of quilt top, with ¼″ seam allowance overlapping appliquéd edge of end borders. Transfer Side Border Pattern to side borders, ½″ from long edges and repeating all across border from end to end. Appliqué vine and leaves in same manner as end borders.

Quilt top should measure 58″ x 73¼″. For lining, cut two pieces 29½″ x 73¼″; sew long sides together with ½″ seams. Cut batting same size as lining and quilt top.

Quilting: Enlarge Wreath Quilting Pattern on paper ruled in 1″ squares. Transfer pattern to plain white squares of quilt top, using dressmaker's carbon and tracing wheel. In all plain white triangles of quilt top (including D triangles in flower blocks), make a grid pattern by drawing lines ¾″ apart and parallel to both right-angle sides of triangles; use ruler and tailor's chalk. Draw same grid pattern in center of wreaths, keeping lines parallel to sides of square blocks. On end borders, transfer dash-line quilting pattern with dressmaker's carbon and tracing wheel.

Pin and baste quilt top, batting, and lining together, following General Directions. Starting in center and working outward, quilt on all marked lines and around all patch and appliquéd pieces, including each part of flowers; use white thread.

To bind edges of quilt, cut 1¼″-wide strips of red fabric, two 58½″ long and two 73¾″ long (or piece to get these lengths). With right sides together and making ¼″ seams, sew strips to top of quilt, ⅜″ from edges. Turn to back of quilt and slip-stitch to lining, turning in raw edges of strips ¼″. Press edges.

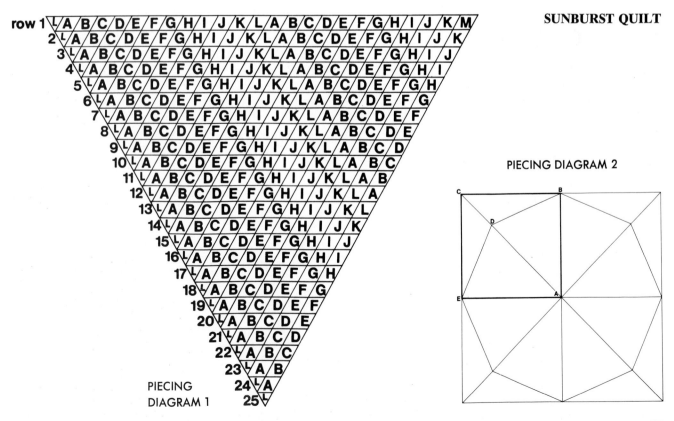

SUNBURST QUILT

PIECING DIAGRAM 1

PIECING DIAGRAM 2

GRANDMA'S GARDEN QUILT

SIZE: Approximately 69" x 99".

EQUIPMENT: Tracing paper. Paper for patterns. Thin, stiff cardboard. Scissors. Light and dark pencils, hard and sharp. Ruler. Sewing and quilting needles. Straight pins.

MATERIALS: Quilt top: Closely woven cotton fabric 36" wide: ¼ yds. peach; a total of 1½ yds. assorted solid colors; a total of 3 yds. assorted prints in colors related to solids; 1⅛ yds. dark green print. Closely woven cotton fabric 60" wide, 2¼ yds. white. Lining: 2¾ yds. white fabric, 72" wide. Edging: Dark green bias binding tape, ½" wide, 9½ yds. Dacron polyester or cotton batting. White sewing thread.

DIRECTIONS: Read General Directions on pages 6 and 7. Quilt is made up of 33 flower blocks of 19 hexagons each; blocks are joined with white hexagons; a border of green hexagons and white scalloped strips finishes quilt. To make quilt top, you will need 1105 hexagons: 33 of peach, 198 of solid colors, 396 of assorted prints, 334 of white, and 144 of dark green print (reserve for border). Trace actual-size pattern for hexagon; complete half-pattern indicated by dash lines. Make several patterns of cardboard (using hexagon outline only) and replace pattern when edges begin to fray. Cut hexagons from fabrics indicated, marking pattern on wrong side of fabric and making sure that two sides of pattern are on straight of goods; add ¼" seam allowances all around each piece. **Note:** Yardage is based on calculating 11 hexagons across 36" width, allowing for seam allowance.

To make a flower block, use one peach hexagon, six hexagons of one solid color, and 12 hexagons of one print in colors related to solid color. Sew solid-color hexagons around the peach, then print hexagons around the solid colors. Make 32 more flower blocks in same manner, combining a print and plain in related colors around a peach center in each block. Arrange

the 33 flower blocks in 13 horizontal rows, alternating a three-block row with a two-block row and starting and ending the work with a three-block row (see Piecing Diagram, which is one-quarter of entire quilt). If desired, make all blocks in each row identical. Join blocks by sewing a row of white hexagons between them, right sides together. When all blocks are joined together, sew a row of white hexagons all around outer edge of work, then a row of green-print hexagons around outer white hexagons. Turn under outer seam allowance of green hexagon border; press and clip so edges lie flat.

White outer border of quilt is cut in 10 pieces: two for each side border, one for each end border, and one for each corner. For each end border, measure quilt top from point A on one side to point A on other side (see Piecing Diagram). From white fabric, cut a 9½"-wide strip this length, plus 1". Place quilt top flat, right side down. Place white end strip, right side down, along edge of quilt top, matching long edge of strip with edges of turned-under seam allowance of green border at its deepest indentation; strip extends ½" beyond point A on each side. Pin in place at points where edges match. Turn quilt top right side up. Continue pinning white strip in place; baste. Slip-stitch (or topstitch) quilt top to white strip along edge of green border, from point A to point A. Turn quilt top to wrong side; trim white border strip ¼" beyond seam line, to match seam allowance of green border.

For each side border, measure quilt top from point B to midpoint of border. From white fabric, cut two 6½"-wide strips this length, plus ¾". Sew strips together at one end, right sides together and with ¼" seam allowance to make one long strip. Pin and sew strip to side of quilt in same manner as for end border, with ½" extending beyond point B on each side.

For each corner, cut a 6¼"-wide piece from white fabric to fit point A to point B, plus 2". Sew to corner as

for side and end strips, with 1" extending beyond points A and B. Press. Sew corner pieces at sides to end and border strips, right sides together; trim seam allowances to ¼".

To scallop border, mark a point for each indentation on outer edge of white fabric (see Piecing Diagram). For each point, mark three more: one 1" above and one 3" to each side of original point. Draw two slightly curving lines to connect the last three points marked; cut out along marked lines. Round border at corners.

For lining, measure quilt, add 1" to width and length, and cut from white lining fabric. Cut batting same size as lining.

Quilting: With ruler and tailor's chalk, transfer quilting lines inside hexagon pattern to each peach hexagon; half-pattern dash-line is also a quilting line. Enlarge End and Side Border patterns on 1" squares; complete half-patterns indicated by dash lines. With dressmaker's carbon and tracing wheel, transfer patterns to border: twice on each end border, ¾" from edge, and six times on each side border, 1¼" from edge. Transfer side border pattern to each corner, centering pattern and reversing direction so petals point outward. Center quilt top over batting and lining and pin and baste together, following General Directions. Starting from center of quilt and working outward, quilt around all seams joining two hexagons of different colors, stitching ¼" from both sides of seam; do not stitch around seams joining hexagons of the same color. Quilt around green hexagon border, ¼" from outer edge on white border. On end borders, quilt two hexagon shapes above each flower design, ¼" from green border. Quilt on all marked lines.

Trim batting and lining to match quilt top. Stitch green binding tape to quilt ¼" from edge of lining. Turn tape to front, and slip-stitch to top.

Press all edges.

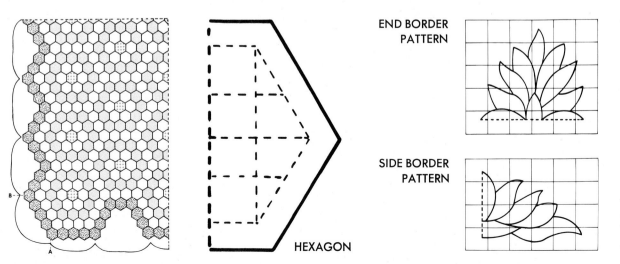

PIECING DIAGRAM

HEXAGON

END BORDER PATTERN

SIDE BORDER PATTERN

Grandma's Garden Quilt, pieced entirely of hexagons, is a later development from the early one-patch mosaic quilts. A scalloped border, quilted in flower motifs, adds an unusually pretty finish.

LOG CABIN COVERLET

SIZE: About 46½″ x 62″.

EQUIPMENT: Scissors. Ruler. Light and dark-colored pencils. Sewing needle.

MATERIALS: Quilt top: Closely woven satin or heavy silk fabrics 45″ wide in a variety of solid colors (with one print) evenly divided between dark and light shades (see Note below) and totaling about 4 yds.; brown velvet, ¼ yd. Lining, 36″ wide, 2¾ yds. Matching sewing thread.

Note: Design will be effective if random colors are used throughout, as long as a sharp contrast is maintained between the light and dark shades. A planned color scheme will create a more formal design. This quilt combines a planned color scheme with random colors (see illustration and Piecing Diagram A, as well as directions).

DIRECTIONS: Read General Directions on pages 6 and 7. Quilt is constructed of 48 pieced blocks arranged to make an overall design, plus a sawtooth edging.

To make each block, cut 16 strips ¾″ wide from satin fabrics (eight in light colors and eight in dark colors); follow Piecing Diagram A for length and color of each strip and add ¼″ seam allowance all around. Cut one piece from brown velvet 1¾″ square, adding ¼″ seam allowance. The colors of pieces A, B, G, H, and I are specified in the color key; pieces C, D, E, and F may vary in color from block to block, as long as the distinction is kept between light and dark shades. With right sides together, sew pieces into a square block; start piecing in the center by sewing the short yellow (B) strip to the brown square, then adding the longer yellow strip, then the short and longer dark print (C) strips, etc., continuing around in a counterclockwise direction until all the pieces are sewn on. Block should measure 7¾″ square, plus outside seam allowance. Make 47 more blocks in same manner.

To construct quilt top, see Piecing Diagram B, which shows upper half of quilt design. Following diagram, sew 24 blocks into six larger blocks (indicated by heavy lines) of four blocks each; then sew the larger blocks into two rows of three blocks each; sew rows together for upper half of quilt top. Sew remaining blocks together in same manner for lower half. Join halves along edge marked "center." Piece should measure about 46½″ x 62″, plus outside seam allowance.

For sawtooth edging, make cardboard pattern 2″ square. Marking pattern on wrong side of fabric and adding ¼″ seam allowance all around, cut about 200 squares from remaining satin fabrics. Keeping right side of fabric outside, fold each square in half diagonally to form a triangle; press lightly. Then fold triangle in half for a smaller triangle; press again to hold shape. Pin folded triangles to right side of quilt top, overlapping corners slightly and matching longest side of each triangle to edge of quilt top. Baste, then stitch on outside seam line of quilt top. Turn seam allowance to wrong side of quilt top, so that triangles point outward; press.

For lining, cut two pieces 31¾″ x 47″. Sew together on long sides with ½″ seam, to make piece 47″ x 62½″. Turn in edges of lining ¼″ all around; press. Wrong sides together, pin lining to quilt top, matching folded edge of lining to outer seam of quilt top; slipstitch pieces together. Tack through both layers wherever four blocks meet, tying on lining side. Press edges.

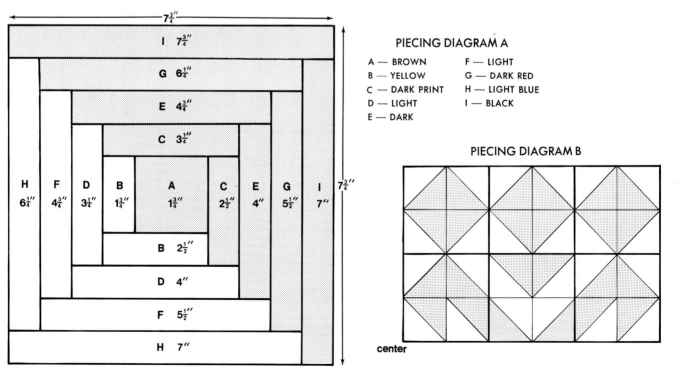

PIECING DIAGRAM A

A — BROWN   F — LIGHT
B — YELLOW   G — DARK RED
C — DARK PRINT   H — LIGHT BLUE
D — LIGHT   I — BLACK
E — DARK

PIECING DIAGRAM B

center

*An unusual variation of log cabin patchwork. Each
quilt block is composed of satin strips in light and dark
shades, sewn around a brown velvet square. New England; circa 1890.*

"CRAZY QUILT" RUNNER

SIZE: 34" x 79".

EQUIPMENT: Scissors. Ruler. Thin, stiff cardboard. Tailor's chalk. Pins. Sewing needle. Pencil.

MATERIALS: Scraps of fabrics totaling about 2¼ yds. in silk, satin, velvet, taffeta, damask, rayon, and ribbons, including prints, solid colors, and embroidered fabrics. Embroidery threads in silk, rayon, pearl cotton, or embroidery floss, in many colors. Maroon velvet 36" wide, ⅓ yd. Tufted balls from silk ball fringe, 6 gold and 6 maroon. For lining, heavy fabric (such as flannel) 36" wide, 2¼ yds.

DIRECTIONS: Read General Directions on pages 6 and 7. Runner consists of 32 8½"-square blocks, each pieced together with fabric scraps and embroidery; pointed borders are trimmed with balls. Make a cardboard template 8½" square. To make each block, lay out scraps of fabric on a large, flat surface. Choose adjoining colors for a pleasing effect and try to include a variety of fabrics in each square. In our runner, the patches showing flowers, teapots, birds, human figures, etc. are scraps of machine-embroidered fabrics. Patches were also combined to create shapes such as stars and fans. Cut patches where necessary to fit together, making squares, rectangles, triangles, and other shapes to form a piece that will allow a 9" square and using about 10 to 15 patches for each square. Overlap the patches about ½" and turn in raw edges of top patch (finished ribbon edges do not have to be turned under). Baste the patches together. Lay cardboard template on right side of assembled piece, centering as much as possible, and mark around with tailor's chalk. Trim piece to ¼" outside marked line, for seam allowance. To join patch pieces, use decorative embroidery stitches in silk, rayon, cotton, or embroidery floss. Choose floss in colors that contrast with the colors of patches to be joined. One or more colors may be combined to enhance the decorative effect. Use stitches singly or in combination over seams and also to decorate some patch pieces, if desired. The main object, however, is to have the embroidery hold the pieces together; at least part of the stitching must go over the seam. Details on this page show some of the many stitches used in the runner; see also the closeup in illustration on opposite page. You may, of course, use any embroidery stitches you like. Embroider only up to marked lines at edge of squares.

Right sides together and with ¼" seams, sew embroidered squares into eight horizontal rows of four squares each; press seams open. Embroider on right side over seam lines, using a variety of stitches. Join rows, again varying seams from square to square. Piece should measure 34" x 68".

For borders, cut two pieces from maroon velvet 5½" x 34", adding ¼" seam allowance all around. On wrong side of each piece, mark a line 2⅞" below seam line on one long side. To make pointed edges, cut a triangular cardboard template by cutting half of a 4" square. Mark points on wrong side of fabric by laying template with base of triangle on marked line and right-angle point at seam line; draw around right angle of triangle. Mark point six times across each border piece.

Trim fabric to ¼" from points for seam allowance. Join straight edge of border pieces to top and bottom of patchwork piece in same manner as for joining squares.

For lining, cut a piece same size and shape as patchwork front with border, including ¼" seam allowance all around. Right sides together, sew patchwork front and lining together on two long sides; turn to right side, press edges. Turn in seam allowance of border and lining at pointed edges and slip-stitch together.

To finish runner, sew a gold or maroon ball cut from silk ball fringe to each point, alternating colors.

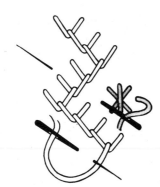

ZIGZAG FEATHERSTITCH WITH STAR FILLING

BLANKET STITCH

WIDE CRETAN STITCH

HERRINGBONE STITCH

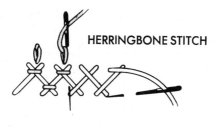

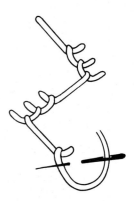

TRIPLE FEATHERSTITCH

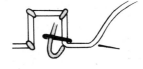

COUCHING

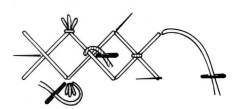

DIAMOND STITCH WITH COUCHING AND STRAIGHT STITCHES

This magnificent example of
Victorian "crazy quilting" was
undoubtedly a table runner.
Today, it might make a handsome
wall hanging. Crazy quilts
were made with luxurious bits
of fabric, joined with embroidery
in a kaleidoscopic design.
Directions are at left.

COLLECTION OF
RHEA GOODMAN-QUILT GALLERY, INC.

BOSTON COMMON QUILT

SIZE: About 75″ square.

EQUIPMENT: Ruler. Scissors. Thin, stiff cardboard. Light and dark colored pencils. Tailor's chalk. Sewing and quilting needles. Quilting frame (optional).

MATERIALS: Closely woven cotton fabric 36″ wide: medium blue, ½ yd.; random colors (both small prints and solid colors), totaling about 2½ yds.; fuchsia (for binding) ⅓ yd. (or use bias binding tape, 9 yds.). White cotton fabric 44″-45″ wide, 6¾ yds. (includes lining). Dacron polyester or cotton batting. White sewing thread.

DIRECTIONS: Read General Directions on pages 6 and 7. Make cardboard patch pattern 1⅝″ square. Cut 877 square patches as follows, marking pattern on wrong side of fabric and adding ¼″ seam allowance all around: cut 112 from medium blue fabric and 765 from random colors (both prints and plain). Cut cardboard pattern in half diagonally to make triangle pattern, and cut 116 triangle patches from white fabric in same manner as for squares. Cut triangle pattern in half and cut four small triangle patches from white fabric.

To make center-square block, sew square patches together in 23 straight rows, making first and last squares in each row blue and the remaining squares in random colors. Make one row of 23 squares, two rows of 21 squares, two rows of 19 squares, two rows of 17 squares, etc., until arriving at two rows of one blue square each. Sew rows together to make center-square block as follows: sew a 21-square row to the 23-square row, matching corners carefully and centering the shorter row on the longer row so that a blue square extends at each end of the longer row. Sew a 19-square row to the 21-square row in

the same manner. Continue sewing on progressively shorter rows until the last row of one blue square is reached, forming a triangle. Starting with the 23-square row again, sew a 21-square row to the other side. Continue sewing on rows in same manner as before until the last row of one blue square is reached, forming a stepped-edge square with a blue border all around. To straighten edges of square, sew a white triangle patch in each right-angle space formed by blue border squares; sew a small triangle patch at each end of the two longest horizontal and vertical rows, completing center-square block. Piece should measure about 28″, plus outside seam allowance.

To make a triangular corner block, sew square patches together in 17 straight rows, starting each row with a blue square and using random colors for all other squares. Make one row of 17 squares, one row of 16 squares, one row of 15 squares, etc., until arriving at row of one blue square. Join rows as follows: sew 16-square row to 17-square row, 15-square row to 16-square row, etc., making random-color end of rows flush with each other and blue end of rows one square shorter with each successive row. Last row will be one blue square, making a triangular block with a blue stepped edge on longest side. To straighten stepped edge, sew white triangle patches in spaces as for center-square block, ending with a white triangle at each end. Make three more triangular corner blocks in same manner.

For white center borders, cut four pieces 8″ x 42″ (measurements include ¼″ seam allowance). Sew a border piece to each side of center block, centering border piece so that an equal amount extends at each corner. To miter corners of borders, lay piece flat, right side down. Hold adjacent ends at

corners together with right sides facing. Keeping border flat, lift up inner corners and pin together diagonally from inner corners to outer corners; baste, then stitch on basting line. Cut off excess fabric to make ¼″ seam; press seam open. Sew the long side of a triangular corner block to each white inner border, to make center piece 58½″ square, plus outside seam allowance.

For outer borders, cut four pieces 8½″ x 75″ (measurements include ¼″ seam allowance). Sew to sides of center piece in same manner as for inner border, mitering corners. Quilt top should measure 75″ square.

For lining, cut two pieces 38″ x 75″ Sew together on long edges, right sides together, with ½″ seams. Press seams open. Cut batting same size as lining and quilt top.

Quilting: On pieced center square and four corner triangles, mark diagonal lines in both directions, going through corners of squares to make an "X" pattern on squares; use ruler and tailors' chalk. To mark borders, extend the diagonal lines in one direction over both inner and outer borders, making all lines parallel; then mark straight lines 1⅝″ apart over all borders, parallel to top and bottom of quilt; this makes a diamond pattern on borders.

Pin and baste lining, batting, and quilt top together, following General Directions. Quilt on all marked lines, starting in center and working around and outward.

To bind edges of quilt, cut four 1½″-wide strips from fuchsia fabric, 75½″ long, piecing together to get these lengths (or use a 1″-wide seam binding). Right sides together and making ¼″ seams, sew strips to front of quilt. Turn strips to back and slipstitch to lining, turning in edges ¼″. Press edges of quilt.

PINWHEEL QUILT

SIZE: About 62″ x 80½″.

EQUIPMENT: Thin, stiff cardboard. Paper for pattern. Light and dark pencils. Glue. Ruler. Tailor's chalk. Compass. Tracing wheel. Dressmaker's (carbon) tracing paper. Straight pins. Sewing and quilting needles. Quilting frame (optional).

MATERIALS: Closely woven cotton fabric 36″ wide: random colors (both prints and solid color), totaling about 3 yds. Cotton fabric 44″-45″ wide: yellow, ¾ yd.; white, 5¾ yds. (includes lining). Dacron polyester or cotton batting (Taylor Bedding). White

sewing thread.

DIRECTIONS: Read General Directions on pages 6 and 7. Quilt is made up of 30 pieced blocks, plus a two-color border quilted in a cable pattern. To make block, see Piecing Diagram, which is one-quarter of finished block. Draw an actual-size pattern of quarter-block, following dimensions on Piecing Diagram. Glue paper pattern to thin cardboard; cut out individual patterns for patch pieces A, B, C, D, E. Marking patterns on wrong side of fabric and adding ¼″ seam allowance all around, cut patches for entire quilt as follows: from random
continued on page 46

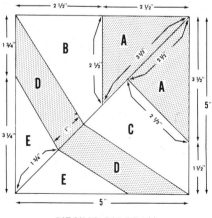

PIECING DIAGRAM

*Square-in-square: a good
design for the beginner! Sew
scraps into triangles and a big
square, add plain white borders.
Straight quilting lines make
X's and "hanging diamond"
patterns. From Indiana.
Boston Common Quilt, left.*

QUILT FROM MARGARET PENNINGTON

*A swirl of triangles makes
the lively pinwheel pattern.
When blocks are joined, a second
pattern of stars appears.
Patchwork design suggests the
quilting; cables trim border.
Pinwheel Quilt at left.*

PINWHEEL QUILT

continued from page 44

colors (both prints and plain), cut 240 A pieces and 240 D; from white fabric, cut 120 B pieces, 120 C, and 240 E. Following Piecing Diagram, join eight pieces to make a quarter-block, using a different color for each A and D piece. Make three more quarter-blocks in same manner, varying colors as much as possible. Join the four quarter-blocks to make a complete block, placing them so that the A pieces all meet in the center to form a pinwheel design; block should measure 10″ square, plus outside seam allowance. Make 29 more complete blocks in same manner. Sew blocks together in six horizontal rows of five blocks each. Sew rows together to complete center of quilt top; piece should measure about 50″ x 60″, plus outside seam allowance.

For inner border, cut four strips from yellow fabric: two 3¼″ x 60½″ and two 5¼″ x 56″, piecing to get lengths (measurements include ¼″ seam allowance all around). Sew the longer strips to long sides of quilt top, right sides together and with ¼″ seams. Sew remaining strips to top and bottom of quilt top in same manner. For outer border, cut four strips from white fabric: two 3½″ x 70″ and two 5¾″ x 62″. Sew to sides, top, and bottom of quilt top in same manner as for yellow border. Quilt top should measure 62″ x 80½″.

For lining, cut two pieces 32″ x 63″. Sew together on long sides with ½″ seams; press seam open. Lining will measure ½″ larger all around than quilt top. Cut batting same size as quilt top .

Quilting: Using ruler, compass, and tailors' chalk, mark quilting lines as follows: On pinwheels, mark straight lines on each A patch, ¼″ in from seam lines. On stars (between pinwheels), mark a straight line in center of each D patch, to form a star shape. On white area within stars, mark lines ¼″ from inner seam line of star; mark a circle 1¾″ in diameter in center of white area. In white area around pinwheels, mark lines ¼″ and 1″ from outer seam line of stars. Using tracing wheel and dressmaker's carbon, transfer Larger Quilting Pattern of Ribbon-Stripe Quilt (see page 8) to wider white and yellow borders at top and bottom of quilt. Transfer inner cable of same quilting pattern to white and yellow borders at sides.

Pin and baste lining, batting, and quilt top together, following General Directions; center top layers so that lining extends ½″ all around. Quilt on all marked lines.

To bind edges, turn excess lining to front of quilt, turn in raw edges ½″, and slip-stitch to quilt top.

BEAR'S PAW QUILT

SIZE: About 75″ x 86″.

EQUIPMENT: Thin, stiff cardboard. Pencil. Ruler. Scissors. Straight pins. Sewing and quilting needles. Tailor's chalk.

MATERIALS: Quilt top: 36″-wide cotton fabric, 3½ yds. dark-patterned and 3⅜ yds. light-patterned (use all one color for each or various colors to add up to these amounts); 2½ yds. navy with a small white figure. Quilt lining: 40″-wide cotton fabric, 5 yds. Black and white sewing thread. Dacron polyester or cotton batting, 81″ x 96″.

DIRECTIONS: Read General Directions on pages 6 and 7. Quilt is made up of 42 blocks, each 10¾″ square. Dimensions and shape of each patch are given in Piecing Diagram. Following General Directions, make a cardboard pattern for patches A, B, C, D, and E. Shaded areas indicate those patches to be cut from dark-patterned fabric and unshaded areas those patches to be cut from light-patterned fabric. For each block, cut the following patches, marking on wrong side of fabric and adding ¼″ seam allowance: four of A (3″ square), four of B (1½″ square), one of C (1¾″ square), 32 of D (half of a 1½″ square; 16 light, 16 dark), and four of E (strip 1¾″ x 4½″). Follow General Directions for sewing patches together to form block 11¼″ square (includes outside seam allowance). Make 42 blocks. Cut six strips of navy fabric (with pattern running lengthwise), each 2¼″ wide, 11¼″ long. Arrange seven blocks into one long strip with navy strips between blocks; sew together, right sides facing, with ¼″ seams. Repeat to make five more strips of seven blocks with navy strips between. Cut five navy strips, again with pattern running lengthwise, each 2¼″ wide, 86¼″ long (or piece to make this length). Arrange the quilt-block strips together side by side with a navy strip between; sew together, right sides facing and with ¼″ seams. Quilt top should measure 73¾″ x 86¼″. Press all seams of quilt top in one direction; do not press seams open.

For lining, cut two pieces, each 39½″ x 88½″; sew long edges together, right sides facing and with ½″ seams, to make piece 78″ x 88½″. Press seam open.

Cut batting the size of quilt top, plus ¾″ on three edges for border.

Place lining wrong side up on flat surface; place batting on top with shorter edges flush on one side and ¾″ of batting extending on all other edges. Place quilt top on batting, again one edge flush and an even margin on other edges. Pin and baste quilt top, batting, and lining together, following General Directions.

Quilting: Mark diagonal lines across entire quilt in one direction only, spacing lines about 1¾″ apart; use a ruler and tailor's chalk. Hand-quilt along these lines with white thread.

To finish quilt at flush edges, trim away ¼″ of batting, turn edge of lining over batting, turn under ¼″ seam allowance on quilt top, and stitch across to close (this will be top of quilt when placed on bed). For each of the remaining edges, turn margin of lining to top of quilt, turn in ¼″ of margin and slip-stitch to top of quilt.

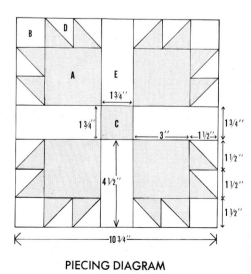

PIECING DIAGRAM

*Plaids, stripes, dots, and
prints — a scrap bag of warm-toned
patches set against pale
makes a cozy Bear's Paw Quilt.
Small triangles sewn around two
sides of square create "paw."*

COLLECTION OF MARGAY FERGUSON

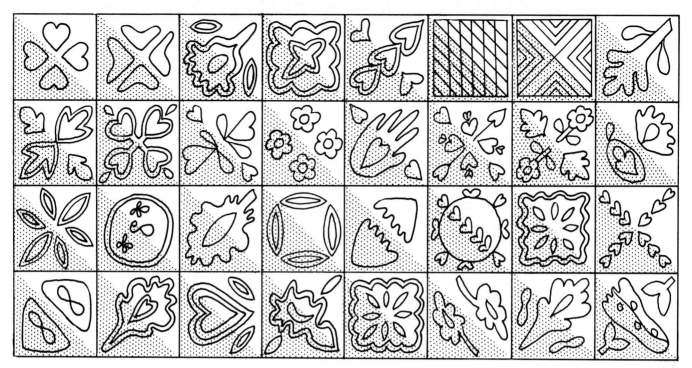

QUILTING DESIGNS

LOST SHIPS QUILT

SIZE: About 69¼″ x 94″.

EQUIPMENT: Ruler. Scissors. Thin, stiff cardboard. Light and dark-colored pencils. Tailor's chalk. Tracing wheel and dressmaker's (carbon) tracing paper (optional). Sewing and quilting needles. Quilting frame (optional).

MATERIALS: Quilt top: Closely woven cotton fabric 36″ wide: a variety of small prints plus one solid color, totaling about 5⅓ yds.; white fabric 45″ wide, 3¾ yds. Lining: Fabric 36″ wide, 5¼″ yds. White thread. White bias binding tape, ½″ wide, 9¼ yds. Dacron polyester or cotton batting.

DIRECTIONS: Read General Directions on pages 6 and 7. Quilt is constructed of 88 pieced blocks, plus a narrow pieced border.

To make block, cut triangle patterns as follows: Draw a 5½″ square on cardboard, connect two opposite corners with a diagonal line and cut on marked lines for large triangle. Cut small triangle in same manner, using a 1⅜″ square. Marking patterns on wrong side of fabric and adding ¼″ seam allowance, cut 88 large triangles from white fabric and 88 from colored fabrics; cut 1760 small triangles from white fabric and 1760 from colored fabrics (20 to match each large colored triangle).

Assemble each block by sewing a large colored triangle to a large white triangle on long sides, to make 5½″ square (plus outside seam allowance). Sew 20 1⅜″ squares in same manner, using 20 small white triangles with 20 small colored triangles (matching color to large triangle). Sew small squares into strips, keeping triangles all pointed in same direction within strip; make two strips of six squares each and two strips of four squares each. Sew strips around large pieced square, keeping all triangles in same direction, to make block 8¼″ square (plus outside seam allowance). Make 87 more blocks in same manner.

Sew blocks into 11 horizontal rows of eight blocks each, then sew rows together for main body of quilt top, always keeping triangles in same direction. For border, cut 232 small triangles from white fabric and 232 from colored fabric, using all colors in quilt. Sew triangles into squares as before, then sew squares into strips, making two strips of 48 squares each and two strips of 68 squares each. Sew shorter strips to top and bottom of quilt top and longer strips to sides. Piece should measure 69¼″ x 94″.

For lining, cut two pieces 35⅛″ x 94″. Sew together on long sides with ½″ seams; press seam open. Cut batting same size as lining and quilt top.

Quilting: The diagram above shows many of the patterns used to quilt the large squares. Adapt these patterns as desired, drawing free-hand, or enlarge each design to actual size of 5½″ square by photostating. Transfer designs to quilt top with tracing wheel and dressmaker's carbon. Or, for simpler quilting, mark a grid pattern over large squares with ruler and tailor's chalk, marking diagonal lines 1″ apart in both directions.

Following General Directions, pin and baste quilt top, batting, and lining together. Starting in center and working around and outward, quilt on all marked lines; quilt on each large triangle and on each small white triangle, ⅛″ in from seams.

Insert edges of quilt into fold of white bias tape and stitch in place.

Simple but effective patchwork design is created with triangles in two sizes. Quilt is a sampler of quilting patterns, however, with about three dozen motifs decorating the large squares. Made around 1860-1870, the quilt was found in New England. In the southern mountains, pattern is also known as Rocky Glen.

THOMAS K. WOODARD AMERICAN
ANTIQUES AND QUILTS

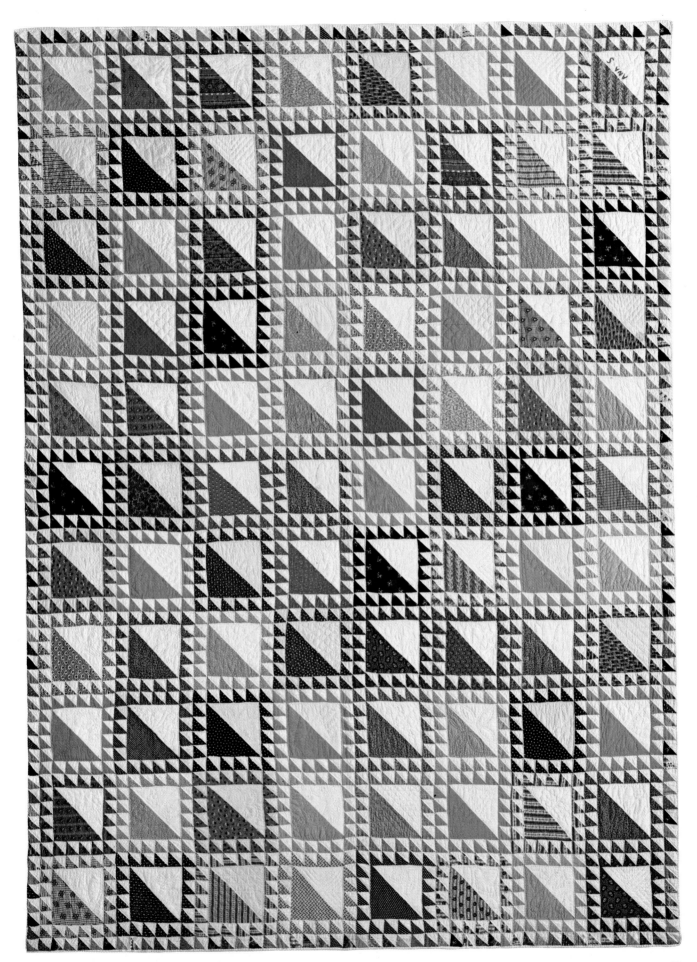

49

WILD GOOSE CHASE QUILT

SIZE: About 89″ square.

EQUIPMENT: Ruler. Scissors. Light and dark-colored pencils. Thin, stiff cardboard. Tailor's chalk. Sewing and quilting needles. Quilting frame (optional).

MATERIALS: Closely woven cotton fabric 36″ wide: assorted prints (with one color predominating) totaling about 5½ yds. White cotton fabric 45″ wide, 8¾ yds. (includes lining). White sewing thread. Dacron polyester or cotton batting (Stearns & Foster).

DIRECTIONS: Read General Directions on pages 6 and 7. Quilt is made up of 36 pieced blocks, set with pieced joining strips. To make patch patterns, see Piecing Diagram, which gives dimensions and shape of each patch. Make cardboard patterns for patches A (3⅜″ square), B (half of 5⅛″ square), C (2⅜″ square), D (half of 2⅜″ square), and E (half of 1-11/16″ square). For each block, cut one of A, four of B, four of C, and eight of D from print fabric (use one print or combine two or three in a block, as desired); cut 24 of E from white fabric. Join patches to make block, starting with smaller pieces; see Piecing Diagram. Block will measure 12″ square, plus outside seam allowance. Make 35 more blocks in same manner.

For joining strips, cut 84 pieces 2⅞″ x 12½″ from white fabric (measurements include ¼″ seam allowance all around). Assemble pieced blocks into six horizontal rows of six blocks each, with a white piece between blocks and at beginning and end of each row. Cut 49 squares from one print fabric, using C pattern. Assemble squares and remaining white pieces into seven horizontal strips, each with seven squares alternating with six white pieces. Assemble quilt top by sewing pieced strips between rows of blocks and at top and bottom of finished piece. Quilt top should measure 89⅛″ square.

For lining, cut two pieces 45″x89⅛″ from white fabric. Sew together on long sides with ⅜″ seams; press seam open. Cut batting same size as lining and quilt top.

Quilting: With ruler and tailor's chalk, mark quilting lines ½″ apart over quilt top: on white pieces of joining strips, mark lines diagonally, alternating direction every other strip, both vertically and horizontally; on print squares of joining strips, mark all lines horizontally; on print triangle patches of blocks, mark lines parallel to long side of triangles; on large squares of blocks, mark lines parallel to two opposite sides, alternating direction of lines every other block across horizontal rows of quilt top; on small squares within each block, mark same pattern as large squares, but alternating direction, moving clockwise around block.

Pin and baste lining, batting, and quilt top together, following General Directions. Starting in center and working around and outward, quilt on all marked lines; quilt on white triangle patches, ⅛″ in from seams.

To bind edges of quilt, cut four 1″-wide strips 89⅝″ long (piece to get lengths) from same print fabric used for squares in joining strips. Right sides together, sew strips to front of quilt with ¼″ seams. Fold strips to back of quilt, turning in raw edges ¼″, and slip-stitch to lining. Press all edges.

PIECING DIAGRAM

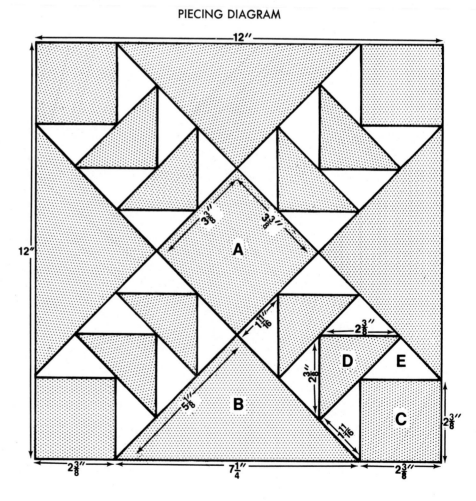

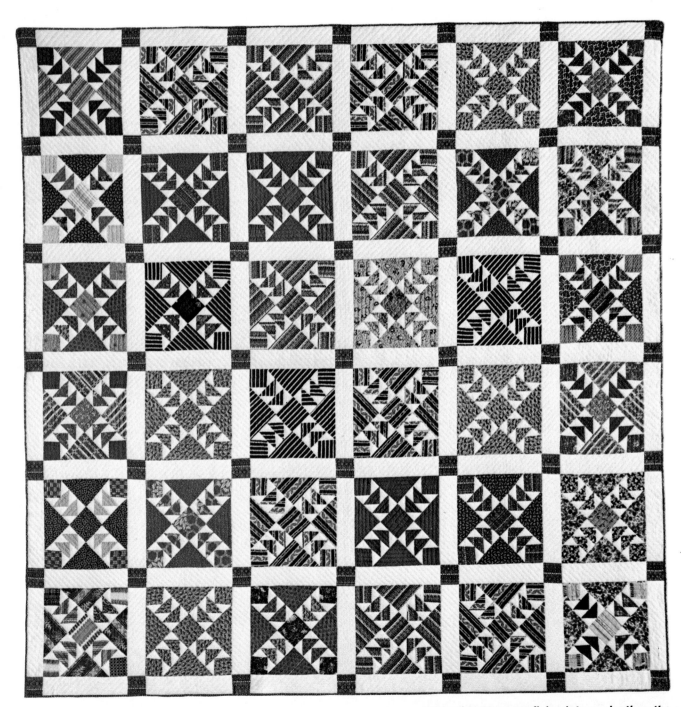

When the geese are flying into each other, the patchwork is called Wild Goose Chase! In this quilt, the fabrics are particularly well chosen, with colors and patterns blending in subtle harmony. Quilt was made in Connecticut, about 1860-1870.

QUILT FROM THOMAS K. WOODARD AMERICAN ANTIQUES AND QUILTS

VARIABLE TRIANGLES QUILT

shown on page 42

SIZE: About 65½" x 77".

EQUIPMENT: Scissors. Ruler. Thin, stiff cardboard. Light and dark-colored pencils. Tailor's chalk. Tracing paper. Dressmaker's (carbon) tracing paper. Tracing wheel. Sewing and quilting needles. Quilting frame (optional).

MATERIALS: Closely woven cotton fabric 36" wide: dark (or medium) prints with brown predominating, totaling about 2 yds.; light prints on white background, totaling about 2 yds. Cotton fabric 45" wide: red, 1 yd.; white, 5 yds. (includes lining). White sewing thread. Dacron polyester or cotton batting (Taylor Bedding).

DIRECTIONS: Read General Directions on pages 6 and 7. Quilt is pieced entirely of triangle patches, including the border.

To make pattern for small triangle, draw a 2" square on cardboard; draw a diagonal line connecting two opposite corners; cut on marked lines. Make patterns for medium and large triangles in same manner, using 4¼" and 6" squares.

Marking patterns on wrong side of fabric and adding ¼" seam allowance all around, cut triangle patches as follows: From red fabric, cut 96 small triangles, 22 medium, and 55 large. From solid white fabric, cut 96 small triangles, 18 medium, and 57 large. From dark print fabrics, cut 576 small triangles. From light print fabrics, cut 576 small triangles.

Sew small red and solid white triangles together on long sides to make 96 red/white 2" squares. Make 512 print squares in same manner, combining a dark-print triangle and a light-print triangle in each square; there will be print triangles left over. To make one block, assemble 16 print squares, three red/white squares, two dark-

print triangles, and two light-print triangles into a hexagon shape (see Piecing Diagram); sew pieces into rows first, then rows into a block, alternating light and dark triangles throughout. Make 31 more blocks in same manner.

To make horizontal row, place four blocks side by side, with red triangles all pointing upward. Sew medium and large red and white triangles to blocks as follows, working left to right: First block: sew a medium white triangle to side A (see Piecing Diagram), medium red triangle to side B, and large white triangle to side D. Second and third blocks: sew large red triangle to side B and large white triangle to side D. Fourth block: sew large red triangle to side B, medium red triangle to side C, and medium white triangle to side D. Sew the four pieced sections into a horizontal row, keeping same order. Make seven more rows in same way.

Sew rows together, keeping all red triangles pointing upward, for main body of quilt top. Piece should measure 56½" x 69", plus outside seam allowance.

For borders, make four strips with remaining triangles: For side borders, make two strips of eight large white triangles and seven large red triangles each, sewing triangles together on short sides; sew medium red triangle to each end, to complete strips. For bottom border*, sew nine large white triangles and eight large red triangles together in same manner, with a medium red triangle at each end. *(**Note:** In bottom border, four of the white triangles will have to be reduced a little in size to fit the bottom of the small-triangle blocks. Cut half of a 4" square of cardboard for new triangle pattern. Place pattern on each of the four white triangles and mark around it. Cut out new triangle, adding ¼" seam allowance. Assemble all triangles into strip as directed above,

alternating larger and smaller white triangles.) For top border*, sew nine large red triangles and eight large white triangles together, with a medium white triangle at each end. *(**Note:** Reduce size of four of the red triangles in same manner as for white triangles in bottom border.) Right sides together and with ¼" seams, sew side borders to main body of quilt top, then top and bottom. Piece should measure about 65½" x 77".

For lining, cut two pieces from white fabric 33¼" x 77". Sew together on long sides with ½" seams; press seam open. Cut batting same size as lining and quilt top.

Quilting: Trace actual-size circle quilting pattern; complete quarter-pattern indicated by dash lines. Using dressmaker's carbon and tracing wheel, transfer pattern to center of all large red/white squares of quilt top, including square shapes that overlap borders; straight lines of quarter-pattern should lie horizontally and vertically. With ruler and tailor's chalk, mark straight vertical lines ¾" apart over main body of quilt top, skipping over large red/white squares; extend pattern onto top and bottom borders in same manner. Mark same pattern horizontally on white triangles of side borders and diagonally on corner triangles of quilt top.

Following General Directions, pin and baste lining, batting, and quilt top together. Starting in center and working around and outward, quilt on all marked lines.

To finish edges of quilt, cut four 1"-wide strips from red fabric, two 66" long and two 77½" long; piece to get these lengths. Sew strips to front of quilt, right sides together and with ¼" seams. Fold strips to back of quilt, turn in raw edges ¼", and slip-stitch to lining. Press edges.

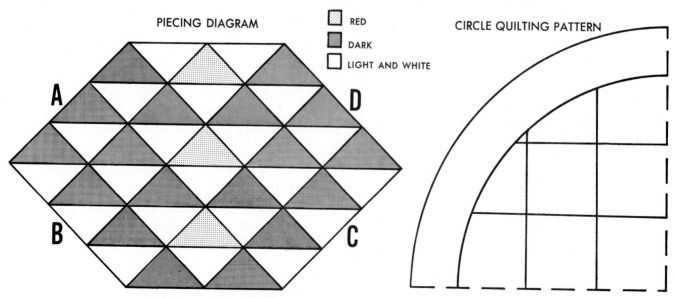

PIECING DIAGRAM

▨ RED
▨ DARK
☐ LIGHT AND WHITE

CIRCLE QUILTING PATTERN

The quilt we call "Variable Triangles" is an unusual design, possibly the invention of its maker. Entire quilt top, including border, is pieced with large and small triangles (compare with another large-small triangle design on page 49). The muted prints of smaller patches soften the red-white sharpness of larger patches. Pennsylvania, 1890.

COLLECTION OF TONY ELLIS AND BILL GALLICK

TRIPLE IRISH CHAIN QUILT
continued from page 67

lines over red/green areas of main body of quilt top, making all lines parallel to first group; mark three groups from left side to bottom and three groups from top to right side. Mark same pattern of seven groups of nine lines each in opposite direction, starting with a line from top right corner to lower left corner. Lines will cross to form a diamond pattern around each gold piece, touch-ing corners. Mark a second diamond inside first diamond, with parallel lines ⅝″ away and cutting across corners of gold center.

Using dressmaker's carbon and tracing wheel, transfer center-piece quilting pattern to gold pieces. Enlarge border quilting pattern on paper ruled in 1″ squares. Transfer pattern to border with inner lines touching inner seam line of gold border; start in corners and repeat cable pattern on each side.

Following General Directions, pin and baste lining, batting, and quilt top together. Quilt on all marked lines, starting in center and working around and outward. Trim corners to a slightly rounded shape.

To finish edges, cut four strips 1¼″ x 81″ from red fabric (piece to get lengths). Sew strips to front of quilt ⅜″ from edges, right sides together and with ¼″ seams. Fold strips to back of quilt, turn in edges ¼″, and slip-stitch.

TRIANGLES QUILT

SIZE: About 77½″ x 79″.
EQUIPMENT: Ruler. Scissors. Tracing paper. Thin, stiff cardboard. Light and dark-colored pencils. Tailor's chalk. Sewing and quilting needles. Quilting frame (optional).
MATERIALS: Closely woven cotton fabric 36″ wide: a wide variety of dark and light prints, plus a few solid colors, totaling about 6¾ yds.; red with a small black print, 2 yds.; tan with a soft red print, 2¼ yds. Lining, 45″ wide, 4½ yds. Dark gray sewing thread. Dacron polyester or cotton batting (Stearns & Foster).

DIRECTIONS: Read General Directions on pages 6 and 7. Trace actual-size pattern as it is for small triangle. Trace pattern again and complete half-pattern indicated by dash lines, for large triangle. Make cardboard patterns for small and large triangles. Marking patterns on wrong side of fabric and adding ¼″ seam allowance all around, cut 300 large triangles and 24 small triangles from various print and plain fabrics. Sew large triangles into 12 horizontal rows of 25 triangles each, joining them on their long sides and alternating light and dark triangles*; begin and end six rows with dark triangles and six rows with light triangles. To complete rows, sew a small triangle to each end. Join rows of triangles for main body of quilt top, again alternating light and dark colors; position rows so that points of adjacent triangles touch. Piece should measure 55½″ x 57″, plus outside seam allowance.

*(**Note:** If desired, pattern can be varied by occasionally using a dark triangle in place of a light triangle, so that there are three dark triangles together in a row. This will create a large dark triangle in the finished quilt design; see illustration.)

For first border, cut four strips 6″ wide from red print fabric, two 56″ long and two 68½″ long (measurements include ¼″ seam allowance). Sew shorter strips to top and bottom of main body of quilt top, then longer strips to sides. For second border, cut four strips 6¼″ wide from tan print fabric, two 67″ long and two 79½″ long. Sew shorter strips to sides, then longer strips to top and bottom. Piece should measure 78½″ x 80″.

For lining, cut two pieces 39¼″ x 79″. Sew together on long sides with ½″ seams, to make lining 77½″ x 79″. Cut batting same size as lining.

Quilting: With ruler and tailor's chalk, mark a diagonal line in each corner of quilt top, connecting main body of piece with outermost corner of border. On inside edges of red border, mark two points on each of the four sides, to divide each side into three even sections. On outside edges of tan border, mark a line ½″ from each edge (for fold line), then mark three points on each fold line, to divide each side into four even sections. To make zigzag pattern, draw line connecting inner end of a corner line to first point marked on outer border, then another line from outer border to first point on inner border, then back to outer border, etc., continuing around quilt with a zigzag pattern of triangles over entire border. Mark another set of triangles, 1″ away and parallel to first lines. Continue to mark lines until entire border is covered with a pattern of parallel triangles.

Following General Directions, pin and baste lining, batting, and quilt top together, centering pieces so that quilt top extends ½″ beyond other two layers. Starting in center and working around and outward, quilt on each triangle patch, ⅛″ from seam lines. Quilt on all marked lines of border, except for fold line.

To finish quilt, fold excess fabric of quilt top to back, turn under edge ¼″, and slip-stitch to lining. Press edges.

TRIANGLE PATTERN

Triangles, the simplest of motifs, are juxtaposed for a surprisingly beautiful effect. The simple light-dark scheme is varied by using an occasional dark triangle out of sequence, thus creating images of larger triangles (or "pyramids") in the quilt's overall design. From Pennsylvania; made around 1895.

FLYING GEESE QUILT

SIZE: Approximately 79" x 85".

EQUIPMENT: Thin, stiff cardboard. Light and dark-colored pencils. Tailor's chalk. Ruler. Scissors. Sewing and quilting needles. Straight pins. Compass. Quilting frame (optional).

MATERIALS: Quilt top: closely woven cotton fabric 36" wide: rust/orange/brown stripe, 3½ yds.; scraps of small prints in colors coordinating with the striped material amounting to 2 yds.; small-print white fabric, ⅔ yd.; striped white fabric, 1⅔ yds. Lining: cotton fabric 45" wide, 5 yds. Dacron polyester or cotton batting (Taylor Bedding). White thread.

DIRECTIONS: Read General Directions on pages 6 and 7. Quilt is constructed of eight solid strips alternating with seven pieced strips. To make patterns for pieced strips, draw a rectangle on cardboard, 5" x 2½"; mark a point midway on one long side; draw diagonal lines from this point to the two opposite corners. Cut on marked lines to make patterns for small and large triangles. Cut several patterns, and re-place pattern when edges begin to fray. Cut patches, marking pattern on wrong side of fabric and adding ¼" seam allowance on all sides. Cut 136 small triangles from the small-print white fabric and 340 from the striped white fabric. Cut 238 large triangles from the scraps of colored fabrics.

To make block, join two small triangles to one large triangle by matching the long side of each small triangle with short sides of the large triangle. Make 238 blocks in this manner, 68 of them with small-print white triangles and 170 with striped white triangles. Using blocks made with same white fabric and keeping large triangles pointed in the same direction, join blocks on long sides to form five long strips of striped white and two strips of printed white, 34 blocks to each strip. Strips will measure 5" x 85" plus outside seam allowance. Cut eight strips from striped brown fabric, each 6" x 85½" (measurements include ¼" seam allowance all around).

To make quilt top, sew long sides of strips together, alternating solid strips with pieced strips and keeping large triangles pointed in same direction; place strips made with small-printed white triangles first and last of the pieced strips. Quilt top should measure 79" x 85", plus outside seam allowance.

For lining, cut two pieces of fabric 40½" x 86". Right sides together, join pieces on long edges with ½" seams, to make piece 80" x 86". Cut batting 79" x 85". Pin and baste lining and batting together, centering pieces; lining will extend ½" on all sides. Fold excess lining over edge of batting; pin and baste the two pieces together. Turn ¼" outside seam allowance of quilt top to insides; baste.

Quilting: With compass, draw a semicircle with 5½" diameter on cardboard; cut out. Using edge of circle as a guide, mark curved lines with tailor's chalk 1" apart across striped fabric strips. On pieced strips, mark a line on large triangles ½" in from side seams and another 1" in from marked lines, continuing lines across small triangles out to sides of strip. Pin and baste quilt top to batting and lining. Starting in the center and working around and outward, quilt on all marked lines.

To finish edge, slip-stitch quilt top to lining along edges.

CLAMSHELL QUILT

SIZE: About 77" x 85½".

EQUIPMENT: Scissors. Tracing paper. Thin, stiff cardboard. Dark and light-colored pencils. Tailor's chalk. Sewing and quilting needles. Quilting frame (optional).

MATERIALS: Closely woven cotton fabrics 36" wide: scraps of various prints totaling about 6¾ yds. White fabric, 45" wide: 10 yds. (includes lining). White sewing thread. White double-fold bias binding tape ½" wide, 9⅛ yds. Dacron polyester or cotton batting (Stearns & Foster).

DIRECTIONS: Read General Directions on pages 6 and 7. Quilt is constructed entirely of clamshell patches, arranged in alternating rows of white and colored clamshells.

Trace actual-size clamshell pattern as is, for half-shell pattern. Trace pattern again and complete half-pattern indicated by dash lines, for whole shell pattern. Make several pattern pieces of cardboard and replace when edges begin to fray. Marking pattern on right side of fabric* and adding ¼" seam allowance all around, cut 612 whole shells from print fabrics and 595 from white fabric; cut 70 half-shells from white fabric.

On each shell patch, mark midpoint of top curve on ¼" seam line. Starting at midpoint and working out to both sides, clip top curve just to seam line every ⅜". Fold clipped edge on seam line to wrong side of piece; press fold carefully without stretching fabric. With right sides up, join two print shells and one white shell, placing upper folded edge of each print shell on a lower seam line of white shell; at each side point of white shell, seam line should match midpoint of a print shell. Pin shells in place. Continue pinning shells together until 17 white and 18 print shells have been joined in two rows; add a white half-shell to each end of white row. Slip-stitch pieces together on folded seam line of colored shells.

*(**Note:** An alternate method of joining shells: When cutting patches, mark pattern on wrong side of fabric. Mark midpoint on upper curve of shells as in first method. Hold two shells with right sides together, easing the top curve of print shell into a lower curve of white shell and matching midpoint of print shell to side point of white shell; stitch on seam lines.)

Using first two rows as top of quilt, continue to add shells a row at a time, alternating a white row with a print row, until 69 rows are joined. To trim top and bottom edges, cut off white shells of first and last rows to within ¼" of print shells. Piece should measure about 77" x 85½".

For lining, cut two pieces 39" x 85½". Sew together on long sides with ½" seams; press seam open. Cut batting same size as lining and quilt top.

Quilting: With tailor's chalk, mark each print shell with outline of shell shape, ½" in from edges. On each white shell, mark a curved grid pattern, using lower curves of cardboard shell pattern as template; mark two lines in each direction approximately ¾" apart, curving from a lower edge to upper edge of opposite side.

Following General Directions, pin and baste lining, batting, and quilt top together. Starting in center and working around and outward, quilt on all marked lines.

To finish quilt, insert raw edges into ½" white binding tape; stitch edges of tape to lining and quilt top; press.

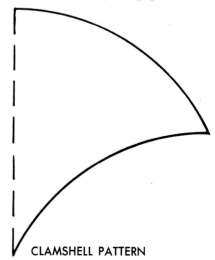

CLAMSHELL PATTERN

Flying Geese seems an apt name for a pattern of triangles all set in the same direction. Quilt is a series of plain and pieced strips; no border. Pennsylvania, 1870.

THOMAS K. WOODARD AMERICAN ANTIQUES AND QUILTS

Clamshells, row upon row, create a very lovely pattern. Quilt is not an easy one to piece, however, as all patches curve and must be joined on the bias. 1865-1875.

QUILT FROM AMERICA HURRAH ANTIQUES, N.Y.C.

Twenty little stars of Bethlehem, pieced from warm-toned prints, are unified by centers of yellow calico. A nice example of the dark quilt, which was made for comfort more than show, but often with quite lovely results. Pennsylvania. Directions below.

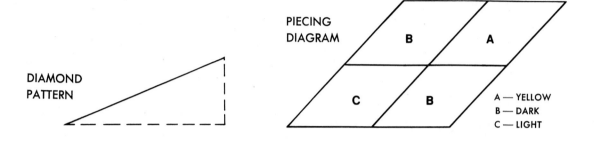

DIAMOND PATTERN

PIECING DIAGRAM

A — YELLOW
B — DARK
C — LIGHT

TWENTY STARS QUILT

SIZE: 78½″ x 94″.

EQUIPMENT: Thin, stiff cardboard. Scissors. Ruler. Tailor's chalk. Light and dark-colored pencils. Sewing and quilting needles. Straight pins. Tracing paper. Quilting frame (optional).

MATERIALS: Quilt top: Closely woven cotton fabric, 36″ wide, in small or medium-size prints: yellow, 2 yds.; green, 3¼ yds.; scraps of 40 dark prints totaling about 3¼ yds.; scraps of 20 light prints totaling about 1 yd. Lining: Cotton fabric, 44″-45″ wide, 5¼ yds. Dacron polyester or cotton batting. White sewing thread.

DIRECTIONS: Read General Directions on pages 6 and 7. Quilt is constructed of 20 pieced star blocks, set with joining strips and squares, plus a two-color border.

To make star blocks, trace actual-size diamond pattern; complete quarter-pattern indicated by dash lines. Following General Directions for cutting diamond patches from fabric, cut 160 patches from yellow fabric, 320 from dark fabrics (16 from same fabric for each star), and 160 from light fabrics (8 from same fabric for each star). Each star is made up of 32 diamond patches arranged in eight diamond-shaped sections radiating from center, and each section is made up of two rows of two diamond patches each. (For Joining Diamonds, see page 10.) Referring to Piercing Diagram, make a diamond-shaped section, using one yellow, two dark, and one light patches. Make seven more diamond-shaped sections in same manner, using the same colors. Join four sections for each half of star, with yellow points meeting in center, then join halves for complete star. Star should measure 12″ across in either direction, point to point, plus outside seam allowance. For background, use another dark fabric. Cut cardboard pattern 3½″ square. Marking on wrong side of fabric and adding ¼″ seam allowance, cut four squares from background fabric. Cut cardboard pattern in half diagonally and cut four triangles in same manner from same fabric. Sew the squares and triangles alternately between the star points, to make piece 12″ square, plus outside seam allowance. Make 19 more star blocks in same manner, combining other light and dark prints around a yellow center.

To complete center of quilt top, cut 31 pieces 12½″ x 4″ from green fabric; cut 12 4″-square pieces from yellow fabric (measurements include ¼″ seam allowance). Before joining pieces, lay star blocks out in shape of quilt, i.e., five horizontal rows of four blocks each; arrange blocks so that colors are well balanced. Place a green piece between each block in first row; join the four blocks and three green pieces, right sides together and with ¼″ seams. Sew four more rows in same manner. Make a joining strip by placing four green pieces end to end with a yellow square between them; sew together, with ¼″ seams. Make three more joining strips in same manner. Place a joining strip between rows of blocks and sew together, matching corners of pieced blocks and yellow squares exactly. Completed piece should measure 58½″ x 74″, plus outside seam allowance.

For border, cut four 2½″-wide strips from yellow fabric, two 59″ long and two 78½″ long (piece to get lengths where necessary); measurements include ¼″ seam allowance. Sew shorter strips to top and bottom of quilt top, right sides together and with ¼″ seams. Sew longer strips to sides of quilt in same manner. Cut four 8¼″-wide strips from green fabric, two 63″ long and two 94″ long. Sew to quilt top in same manner as yellow strips. Piece should be 78½″ x 94″.

For lining, cut two pieces of fabric 39¾″ x 94″. Sew together along long edges, right sides together and with ½″ seam allowance. Press seam open. Cut batting same size as quilt top and lining. Pin and baste lining, batting, and quilt top together.

Quilting: With ruler and tailor's chalk, mark straight quilting lines on quilt top as follows: On background of star blocks, mark diagonal lines on corner squares in both directions, 1″ apart. On side triangles of background, mark vertical lines in same manner. On yellow squares, mark diagonal lines as for background squares. On green and yellow border and on green joining strips, mark pairs of diagonal lines ¼″ apart, every ¾″. Starting in center and working outward, quilt on all marked lines and on each diamond patch, close to seam line.

To bind edges, cut four 1½″-wide strips of yellow fabric, two 79″ long and two 94½″ long (piece to get these lengths). Sew strips to top of quilt, right sides together and with ¼″ seam allowance. Turn strips to back of quilt and slip-stitch to lining, turning in raw edges of strips ¼″. Press edges.

BLAZING STAR QUILT

SIZE: Approximately 85¾" square.

EQUIPMENT: Scissors. Ruler. Thin, stiff cardboard. Light and dark-colored pencils. Tailor's chalk. Dressmaker's (carbon) tracing paper. Tracing wheel. Sewing and quilting needles. Quilting frame (optional).

MATERIALS: Quilt top, closely woven cotton fabric: small-size prints, * 36" wide: red (A) ⅞ yd., rust (B) 1 yd., blue (C) 1⅝ yds., medium pink (D) ¼ yd., light pink (E) ½ yd., yellow (F) 1⅔ yds., dark green (G) 1⅛ yds.; plain colors, 45" wide: dark green 2⅔ yds., red ½ yd., yellow ⅓ yd. Lining: 45" wide, 4⅝ yds. White and matching sewing thread. Dacron polyester or cotton batting (Taylor Bedding).

*(Note: Original quilt has two red prints, three blue prints, three yellow prints, and two dark green prints. As the prints in each of these three colors are very similar, we have specified only one print for each. However, use more than one print (one for each row) if desired, to add variety to the design.)

DIRECTIONS: Read General Directions on page 6 and 7. Quilt is constructed of a large eight-pointed star, set with smaller-star blocks and half-star blocks; borders are pieced and plain.

To piece all stars, trace actual-size diamond pattern; cut several diamond patterns from cardboard and replace as edges begin to fray from repeated use. Follow General Directions for cutting diamond patches, marking pattern on wrong side of fabric and adding ¼" seam allowance all around; cut 2336 diamonds from small-print fabrics as follows: red, 272; rust, 328; blue, 544; medium pink, 88; light pink, 136; yellow, 600; dark green, 368. For Joining Diamonds, see directions on page 10.

The large star is made up of 1568 diamond patches, pieced into eight identical diamond-shaped sections radiating from center. Each section is made up of 14 rows of 14 diamond patches each; see Large Piecing Diagram for one section. Following diagram and color illustration, make one section of the large star, starting row 1 with red (A), rows 2, 3, and 4 with blue (C), row 5 with dark green (G), etc. until 14 rows have been pieced together. Matching corners carefully, join the 14 rows for a diamond-shaped section. Make seven more sections in same manner. Join four sections for each half of star, with red points meeting in center, then join halves for complete star. Large star should measure 70" across in any direction, point to point, plus outside seam allowance. Star points should measure about 19¼" on each side, plus seam allowance.

Each complete small star is made of 128 diamond patches, pieced into eight diamond-shaped sections as for large star. Each section is made up of four rows of four diamond patches each; see Small Piecing Diagram. Following diagram, make 48 diamond-shaped sections. Joining sections as before, make four complete stars and four half-stars.

To make patterns for dark green background, cut a 6" square from cardboard. Marking pattern on wrong side of fabric and adding ¼" seam allowance all around, cut 20 squares from plain green fabric. Cut square pattern in half diagonally for triangle pattern and cut 32 green triangles in same manner. To make a small-star block, fit four green squares and four green triangles alternately between the points of a small star; both squares and triangles will extend about ½" beyond star points. Overlap extended ends of triangles with extended edges of squares and stitch in place. Small-star block should measure about 19¾" square, plus outside seam allowance. Make three more blocks in same manner. To make half-star blocks, fit a square between two middle points of a half-star, then fit four triangles between and around the other points to make triangle-shaped block (see illustration for placement of triangles); green pieces will extend about ½" beyond star points. Overlap extended ends of the two inner triangles with extended edge of square and the two outer triangles. Make three more half-star blocks in same manner. Fit small-star blocks and half-star blocks alternately between the points of the large star made; blocks will extend about ½" beyond points of large star. Overlap extended ends of

continued on page 107

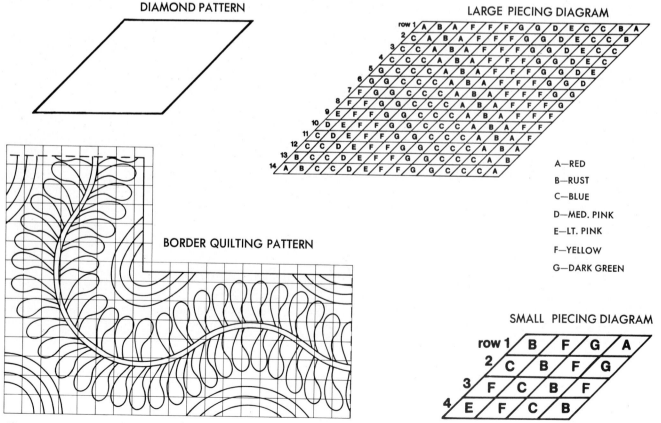

DIAMOND PATTERN

LARGE PIECING DIAGRAM

A—RED
B—RUST
C—BLUE
D—MED. PINK
E—LT. PINK
F—YELLOW
G—DARK GREEN

BORDER QUILTING PATTERN

SMALL PIECING DIAGRAM

row 1	B	F	G	A
2	C	B	F	G
3	F	C	B	F
4	E	F	C	B

Large satellite stars give extra exuberance to this Star of Bethlehem design, in a brilliant display of color. Made in Pennsylvania around 1860. Stars are pieced with diamond patches; the center of quilt is trimmed with a sawtooth border; then the whole is set in a wide border quilted in a graceful plume design.

OCEAN WAVES QUILT

SIZE: 88" square.

EQUIPMENT: Thin, stiff cardboard. Light and dark-colored sharp pencils. Tailor's chalk. Ruler. Scissors. Paper for pattern. Straight pins. Sewing and quilting needles.

MATERIALS: Quilt Top: Closely woven cotton fabric in small-figured prints, 36" wide: 3¼ yds. red with black figure; 2⅛ yds. yellow with red figure; scraps of other light and dark-colored prints (other shades of red and yellow may be included), totaling about 6 yds. Lining: 5 yds. cotton fabric, 45" wide. Dacron polyester or cotton batting. White sewing thread.

DIRECTIONS: Read General Directions on pages 6 and 7. Quilt is made up of 16 eight-sided blocks (see Piecing Diagram for one block), plus connecting squares and triangles and a two-color border. Following General Directions, make cardboard patterns for four patches as follows: 5" squares and small, medium, and large triangles made by cutting half of 1¾", 3½", and 5" squares. Cut all patches, marking pattern on wrong side of fabric and adding ¼" seam allowance: 128 small triangles, four medium triangles, 12 large triangles, and 25 squares from red fabric; 128 small triangles from yellow fabric; 1216 small triangles from other light-colored prints and 1216 small triangles from other dark-colored prints.

Following General Directions for piecing, make 1¾"-square patches by piecing together two small triangles for each patch; combine the red triangles with yellow and 1088 each of the other light and dark triangles; there will be

some light and dark triangles left over. Referring to Piecing Diagram, make the six-sided shape marked off by heavy lines by piecing together two red/yellow squares (indicated by dash lines), 17 other light/dark squares, and two each of separate light and dark triangles. Make three more six-sided shapes in same manner. Piece the four shapes together around a 5" red square in center to make an eight-sided block; note positioning on Piecing Diagram of light and dark triangles adjacent to center square: light triangles are opposite light, dark triangles are opposite dark. Make 15 more blocks in same manner. Place four blocks in a row, long sides together, positioning blocks so that adjacent red/yellow squares contrast to form pinwheel design; sew blocks together, right sides facing, along ¼" seam lines. Make three more rows in same manner. Sew the four rows together, again making sure that adjacent red/yellow squares contrast for pinwheel design; as you sew two rows together, fill in the three square spaces thus formed between rows with 5" red squares, sewing two sides of red square to first row before sewing on second row. When all rows are joined, sew three large red triangles in spaces along each side and a medium red triangle in each corner. Patched piece will measure 70½" square, including outside seam allowance.

For border, cut four 2½"-wide strips of yellow fabric: two 70½" long, two 74½" long. Sew the shorter strips to two opposite sides, right sides together and making ¼" seams. Sew the longer strips to other sides in same manner, joining ends of shorter strips to sides of longer strips. Cut four strips

of red fabric, each 7¾" x 89". Sew a strip to each side of quilt top with ¼" seams, mitering corners. To miter, hold adjacent ends at corners together, right sides facing. Keeping border flat, lift up inner corners and pin together diagonally, from inner corner to outer corner; baste. Stitch on basting line. Cut off excess fabric to make ½" seam.

For lining, cut two pieces 44½" x 88". Sew together with ½" seams to make 88"-square piece. Cut batting same size as lining.

Quilting: For patchwork portion of quilt top, mark intersecting diagonal lines over every row, going through corners of each small square in both directions; as you mark (with ruler and tailor's chalk), extend lines onto yellow border stripe, but skip over all large red squares and the side and corner red triangles. Mark each large red square with a vertical line from top to bottom corner, then an intersecting horizontal line between side corners. Mark three parallel lines on each side of these lines, equidistant from each other. Mark side and corner red triangles in same pattern.

For border, enlarge quilting pattern by copying on paper ruled in 1" squares. Using dressmaker's carbon and tracing wheel, transfer pattern to each corner of quilt top, ½" from side edge. Continue transferring cable design all around border.

Pin and baste quilt top, batting, and lining together and quilt along marked lines as instructed in General Directions, working patchwork section first. Quilt around outside edge of yellow border stripe. Turn excess fabric of quilt top to back; turn raw edge under ¼" and slip-stitch to lining of quilt.

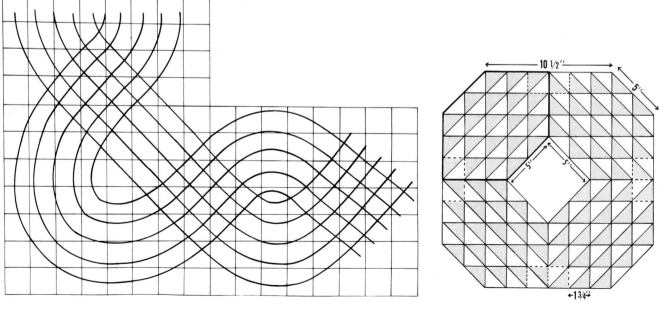

BORDER QUILTING PATTERN

PIECING DIAGRAM

Over 2000 tiny triangles in multi-shades of light and dark create this kaleidoscopic pattern called Ocean Waves. A second motif, Pinwheel, appears when red and yellow triangles are used at regular intervals in the patchwork. Graceful cable-design quilting decorates the red border. Pennsylvania Dutch, dated 1906.

COLLECTION OF TONY ELLIS AND BILL GALLICK

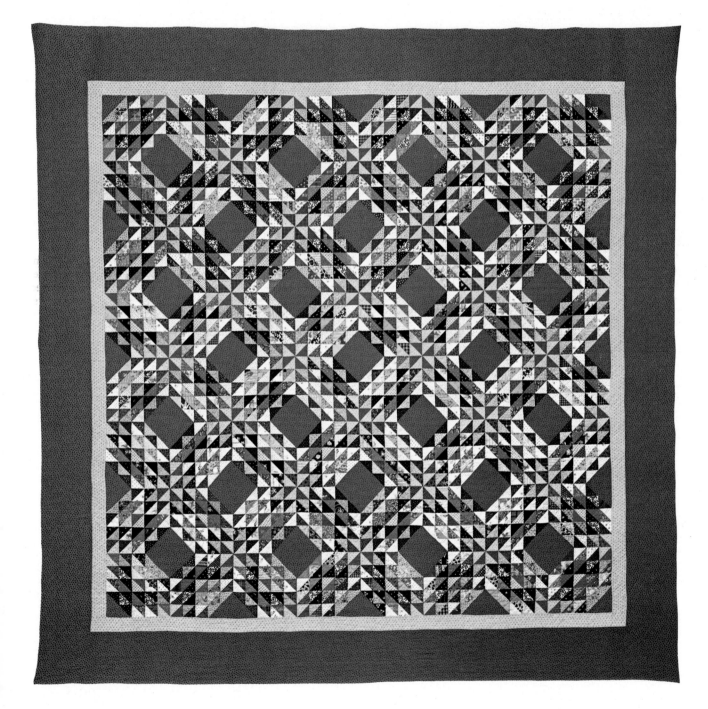

Brilliant three-color quilt, made in Pennsylvania around 1890, has an affinity with contemporary design. The geometrics are softened by graceful cables, quilted on every panel. Coverlet is unusual because of its border, not typical of the Tree Everlasting Quilt. See page 66.

See page 66.

Irish chain, one of the best known of all patchwork patterns, seems intricate at first glance. The triple-chain design above, however, is simply an arrangement of two pieced blocks repeated alternately. Quilting includes wreaths, cables, and straight diagonal lines. Made in Pennsylvania, around 1890. Triple Irish Chain Quilt, page 67.

TREE EVERLASTING QUILT
shown on page 64

SIZE: About 80½" x 85½"

EQUIPMENT: Thin, stiff cardboard. Ruler. Pencil. Paper for pattern. Scissors. Dressmaker's (carbon) tracing paper. Tracing wheel. Sewing and quilting needles. Straight pins. Quilting frame (optional).

MATERIALS: Closely woven cotton fabric 44"-45" wide: dark blue-green, 2 yds.; red, 1¼ yds.; gold, 8¼ yds. (including lining). Dacron polyester or cotton batting (Stearns & Foster). Gold sewing thread.

DIRECTIONS: Read General Directions on pages 6 and 7. Cut nine panels 5¾"x55¾": five from gold fabric and four from green (measurements include ¼" seam allowance). To make pattern for triangles, cut a piece of cardboard 1⅝" square; cut square in half diagonally. Marking pattern on wrong side of fabric and leaving ¼" seam allowance, cut 418 each red and gold triangles. Right sides together, join red and gold triangles to make 418 squares, matching long sides. Join squares, so that colors alternate, into 10 strips of 34 squares each and two strips of 39 squares each.

Lay the nine gold and green panels out vertically, alternating colors; lay the ten 34-square strips between them and at right and left of outer gold panels; alternate direction of red triangles with every other strip. Right sides together, join strips and panels on ¼" seam lines. Sew 39-square strips across top and bottom. Piece should measure 58½" x 63½", plus outside seam allowances.

For border, cut four strips 5¾" wide from green fabric, two 64" long and two 69½" long (piece where necessary); measurements include ¼" seam allowance. Sew shorter strips to top and bottom, right sides together and making ¼" seam allowance. Sew longer strips to sides. From gold fabric, cut four strips 6¼" wide, two 74½" long and two 80½" long (piece where necessary); measurements include ¼" seam allowance. Sew strips to quilt top in same manner as before. Quilt top should measure about 80½" x 85½".

For lining, cut two pieces from gold fabric, each 43¼" x 80½". Join on long edges, right sides together and with ½" seam allowance. Press seam open. Cut batting same size as lining.

Quilting: Enlarge quilting patterns on paper ruled in 1" squares. Using dressmaker's carbon and tracing wheel, transfer smaller pattern to each green and gold center panel, repeating pattern to cover entire length of panel. Transfer larger pattern to green and gold outer border, ¼" outside of center seam, repeating along entire length of shorter sides and between sides on longer ends.

Pin and baste lining, batting, and quilt top together, following General Directions. Starting at center and working outward, quilt along all marked lines; quilt on each side of seam lines joining triangles, ⅛" away; quilt close to seam line on each center panel and around entire pieced center, on green border.

To bind edges, cut four 1½" wide strips from red fabric, two 86" long and two 81" long (piece to get these lengths). Sew strips to quilt top, right sides together and with ¼" seams. Turn strips to back of quilt and slipstitch to lining, turning in raw edges of strips ¼". Press edges of quilt.

QUILTING PATTERNS

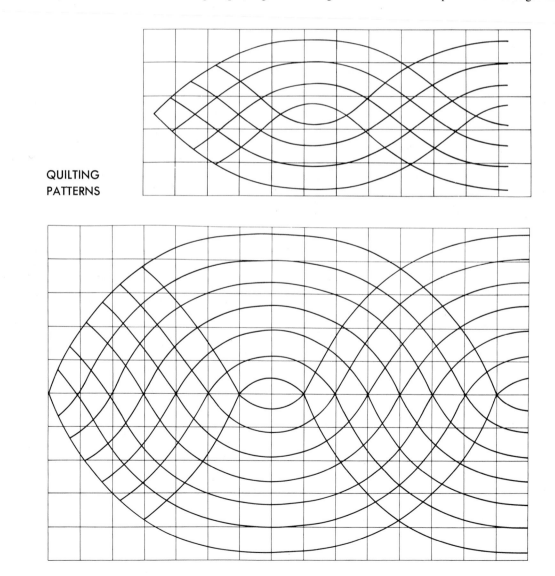

TRIPLE IRISH CHAIN QUILT

shown on page 65

SIZE: Approximately 80½″ square.

EQUIPMENT: Ruler. Scissors. Thin, stiff cardboard. Paper for pattern. Tracing paper. Dressmaker's (carbon) tracing paper. Tracing wheel. Tailor's chalk. Dark and light-colored pencils. Quilting and sewing needles. Quilting frame (optional).

MATERIALS: Closely woven cotton fabric 45″ wide: dark green, 3 yds.; red, 1¾ yd.; gold, 2¼ yds.; lining, 4½ yds. Matching sewing thread. Dacron polyester or cotton batting (Taylor Bedding).

DIRECTIONS: Read General Directions on pages 6 and 7. Quilt is constructed of 49 blocks pieced in two designs and is trimmed with a two-color border. Cut a 1⅞″-square pattern from cardboard. Make several patterns and replace when edges begin to fray. Marking pattern on wrong side of fabric and adding ¼″ seam alowance all around, cut 517 squares from green fabric and 396 from red.

To make Block A, sew 12 red squares and 13 green squares into five rows of five squares each, then sew rows together; see Piecing Diagram A for arrangement of colors. Make 24 more of Block A in same manner.

For Block B, trace pattern for center piece; complete quarter-pattern indicated by long dash lines (short dash lines are quilting pattern). Cut 24 center pieces from gold fabric, in same manner as for squares. Assemble four red squares and eight green squares around a gold center piece for Block B; see Piecing Diagram B. Make 23 more of Block B in same manner.

Sew blocks into seven rows of seven blocks each, alternating Blocks A and B and beginning four rows with Block A and three rows with Block B. With right sides facing, sew rows together for main body of quilt top, alternating Block A rows with Block B rows; see illustration. Piece should measure 65⅝″ square, plus outside seam allowance.

For first border, cut four strips 3½″ wide from gold fabric, two 66⅛″ long and two 72⅛″ long (measurements include ¼″ seam allowance). Sew shorter strips to sides of main body of quilt top, then longer strips to top and bottom. Piece should measure 71⅝″ square, plus outside seam allowance. For second border, cut four strips 4¾″ wide from green fabric, two 72⅛″ long and two 80⅝″ long (measurements include ¼″ seam allowance). Sew strips on in same manner as for gold strips. Piece should measure 80⅝″ square.

For lining, cut two pieces 40¾″ x 80⅝″. Sew pieces together along long sides, right sides facing and with ⅜″ seams. Press seam open. Cut batting same size as lining and quilt top.

Quilting: With ruler and tailor's chalk, mark diagonal lines over main body of quilt top as follows: Mark a line from upper left corner to lower right corner, going through corners of green squares that form a center diagonal row. Mark a parallel line on both sides of first line, going through corners of red squares. Mark parallel lines through next green squares (lines will touch corners of gold center pieces). Mark parallel lines between lines drawn, making nine lines in all, about ⅝″ apart. Mark six more groups of nine diagonal

continued on page 54

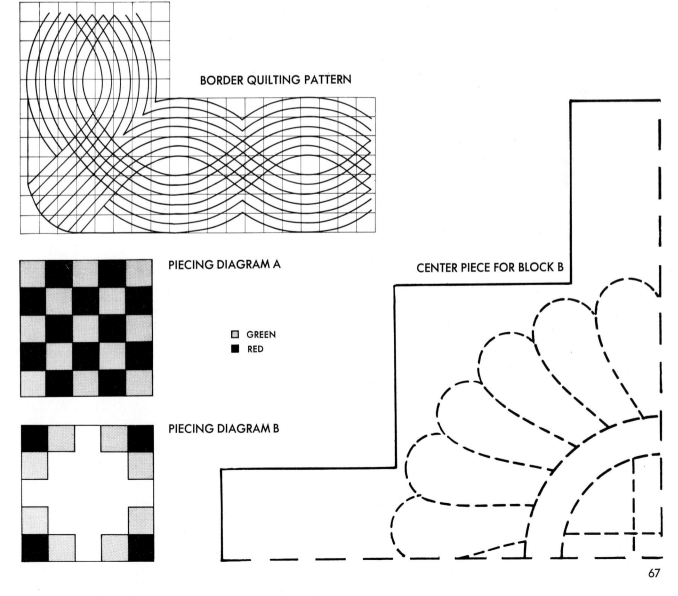

BORDER QUILTING PATTERN

PIECING DIAGRAM A

☐ GREEN
■ RED

PIECING DIAGRAM B

CENTER PIECE FOR BLOCK B

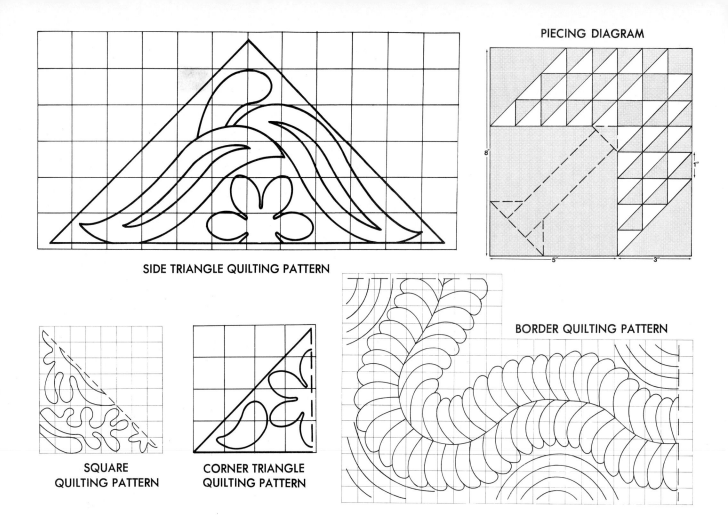

SIDE TRIANGLE QUILTING PATTERN

PIECING DIAGRAM

SQUARE
QUILTING PATTERN

CORNER TRIANGLE
QUILTING PATTERN

BORDER QUILTING PATTERN

TREE OF LIFE QUILT

SIZE: Approximately 75¾" x 87".

EQUIPMENT: Ruler. Scissors. Dark and light-colored pencils. Thin, stiff cardboard. Paper for patterns. Dressmaker's (carbon) tracing paper. Tracing wheel. Tailor's chalk. Sewing and quilting needles. Quilting frame (optional).

MATERIALS: Closely woven cotton fabric 45" wide: gold, 2¼ yds.; red, 8½ yds. (includes lining). Red and gold sewing thread. Dacron polyester or cotton batting (Stearns & Foster).

DIRECTIONS: Read General Directions on pages 6 and 7. Quilt is made up of 30 pieced tree blocks, set with plain blocks and a three-strip border.

To make tree blocks, see Piecing Diagram. Block is made of squares, triangles, and pieced squares; trunk is appliquéd in place. Make patterns for patch pieces as follows: Draw a 5" and a 1" square on cardboard; cut out for large and small square patterns. Draw a 3" and another 1" square on cardboard; draw a line on each square connecting opposite corners; cut out on marked lines for large and small triangle patterns. Cut a cardboard strip 1" x 4⅞". Cut several pattern pieces and replace

pattern when edges begin to fray. Marking patterns on wrong side of fabric and adding ¼" seam allowance all around, cut patch pieces as follows: From red fabric cut 720 small triangles, 60 large triangles, 90 small squares, and 30 large squares. From gold fabric cut 990 small triangles and 30 strips.

On each large red square, appliqué (see directions on page 90) three gold triangles and one gold strip for tree trunk; see Piecing Diagram for position of pieces indicated by dotted lines.

Make 720 patches 1" square by sewing small red and gold triangles together on their long sides.

To assemble tree block, sew one large red appliquéd square, two large red triangles, three small red squares, six gold triangles, and 24 pieced red/gold squares together, following Piecing Diagram; start by sewing smaller pieces into rows, then adding large triangles and square. Tree block should measure 8" square, plus outside seam allowance. Make 29 more blocks in same manner.

For red background blocks, make a cardboard pattern 8" square. Cut 20 red squares, adding ¼" seam allowance all around. Cut pattern in half diagonally, and cut 18 large red triangles in same manner. Cut cardboard triangle

in half and cut four smaller red triangles.

Center of quilt top is assembled by placing tree blocks alternately with red squares in diagonal rows, starting and ending each row with a tree block. All tree blocks are facing in same direction; see illustration. For half of center design, place blocks as follows: Row 1: 1 block. Row 2: 3 blocks. Row 3: 5 blocks. Row 4: 7 blocks. Row 5: 9 blocks. Pin pieces together on seam allowances with right sides facing. Stitch blocks together into rows; stitch rows together. Make second half of center design in same manner, starting with row 5 and ending with row 1. Join the two halves to make a rectangle with serrated edges. To fill out rectangle, place large red triangles around edge of rectangle between tree blocks, four on top and bottom, five on each side; place small red triangle in each corner. Sew triangles in place. Finished center piece should measure 56¼" x 67½", plus outside seam allowance.

For borders, cut 12 strips, each 3¾" wide: from red fabric, cut two strips 63¼" long, two 74½" long, two 76¼" long, and two 87½"; from gold fabric, cut two 70¼" long and two 81" long (measurements include ¼" seam allow-

continued on page 72

Tree quilt is made in the vibrant hues typical of Pennsylvania coverlets of 1890. Graceful quilting patterns offset the precise geometry of the pieced tree blocks (trunks are appliquéd). Tree symbol dates from earliest colonial times, when it appeared on coins and flags as well as in the green-and-white "pine tree" quilts.

THOMAS K. WOODARD AMERICAN ANTIQUES AND QUILTS

CHERRY BASKET QUILT

SIZE: About 73" square.

EQUIPMENT: Scissors. Ruler. Thin, stiff cardboard. Hard, sharp pencils. Tracing paper. Dressmaker's (carbon) tracing paper. Tracing wheel. Tailor's chalk. Sewing and quilting needles. Straight pins. Square. Quilting frame (optional).

MATERIALS: Quilt top: Closely woven cotton fabric, 44"–45" wide: dark blue-green, 2 yds.; red, 1½ yds.; light orange, 1½ yds. Lining: print or plain fabric 44"–45" wide, 4⅛ yds. Dacron polyester or cotton batting (Taylor Bedding). Matching sewing thread.

DIRECTIONS: Read General Directions on page 6 and 7. Quilt is constructed of pieced-and-appliquéd basket blocks set with plain blocks of squares and triangles; four pieced and plain strips make border.

To make basket blocks, see Piecing Diagram. A block is made with 17 patch pieces; handles are appliquéd in place. To make triangular patterns for patch pieces, cut cardboard pieces 6½" square and 1⅝" square; cut squares in half diagonally. Marking on wrong side of fabric and adding ¼" seam allowance all around, cut 36 large triangles and 288 small triangles from red fabric; cut 360 small triangles from light orange fabric. For basket handles, trace actual-size pattern; complete half-pattern indicated by dash lines. Cut 36 orange basket handles, marking on wrong side of fabric and adding ¼" seam allowance all around. Appliqué a handle to each large red triangle, positioning as shown by dash lines on Piecing Diagram; see How to Appliqué on page 90. Piece 10 orange triangles and six small red triangles together as shown in Piecing Diagram to make one large triangle. Sew pieced triangle to large red triangle for one basket block 6½" square, plus outside seam allowance. Sew two small red triangles to base of each block, one on each side of orange corner trangles; see color illustration. Make 35 more blocks in same manner.

For blue-green quilt blocks, make cardboard pattern 6½" square. Cut 25 squares, adding ¼" seam allowance all around. Cut cardboard pattern in half diagonally and cut 20 large green triangles in same manner. Cut cardboard triangle in half and cut four smaller green triangles.

To assemble quilt top, place basket blocks alternating with green blocks in diagonal rows, starting and ending each row with a basket block. At opposite sides of quilt top, position basket blocks around edges so that top of each block is pointed toward the center

of quilt design, to form a border; other basket blocks are all facing in same direction; see illustration. Row 1: 1 block. Row 2: 3 blocks. Row 3: 5 blocks. Row 4: 7 blocks. Row 5: 9 blocks. Row 6: 11 blocks. Row 7: 9 blocks. Row 8: 7 blocks. Row 9: 5 blocks. Row 10: 3 blocks. Row 11: 1 block. Place five large green triangles on each side of quilt top between baskets; place a small triangle in each corner. Pin pieces together on seam allowances with right sides facing; small red triangles at base of each basket will overlap front of adjacent green blocks. Stitch blocks together; appliqué overlapping red triangles in place. Finished piece should measure approximately 55⅛" square, plus outside seam allowance.

To make first border, measure your quilt top precisely along one side, omitting seam allowance, and divide the number by 28. Make a cardboard square, using resulting number for side dimensions. (If the number is difficult to measure on a ruler, such as 1.9", use 10-to-the-inch graph paper to draw a precise square.) Cut square in half diagonally to make triangular patterns. Cut 116 triangles each from red and orange fabrics, marking pattern on wrong side of fabric and adding ¼" seam allowance. Sew triangles together to make 116 red-and-orange squares. Sew squares together, alternating colors, to make four strips of 29 squares each. Sew a strip to each side of quilt top, right sides together and with ¼" seam allowances; make one end of strip flush with one side of quilt top and other end extending one square beyond other side of quilt top.

Measure quilt top again, omitting seam allowances. Cut four orange strips 2¼" wide: two the length of quilt top and two this length plus 4½", adding ¼" seam allowance all around. Sew shorter strips to sides of quilt top, then longer strips to top and bottom. Measure quilt top again and cut four

continued on page 72

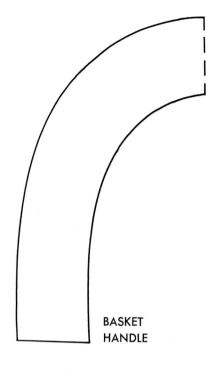

BASKET HANDLE

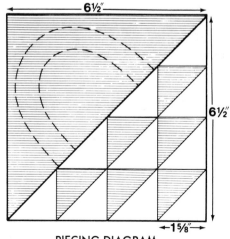

PIECING DIAGRAM

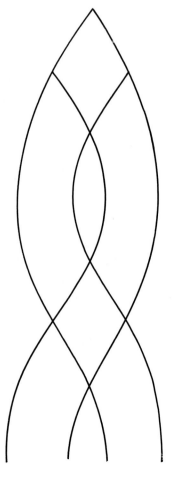

CABLE QUILTING PATTERN

70

Cherry baskets in rows—an all-time favorite pattern! Often seen in one color with white, design is especially lively when made in the "gaudy" hues loved by Pennsylvania quilt makers. Each basket is a pieced block, with handles appliquéd. 1880-1890.

COLLECTION OF GEORGE E. SCHOELLKOPF

TREE OF LIFE QUILT
continued from page 68

ance all around). Sew 63¼" red strips to top and bottom of center piece, centering strips so that an equal amount extends at each corner. Sew 74½" red strips to sides of center piece, centering in same manner. To miter corners, lay piece flat, right side down. Hold adjacent ends together at corners with right sides facing. Keeping border flat, lift up corners and pin strips together diagonally from inner corners to outer corners; baste, then stitch on basting line. Cut off excess fabric to make ¼" seam; press seam open. Sew on gold strips in same manner, then remaining red strips, mitering all corners. Quilt top should measure 75¾" x 87".

For lining, cut two pieces from red fabric 38⅞" x 88". Sew together on long sides with ½" seams, to make piece 76¾" x 88". Press seam open. Cut batting same size as quilt top.

Quilting: Enlarge quilting patterns on paper ruled in 1" squares; complete half-patterns and corner triangle patterns for square indicated by dash lines. With dressmaker's carbon paper and tracing wheel, transfer the square pattern in every other red background square, alternating both horizontally and vertically; transfer corner and side triangle patterns to triangle blocks around edge of quilt center. In remaining background squares, using ruler and tailor's chalk, mark straight lines ¾" apart, both horizontally and vertically, starting in center of squares with corner-to-corner lines. On tree blocks, mark same grid pattern on red triangle shapes in three corners of block; on large red shapes on each side of trunk, mark lines ¾" apart, one set parallel to tree trunk and another set parallel to triangles at bottom of trunk. With tracing wheel, transfer border feather motif around corners, repeating curve to cover length of each border.

Following General Directions, center lining, batting and quilt top together; lining will extend ½" beyond edges of batting and quilt top. Pin and baste layers together. Starting in center and working around and outward, quilt on all marked lines using both red and gold thread. Quilt on small pieces of tree blocks, ⅛" in from seams. Fold excess lining to front of quilt, turn raw edges under ¼", and slip-stitch to quilt top.

CHERRY BASKET QUILT
continued from page 70

red strips 2¼" wide, in same manner as before; sew to sides. Measure again and cut four green strips 2½" wide; sew to sides. Completed quilt top should measure approximately 73" square.

For lining, cut two pieces 73" x 37". Sew together along long edges with right sides together and making ½" seams. Press seam open. Cut batting same size as lining and quilt top.

Quilting: With ruler and tailor's chalk, mark vertical and horizontal quilting lines on green blocks of pieced center; draw lines from corners to corners of squares in both directions, then draw lines parallel to these lines and 1" from each other, to cover squares. Skip over small red triangles at base of basket blocks. Extend lines onto large red triangles of basket blocks, skipping over handles. Continue same pattern in large green triangles at sides. For green corners, mark same pattern on the diagonal. Mark same diagonal pattern on red border.

Trace actual-size cable quilting pattern. Using dressmaker's carbon and tracing wheel, transfer pattern to orange border, repeating all around.

Transfer cable pattern to green border, ⅜" from red border.

Pin and baste lining, batting, and quilt top together, following General Directions. Starting in center and working outward, quilt on all marked lines; quilt around small triangles and handles of basket blocks, 3/16" from seam lines on each side, within basket blocks.

To bind edges, cut four 1¾"-wide strips of green fabric, 73½" long (or piece to get these lengths). With right sides together and making ¼" seams, sew strips to top of quilt. Turn to back of quilt and slip-stitch to lining, turning in edges of strips ¼".

TRIP AROUND WORLD QUILT
shown on opposite page

SIZE: About 80" square.

EQUIPMENT: Scissors. Ruler. Light and dark-colored pencils. Thin, stiff cardboard. Tailor's chalk. Sewing and quilting needles. Quilting frame (optional).

MATERIALS: Closely woven cotton fabric 45" wide: For quilt top, ½ yd. each medium pink, light pink, orange, light gold; ⅜ yd. each medium gold, cream, black, navy, medium blue, light blue, medium green; ¾ yd. red; 2¼ yds. dark green. For lining, 4½ yds. Yellow sewing thread. Dacron polyester or cotton batting (Taylor Bedding).

DIRECTIONS: Read General Directions on pages 6 and 7. Quilt is made up of 1225 squares, plus a plain quilted border. For square patches, make a cardboard pattern 2" square. Cut patches, marking on wrong side of fabric and adding ¼" seam allowance all around. Cut 173 red patches, 92 medium pink, 96 light pink, 96 orange, 84 medium gold, 92 light gold, 88 cream, 84 black, 84 navy, 84 medium blue, 84 light blue, 84 medium green, 84 dark green. Following color illustration, sew the patches together in diagonal rows to make a square block, starting in corner with one cream patch. Next row is two light gold patches; next row is three orange patches, etc. Continue sewing on patches, each row one patch longer than previous row, until you reach light pink row, which will be 18 patches long. Continue adding rows, but with each row one patch shorter than previous row, until you reach the red square that is the center of quilt design. You have now completed slightly more than one-quarter of entire design. Mark off a section on color illustration to correspond to block you have sewn, matching rows exactly. Extend your lines on illustration to divide design into four sections; you will note that the three new sections are not identical to the first one marked. Piece three more blocks to correspond to these three sections. Join the four blocks, with red cross in center, to make patchwork design about 70" square.

For border, cut four 5¾"-wide strips from dark green fabric, two 70½" long and two 81" long (measurements include ¼" seam allowance). Sew shorter strips to top and bottom of patchwork design, then longer strips to sides.

For lining, cut two pieces 40½" x 80". Sew together on long sides with ½" seams, to make piece 80" square. Cut batting same size as lining.

Quilting: With ruler and tailor's chalk, mark diagonal quilting lines 1¼" apart on border of quilt top; mark all lines in same direction. Following General Directions, pin and baste quilt top, batting, and lining together, centering layers so that quilt top extends ½" all around beyond edges of batting and lining.

Starting in center and working around and outward, quilt on each square patch, ⅛" in from seams, using yellow thread. Quilt on marked lines of border.

To finish edges, fold excess fabric to back of quilt, turn in raw edge ¼", and slip-stitch to lining. Press all edges.

*Trip Around the World (also Grandma's Dream or Checkerboard)
displays a rainbow of exhuberant colors—from Pennsylvania, of course!
Construction of quilt is easy: 2"-square patches are sewn
in diagonal rows; use illustration for pattern. The quilting follows
the patchwork, with diagonal lines on plain border. Around 1910.*

BARN RAISING QUILT

SIZE: 44½″ square.

EQUIPMENT: Scissors. Ruler. Light and dark-colored sharp pencils. Paper for pattern. Dressmaker's (carbon) tracing paper. Tracing wheel. Sewing and quilting needles.

MATERIALS: Quilt top: Closely woven cotton fabric, 36″ wide: a variety of print fabrics, evenly divided between dark colors and light colors, totaling about 2 yds. (see Note below); 1¼ yds. of solid dark green. Lining: 2⅝ yds. of 50″-wide dark red print fabric. Dacron polyester or cotton batting. Sewing thread in gray and to match fabrics.

Note: Design will be effective if random colors are used throughout, as long as a sharp contrast is maintained between the light and dark shades. A planned color scheme will create a more formal design. This quilt combines a planned color scheme with random colors (see illustration and Piecing Diagram, as well as directions).

DIRECTIONS: Read General Directions on page 6 and 7. Quilt consists of 36 pieced squares arranged to make an overall design, plus a border. For each square, cut 16 ⅝″-wide strips (eight in light colors, eight in dark colors) and a 1″ square, adding ¼″ seam allowance on all sides. See First Piecing Diagram for length and color of strips. The colors of the inner pieces (A, B, C, D, E) are specified on the diagram; the colors of the outer pieces (F, G, H, I) may vary from square to square. Cut the dark green strips from solid green fabric; the other pieces are prints. With right sides together, sew pieces into a 6½″ square, including outside seam allowance; start piecing from the center and work around and outward. Make 35 more squares in same manner. For four of these squares, use the same fabric for all G pieces; these will be Corner Squares. For four other squares, use the same fabrics for all except H pieces; use one fabric for H pieces on two squares and another fabric for H pieces on the other two; these will be the four Center Squares.

Sew nine squares into a block 18½″ square, with right sides together and following Second Piecing Diagram; place one Corner Square at upper left and one Center Square at lower right. Make three more blocks in same manner. Sew the four blocks together to make a 36½″ square piece, joining Center Squares as shown in illustration.

For border, cut four strips 4½″ wide, two 36½″ long and two 44½″ long. Sew shorter strips to opposite sides of pieced square, right sides together and with ¼″ seam allowances. Sew longer strips to other ·sides of square in same manner, sewing sides of longer strips to ends of shorter strips. Cut batting same size as quilt top. For lining, cut two pieces 46½″ x 45½″; sew longer sides together with ½″ seams to make piece 45½″ square.

Quilting: Enlarge Border Quilting Pattern by copying on paper ruled in 1″ squares. Transfer pattern to each corner of quilt-top border, ¼″ from outside edge, using dressmaker's carbon and tracing wheel. Repeat design all around quilt, alternating triangles and curves.

Following General Directions, center batting and quilt top over lining; pin and baste together. Quilt around all seams of pieced top and marked lines of border, using gray thread. Finish quilt by turning margin of lining to front; turn in raw edges ¼″ and slipstitch to top. Press all edges.

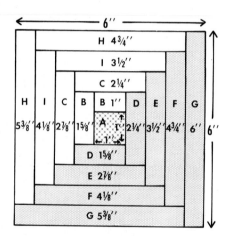

FIRST PIECING DIAGRAM

A — RED
B — YELLOW-GREEN
C — RED/WHITE STRIPE
D — DARK GREEN
E — NAVY
F, G — RANDOM DARK COLORS
H, I — RANDOM LIGHT COLORS

BORDER QUILTING PATTERN

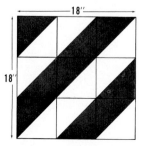

SECOND PIECING DIAGRAM

Barn Raising is one of the intricate and fascinating "log cabin" patchwork designs. All log cabin quilts are composed of narrow strips, half light and half dark; how they are assembled determines the final design. Pennsylvania Dutch crib quilt, about 1900.

COLLECTION OF TONY ELLIS AND BILL GALLICK

STRAIGHT FURROW QUILT

SIZE: About 55½″ x 60½″.

EQUIPMENT: Ruler. Scissors. Light and dark pencils. Sewing needle.

MATERIALS: Closely woven cotton fabric, 36″ wide: orange, ⅛ yd.; black and tan, ¼ yd. each; a variety of print fabrics evenly divided between dark and light colors, totaling about 4 yds. (see note below); 4 yds. for lining. Orange binding, ½″ wide, 8½ yds. Sewing thread to match lining.

Note: Design will be effective if random colors and prints are used throughout, as long as a sharp contrast is maintained between light and dark shades. This quilt combines a planned color scheme with random colors (see illustration and Piecing Diagram as well as directions).

DIRECTIONS: Read General Directions on pages 6 and 7. Quilt is made up of 90 pieced blocks arranged in an overall striped design, plus a striped pieced border. As each block is constructed it is sewn to a separate square of lining fabric; there is no batting. Cut a cardboard pattern 5″ square. Marking on wrong side of fabric and adding ¼″ seam allowance all around, cut 90 squares from lining fabric. With ruler and sharp pencil, mark two diagonal lines corner to corner on wrong side of each lining square; lines will cross in exact center of square.

To make each block, see Piecing Diagram for dimensions of each piece. Cut one orange center square (A) and 20 strips: 10 in light colors (tan, strips C, plus four other colors, strips E, G, I, K) and 10 in dark colors (black, strips B, plus four other colors, strips D, F, H, J), marking outlines on right side of fabric and adding ¼″ seam allowance all around. There will be two strips in each color, the same in width but differing in length. Be sure to cut edges of pieces perfectly straight.

Place orange square in exact center of lining square, wrong sides together and matching corners of orange square to lines drawn on lining square; pin in place and sew down edges without turning under. Place the shorter black (B) strip horizontally on orange square, right sides together and matching bottom edge of black strip to bottom edge of orange square; pin and sew in place, about ⅛″ from bottom edge. Fold black strip back on marked line just above stitching, so that right side of fabric is facing upward; press lightly, making a ⅛″ pleat, so that strip will remain in place as folded. Folded edge of black strip should just cover marked line on bottom of orange square. Place remaining black strip vertically over orange square and end of first

strip, right sides together and matching edges along right sides. Pin, sew, turn, and press as for first strip. Continue across top side of orange square with shorter tan strip, then on left side with longer tan strip to complete a pieced square of overlapping strips, with a ½″ orange square showing in center. Following Piecing Diagram, sew the shorter of the two D strips across the bottom of the pieced square in same manner, sewing down edges of three overlapped strips at the same time. Sew the longer D strip to the right side of pieced square, etc. Continue adding strips, working in a counterclockwise direction, until all strips are used. Finished block should measure 5″ square, plus outside seam allowance. Make 89 more blocks in same manner.

Mark ¼″ seam line all around blocks, on wrong side. To join two blocks, place them side by side so that either their dark sides or their light sides are adjacent where seam will join. Turn one block over the other so that blocks have right sides together; pin and stitch on marked seam line. Turn top block back and press lightly along seam line on right side. On wrong side, fold raw edges under and whip together along folded edge. Sew blocks together in nine horizontal rows of 10 blocks each, matching dark sides against dark and light sides against light in adjacent blocks. Sew rows together, again matching dark against dark and light against light in adjacent blocks to make an overall design of diagonal stripes. Piece should measure 45″ x 50″, plus outside seam allowance.

For border, cut about 280 strips ½″ x 8″, marking on right side of fabric and adding ¼″ seam allowance all

around; use all the fabrics of quilt center. Cut four 5¾″-wide pieces from lining fabric, two 56″ long and two 61″ long (measurements include ¼″ seam allowance). Place quilt center right side up. Place lining pieces, wrong side up, one at a time around quilt center, centering each piece carefully so there is an equal amount extending at each end. To miter corners, draw a diagonal line from each of the two outer corners of lining piece to nearest corner of quilt center. These lines will be seam lines when border is sewn to quilt center, and they also serve as beginning guide lines for sewing strips to border pieces. While each border piece is still in place, mark beginning point with a pin: left border at lower line; right border at upper line; bottom border at left line; top border at right line. Sew strips to each border piece in overlapping fashion as for quilt center; fold of first strip should meet starting corner line. Continue to sew on strips until corner line at opposite end of lining piece is half covered (corner will be completed after quilt is assembled). Trim ends of strips to match side edges of border pieces.

Sew border pieces to quilt center with ¼″ seams, finishing seams on wrong side in same manner as for blocks. To miter corners, turn quilt wrong side up; keeping border flat, lift up corners and pin together diagonally from inner corner to outer corner; check front to see that stripes in adjacent borders meet. Baste; stitch on basting line, and cut off excess fabric to make ¼″ seams. Finish seams on back. Turn quilt right side up. Sew strips all the way across the two unfinished corners. To finish edges of quilt, bind with orange tape all around.

PIECING DIAGRAM

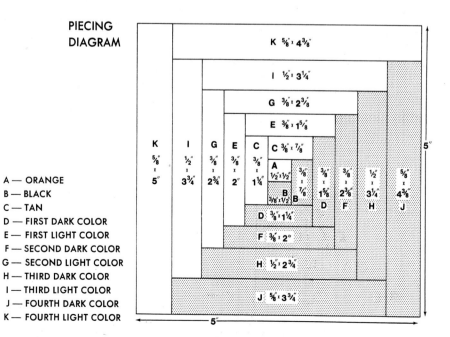

A — ORANGE
B — BLACK
C — TAN
D — FIRST DARK COLOR
E — FIRST LIGHT COLOR
F — SECOND DARK COLOR
G — SECOND LIGHT COLOR
H — THIRD DARK COLOR
I — THIRD LIGHT COLOR
J — FOURTH DARK COLOR
K — FOURTH LIGHT COLOR

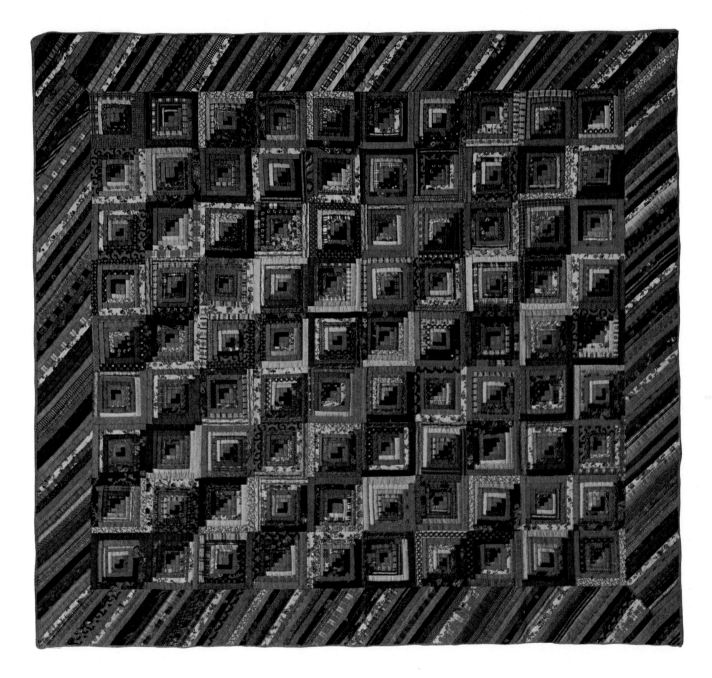

"Straight furrow" has basically the same construction
as the Barn Raising Quilt on page 75, i.e., each block is composed of
half light and half dark strips. Here, though, the ninety
light-dark blocks are assembled for a design of diagonal stripes
that continues onto the border. Pennsylvania; around 1860.

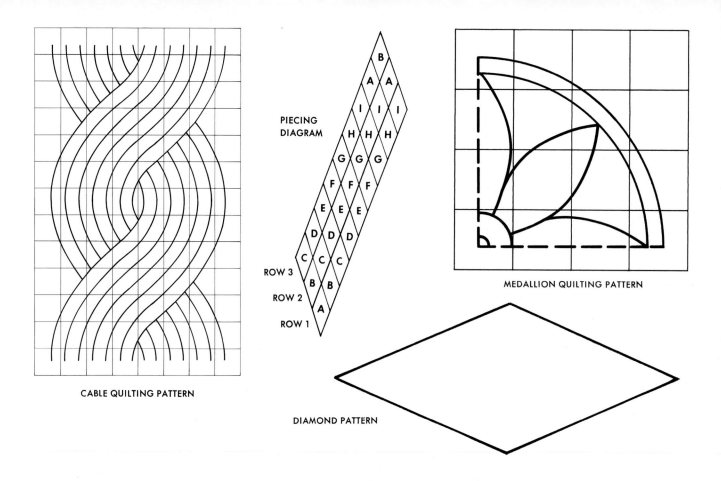

CABLE QUILTING PATTERN

PIECING DIAGRAM

ROW 3
ROW 2
ROW 1

MEDALLION QUILTING PATTERN

DIAMOND PATTERN

STAR OF BETHLEHEM QUILT

SIZE: About 79½" square.

EQUIPMENT: Ruler. Pencils. Thin, stiff cardboard. Tracing paper. Scissors. Dressmaker's carbon (tracing) paper. Tracing wheel. Tailor's chalk. Sewing and quilting needles. Quilting frame (optional).

MATERIALS: Closely woven cotton fabric 45" wide: ½ yard each dark gold (A), medium gold (B), light gold (C), heather (D), dusty rose (E), muted pink (F), grayish lavender (G), lavender (H), pale gray (I); 3⅜ yds. blue; 4¾ yds. deep pink (includes lining). Matching sewing thread. Dacron polyester or cotton batting.

DIRECTIONS: Read General Directions on pages 6 and 7. Quilt is made up of a large eight-pointed star, set with small-star and half small-star blocks, plus narrow and wide borders. To piece all stars, trace actual-size diamond pattern. Cut several patterns from cardboard and replace as edges begin to fray from repeated use. Follow General Directions for cutting diamond patches, marking pattern on wrong side of fabric and adding ¼" seam allowance all around. For large center star, cut 72 diamond patches each of all colors except blue and deep pink. For Joining Diamonds, see directions on page 10.

The large star consists of 648 diamond patches, pieced into eight identical diamond-shaped sections radiating from center. Each section is made up of nine rows of nine diamonds each. Referring to color illustration opposite and to the Piecing Diagram (which shows first three rows of section joined) for color placement, make each section as follows: Piece patches together in rows of nine, starting first row with dark gold (A); start second row with medium gold (B), third row with light gold (C); fourth row with heather (D), fifth row with dusty rose (E); sixth row with muted pink (F); seventh row with grayish lavender (G); eighth row with lavender (H); and ninth row with gray (I). Matching corners carefully, join the nine rows to form a diamond-shaped section. Make seven more sections in same manner. Join four sections for each half of star, having all dark gold points meeting in center; then join star halves for complete star. When star is complete, the points should measure 18" (plus outside steam allowance) on each side. Check measurements before cutting background pieces.

For blue background of quilt top, make cardboard pattern 18" square. Marking pattern on wrong side of fabric and adding ¼" seam allowance all around, cut four squares from blue fabric. Cut cardboard pattern in half diagonally for triangle pattern. Cut four triangles from blue fabric in same manner as for squares.

For small stars and half-stars, cut 48 diamond patches from leftover fabrics, cutting six patches each from eight colors. Join patches into four stars of eight diamonds each and four half stars of four diamonds each. Prepare edges of stars and half-stars for appliqué (see page 90); leave the straight edges of half-stars flat. Appliqué stars to center of blue background squares and half-stars to triangles, with raw edges even. Sew the squares and triangles alternately between the star points, to complete center of quilt top. Piece should measure 61½" square, plus outside seam allowance.

For pink border, cut two strips 2½" x 62" (measurements include ¼" seam allowance all around). Sew to top and bottom of quilt center. Cut two more pink strips 2½" x 66" and sew to sides. For blue border, cut two strips 7¾" x 66". Sew to top and bottom of quilt top, with ¼" seams. Cut two more blue strips 7¾" x 80½" and sew to sides of quilt top: Piece should now measure 80½" square.

For lining, cut two pieces from deep pink fabric 40¾" x 80½". Sew together on long sides with ½" seams to make lining 80½" square. Cut batting same size as lining and quilt top.

Quilting: With ruler and tailor's chalk, draw diagonal lines 1" apart in both directions on the blue squares and triangles, skipping over stars; on tri-
continued on page 136

A delicate balance of colors, shading golds into roses into lavenders, creates the beauty of this Star of Bethlehem. Small diamonds are pieced together to make eight identical sections, which are then joined for the eight-pointed star. Little satellite stars, pieced and appliquéd, decorate background. Border is quilted with cables and medallions.

QUILT COURTESY OF GEORGE E. SCHOELLKOPF

AMISH DIAGONAL QUILT

SIZE: About 66¾″ x 74½″.

EQUIPMENT: Thin, stiff cardboard. Light and dark-colored pencils. Ruler. Scissors. Paper for pattern. Dressmaker's (carbon) tracing paper. Tracing wheel. Quilting and sewing needles. Quilting frame (optional).

MATERIALS: Quilt top: Closely woven cotton fabric 44″-45″ wide: ½ yd. each dark blue-green, dusty pink, rose pink, light pink, golden brown, and olive drab; ¼ yd. each black and white; 2 yds. tan. Lining: fabric 44″-45″ wide, 4⅛ yds. Dacron polyester or cotton batting (Stearns & Foster). White sewing thread.

DIRECTIONS: Read General Directions on pages 6 and 7. Any combination of colors may be used, as long as a contrast is kept between light and dark colors for the shadowed effect. Quilt is made up of 728 squares sewn together, plus a solid-color border quilted in a cable pattern.

Make patch pattern by cutting a 1⅞″ square from cardboard. Cut square patches as indicated in General Directions, marking pattern on wrong side of fabric and adding ¼″ seam allowance all around. Cut 104 patches each of blue-green, dusty pink, rose pink, light pink, golden brown, and olive drab; cut 52 patches each of black and white. Following color illustration, sew patches together in diagonal rows to make a square block (one-quarter of patched top), starting in corner with one blue-green patch. Add 2 dusty pink patches for second row, joined to adjacent sides of blue-green patch. Continue with 3 rose pink; then 4 light pink; 5 golden brown; 6 white; 7 golden brown; 8 light pink; 9 rose pink; 10 dusty pink; 11 blue-green; 12 olive drab; 13 black; 13 olive drab; 12 blue-green; 11 dusty pink; 10 rose pink; 9 light pink; 8 golden brown; 7 white; 6 golden brown; 5 light pink; 4 rose pink; 3 dusty pink; 2 blue-green; 1 olive drab. Make three more pieced blocks in same manner. Join the four blocks into an overall design, turning two blocks halfway around to match colors and to form diagonal rows as shown in illustration; each of the four corner patches will match its diagonal opposite. Piece should measure 48¾″ x 52½″, plus outside seam allowances.

For border, cut two pieces 9½″ x 53″ and two pieces 11½″ x 67¼″, all from tan fabric; measurements include ¼″ seam allowance. Right sides together, sew shorter pieces to sides of pieced center; sew longer pieces to top and bottom. Quilt top should measure about 66¾″ x 74½″.

For lining, cut two pieces 34″ x 74½″. Sew together along long edges, right sides together and making ½″ seam allowances. Press seam open. Cut batting same size as quilt top.

Quilting: Enlarge Border Quilting Pattern on paper ruled in 1″ squares. Using dressmaker's carbon and tracing wheel, transfer pattern to top and bottom borders of quilt top, 1¼″ from patchwork center; start at midpoint of borders with part of design where quilting lines intersect, and repeat design all the way across to each side. Repeat on side borders, leaving no space between quilting design and patchwork center; start at midpoint with intersecting lines and work out to seam lines between side and end borders.

For patchwork center, mark intersecting diagonal lines over every row of squares, going through corners of squares; use ruler and tailor's chalk. Extend marked lines onto top and bottom borders, up to edges of marked border design.

Pin and baste quilt top, batting, and lining together, and quilt along marked lines as instructed in General Directions, starting in center and working outward.

Trim corners of quilt for a slightly rounded shape. To bind edges, cut four 1½″ strips from tan fabric, two 67¼″ long and two 75″ long (piece to get these lengths). Sew strips to front edges, right sides together and with ¼″ seam allowances. Turn strips to back of quilt, turn edges under ¼″, and slip-stitch to lining. Press all edges.

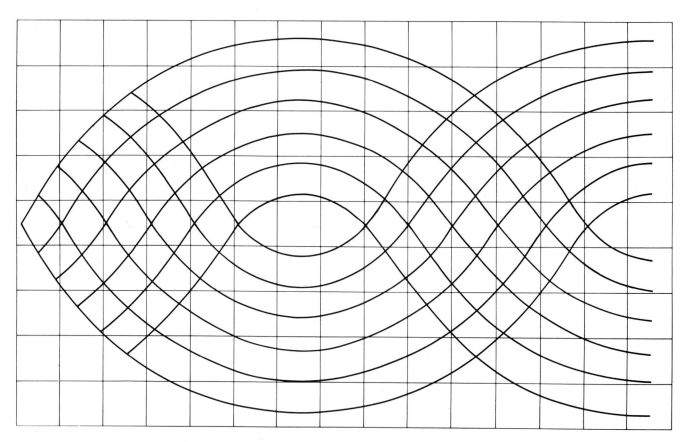

BORDER QUILTING PATTERN

A diagonal version of the traditionally Amish sunshine and shadow theme, circa 1910. More than 700 square patches create the softly colored design, framed with a wide cable-quilted border.

COLLECTION OF PHYLLIS HADERS, AMERICAN QUILTS

*A most unusual turn-of-the-century Amish quilt can be made
with fabric strips or ribbons—or both.
To sew by hand or machine. The easy piecing pattern and straight-line
quilting make it a perfect first project for beginning quilters.*

For Ribbon-Stripe Quilt, turn to page 84.

COLLECTION OF TONY ELLIS AND BILL GALLICK

*In typical Amish fashion, a simple geometric design is
worked in a sophisticated blend of colors, then elaborately finished
with several exquisite quilting patterns.
Made in Pennsylvania around 1905.
Directions for Amish Diamond Quilt start on page 85.*

RIBBON-STRIPE QUILT

shown on page 82

SIZE: About 78½" x 79½".

EQUIPMENT: Ruler. Tailor's chalk. Scissors. Tracing paper. Dressmaker's (carbon) tracing paper. Tracing wheel. Sewing and quilting needles. Straight pins. Sewing machine (optional). Pencil. Quilting frame (optional).

MATERIALS: For stripes, use yard goods, seam binding, or ribbons in seven plain colors, plus one striped and one checked print; see directions for colors and individual amounts. For borders, 36"-wide fabric: ⅔ yd. light navy print, 1 yd dark navy print, scraps of light brown. For lining, 44"-45" wide fabric, 4½ yds. Navy bias tape, 9 yds. Dacron polyester or cotton batting. White sewing thread.

DIRECTIONS: Read General Directions on pages 6 and 7. Quilt is constructed of 63 stripes plus side panels and a narrow border with contrasting corners. Cut stripes 1½" wide x 71½" long (includes ¼" seam allowance all around) or cut stripes into random widths (¾", ⅝", 1", 1½", plus seam allowance) as in original quilt. Piece to get length, where necessary. Original quilt has some stripes cut on the bias and some on the straight of fabric. Use either all cut on the straight, or some bias and some straight, but not all bias. Cut 4 aqua stripes, 8 blue, 11 pink, 6 navy, 10 red, 4 tan, 4 light green, 8 green striped, 8 purple checked. Join stripes on long edges, right sides together and with ¼" seam allowance; stripes can be sewn on the machine, if desired. Starting in center of quilt with pink stripe and working to right, join stripes as follows: purple checked, green striped, navy, aqua, blue, pink, red, tan, red, pink, blue, aqua, navy, green striped, purple checked, red, purple checked, green striped, navy, light green, blue, pink, red, tan, red, pink, blue, light green, purple checked, green striped, pink. Starting from center pink stripe again, join remaining stripes, working to left and repeating design.

For side panels, cut two pieces 5" x 71½" from light navy print and sew them to each side of striped center, right sides together and with ¼" seam allowance. Cut two stripes from tan 1¼" x 71½" and sew to side panels in same manner. Cut two stripes 1¼" x 74" from blue fabric and sew across top and bottom of quilt top.

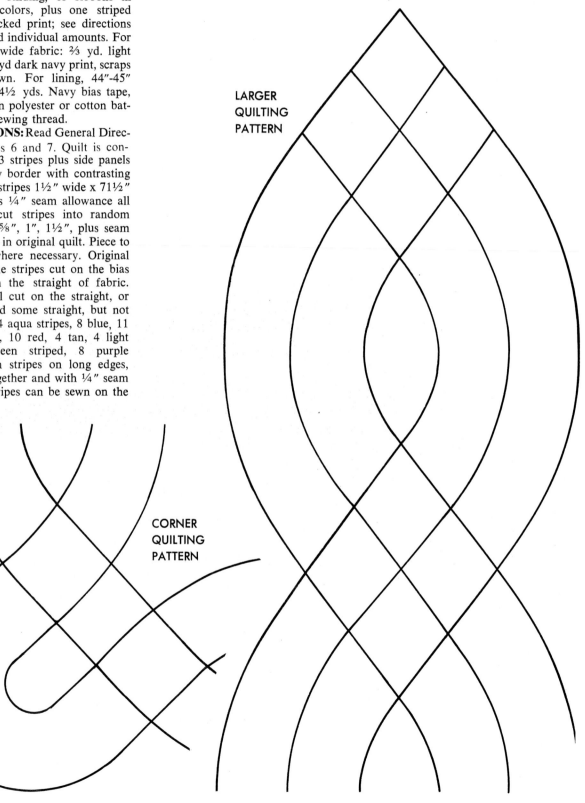

LARGER QUILTING PATTERN

CORNER QUILTING PATTERN

Cut four 3¼"-wide pieces from dark navy print, two 73" long and two 74" long. Sew the 73" pieces to sides of quilt top. Cut four pieces from light brown fabric 3¼" square; sew one to each end of 74" pieces. Sew pieces to top and bottom of quilt top. Quilt top should now measure about 78½" x 79½".

For lining, cut two pieces 40¼" x 78½"; sew together along long sides, right sides together and with ½" seam allowance. Press seam open. Cut batting to match quilt top and lining.

Quilting: With ruler and tailor's chalk mark straight quilting lines on striped center of quilt top and on narrow stripes of border. Mark lines ¼" from seam lines on each side; on narrow border stripes (and if using some narrow stripes in center of quilt top), mark one line down center. Using dressmaker's carbon and tracing wheel, transfer larger quilting pattern to light navy side panels, repeating design to cover panels. Transfer corner quilting pattern to each corner of border, ½" from outer sides; repeat single cable design from inside of larger pattern across each border.

Pin and baste quilt top, batting, and lining together, following General Directions. Quilt on all marked lines.

Insert edges of quilt into fold of bias tape and sew edges of tape to top and lining of quilt. Press all around.

AMISH DIAMOND QUILT

shown on page 83

SIZE: About 76" square.

EQUIPMENT: Tracing paper. Paper for patterns. Dressmaker's (carbon) tracing paper. Ruler. Yardstick. Scissors. Pencil. Tracing wheel. Tailor's chalk. Sewing and quilting needles. Straight pins. Large compass or piece of string. Quilting frame (optional).

MATERIALS: Quilt top: Closely woven cotton fabric, such as broadcloth, 44"-45" wide: dark purple, 3 yds.; deep turquoise, 1½ yds.; bright pink, ⅞ yd.; dark maroon, ⅞ yd. Lining: Closely woven cotton fabric, 44"-45" wide, 2¼ yds. Black sewing thread and threads to match fabrics. Dacron polyester or cotton batting (Stearns & Foster).

DIRECTIONS: Read General Directions on pages 6 and 7. Mark strips, squares, and triangles on wrong side of fabric, the lengths and widths indicated on Piecing Diagram. Cut out pieces, adding ¼" all around for seam allowance. (**Note:** Pieces may be cut before beginning construction of the quilt top; however, since seam allowances may vary slightly in the sewing, pieces may also be measured and cut as you progress, for greater accuracy.)

If this alternate method is selected, be sure to measure accurately each side of the completed square before cutting the adjoining strips. The strips to be joined should be the exact length (including ¼" seam allowance at each end) as the pieces to which they are being joined.)

Following Piecing Diagram and beginning with center square, begin joining pieces as follows. With right sides together and using marked line as seam line, sew a purple square in place at each end of two of the 3"-wide pink strips. Join these strips to opposite sides of center square. Sew remaining 3" strips in place, completing center square. Press seam allowances flat. Continue adding pieces in this manner until quilt top is complete. Piece should measure 73½" square, with outside seam allowance.

For lining, cut two strips of lining fabric, each 36¾" x 73½". Sew the two long edges together with ½" seam allowance. Press seam open. Cut batting same size as lining and quilt top.

Quilting: Quilting patterns are on pages 86 and 87. Trace actual-size patterns for Princess Feather and center Star; complete quarter-pattern of the star indicated by dash lines. Using compass and tailor's chalk, mark two concentric circles in center of center square: outer circle, 19½" in diameter; inner circle, 12½" in diameter. (**Note:** If large enough compass is not available, the following method may be used: Tie one end of string securely to pencil. Pin other end of string to center of square, leaving 9¼" of string between pencil and pin. Swing pencil around fabric to mark 19½" outer circle. Using same center point and

leaving 6¼" of string between pencil and pin, mark 12½" inner circle.)

Place center line of princess feather motif on each drawn circle. Using dressmaker's carbon and tracing wheel, repeat feather pattern until each circle is complete. Marking with tailor's chalk, divide center of quilt top into eight equal sections; place a diamond in each section for an eight-pointed star. Enlarge remaining quilting patterns on paper ruled in 1" squares. Using dressmaker's carbon and tracing wheel, transfer motifs to remaining areas of quilt, reversing patterns as needed to complete scallops of each motif. Transfer Purple Border Pattern to each corner of quilt, as basis for feather design; then transfer Princess Feather Pattern over lines, as for wreath design in center of quilt.

Pin and baste quilt top, batting, and lining together; quilt along marked lines as instructed in General Directions. Begin quilting from center motif and work outward.

For edging, cut eight 3½"-wide strips from dark maroon fabric, across the 44" width of fabric. Sew two short ends together to make four 87½"-long strips. Place center seam of one strip at center of one side edge of quilt. Trim strip to match side edge of quilt top, plus ¼" at each end. With right sides facing, stitch strip to one side edge of quilt top with ¼" seams.

Fold strip in half to back of quilt; turn in long edge ¼" and slip-stitch to back of quilt. Repeat on opposite side of quilt. For remaining two sides, trim binding strips to match side of quilt, including bindings already in place and adding ¼" at each end. Stitch in place, overlapping ends.

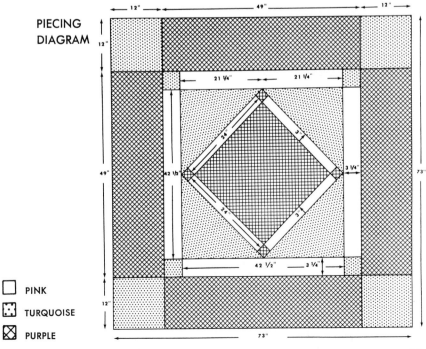

PIECING DIAGRAM

☐ PINK
▨ TURQUOISE
⊠ PURPLE

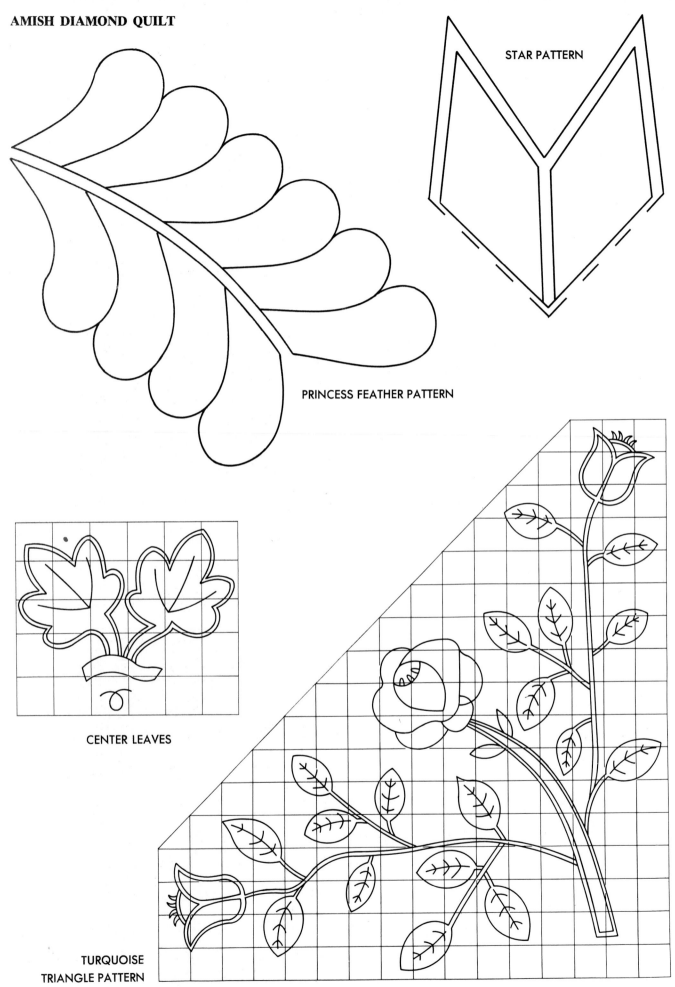

AMISH DIAMOND QUILT

STAR PATTERN

PRINCESS FEATHER PATTERN

CENTER LEAVES

TURQUOISE
TRIANGLE PATTERN

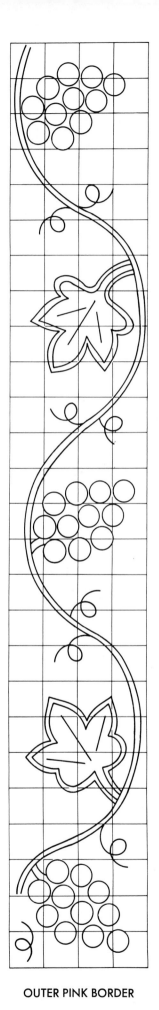

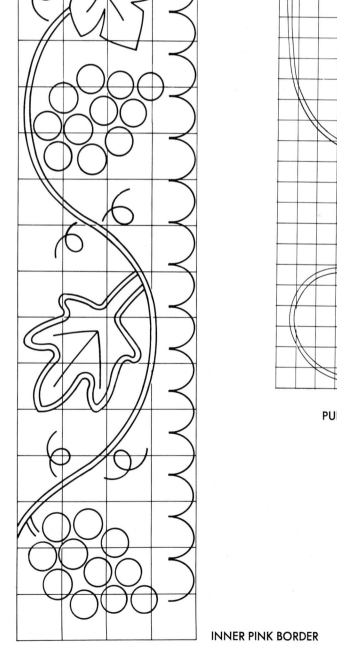

PURPLE BORDER

OUTER PINK BORDER

INNER PINK BORDER

SUN AND SHADOW QUILT

SIZE: About 85″ square.

EQUIPMENT: Thin, stiff cardboard. Pencil. Ruler. Scissors. Straight pins. Sewing needle. Paper for pattern. Tailor's chalk. Dressmaker's carbon paper. Tracing wheel. Quilting frame (optional). Quilting needle.

MATERIALS: Use a closely woven cotton, rayon, silk, or crepe fabric. Border: 36″ to 45″-wide royal blue, 4¾ yds. (or 54″-wide fabric, 2⅝ yds.) Lining: 44″-wide medium blue, 4¾ yds. Squares: 45″-wide fabric in following colors: ¼ yd. each yellow-green, cornflower blue, black; ⅜ yd. each light green, shocking pink, mauve, turquoise, midnight blue, royal blue, dark purple, light purple, lavender; ½ yd. each wine, dark green, olive. Black sewing thread. Cotton or dacron quilt batting.

DIRECTIONS: Read General Directions on pages 6 and 7. Any combination of colors may be substituted for the ones given above; the colors must progress in the design from light to dark to retain the shadowed effect. The quilt is made up of 1,089 squares sewn together, plus a wide quilted border of solid color fabric.

Make pattern template by marking a 1⅞″ square on cardboard; cut out. Cut square patches as indicated in General Directions, marking on wrong side of fabric and adding a ¼″ seam allowance. Cut 85 shocking pink patches, 88 mauve, 92 wine, 96 dark green, 96 olive, 32 yellow-green, 24 cornflower blue, 84 turquoise, 80 midnight blue, 64 royal blue, 36 black, 84 dark purple, 84 light purple, 84 lavender, 60 light green. Following color illustration, sew the patches together in diagonal rows to make a square block, starting in corner with one turquoise patch. Next row is two royal blue patches; next row is three yellow-green patches, etc. Continue sewing on rows of patches, each row one patch longer than previous row, until you reach bottle green row, which will be 17 patches long. Continue sewing on rows, but with each row one patch shorter than previous row, until you reach one shocking pink patch, which is the center of quilt. You have now completed slightly more than one-quarter of entire square design. Mark off a section on color illustration to correspond to block you have sewn, matching rows exactly. Extend your lines on illustration to divide square design into four sections; you will note that the three new sections are not identical to the first one marked. Piece three more blocks to correspond to these three sections. Join the four blocks, with single shocking pink patch in center, to make patchwork design about 62″ square.

For border, cut four pieces of royal blue fabric, each 12¼″ wide: two 85½″ long and two 62″ long; these measurements allow for ¼″ seams. With right sides facing, sew the two shorter strips to opposite sides of patchwork square and the two longer strips to remaining sides, joining ends of shorter strips to sides of longer strips.

For lining, cut two strips of blue fabric, each 43¼″ x 85½″. Sew the two long edges together with ½″ seams, making an 85½″ square. Cut batting the size of lining.

Quilting: For patchwork square, mark intersecting diagonal lines over every row, going through corners of each patch in both directions; use ruler and tailor's chalk. For border, enlarge quilting pattern by copying on paper ruled in 2″ squares. Using dressmaker's carbon and tracing wheel, transfer pattern to each corner of quilt top, 1¼″ from edge. Continue design all around border by repeating oval segment of pattern twice more on each side, overlapping flowers at sides of oval.

Pin and baste quilt top, batting, and lining together, and quilt along marked lines as instructed in General Directions, quilting the patchwork center first. To bind edges of quilt, cut four strips of royal blue fabric, each 2½″ x 86″. Sew a strip to one side edge of quilt top, with seam line 1″ from edge of quilt and ¼″ from edge of strip, right sides together; turn in ends. Fold strip to back of quilt; turn in edge of strip ¼″ and slip-stitch to back. Repeat on opposite side of quilt, then on two remaining sides, overlapping ends of strips. Press all edges of quilt.

BORDER QUILTING PATTERN

Sunshine and Shadow (other names are Trip Around the World and Grandma's Dream) is a beautiful display of the Amish sense of design. The colors of the quilt, made in the 1930's or early 40's with modern dress fabrics, seem to shimmer with a neon glow. The wide, plain border has a floral-wreath quilting pattern, in contrast to the geometry of the patchwork center.

QUILT FROM GEORGE E. SCHOELLKOPF

Appliqué Quilts

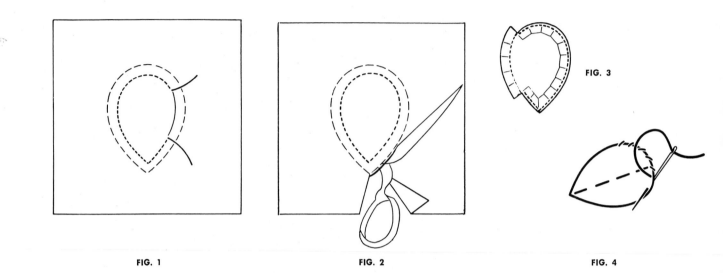

FIG. 1   FIG. 2   FIG. 3   FIG. 4

HOW TO APPLIQUE

Choose a fabric that is closely woven and firm enough so a clean edge results when the pieces are cut. Cut a pattern piece for each shape out of thin, stiff cardboard, and mark the right side of each piece. Press fabric smooth. Place cardboard pattern, wrong side up, on wrong side of fabric. Using sharp, hard pencils (light-colored pencil on dark fabric and dark pencil on light fabric), mark the outline on the fabric. When marking several pieces on the same fabric, leave at least ½″ between pieces. Mark a second outline ¼″ outside the design outline. Using matching thread and small stitches, machine-stitch all around design outline, as shown in Fig. 1. This makes edge easier to turn and neater in appearance. Cut out the appliqué on the outside line, as in Fig. 2. For a smooth edge, clip into seam allowance at curved edges and corners. Then turn seam allowance to back, just inside stitching as shown in Fig. 3, and press. Pin and baste the appliqué on the background, and slip-stitch in place with tiny stitches, as shown in Fig. 4.

DESIGNING APPLIQUES

It's easy to design your own appliqué pattern with paper and scissors. First, fold a square of paper into quarters or eighths, then cut away the center point and the edges in a design as simple or elaborate as you like. Continue cutting out paper designs until you find the pattern or patterns that please you most. It was with this simple method that the quilt on opposite page was created.

This beautiful Bride's Quilt is made up of 64 appliquéd blocks, many of them probably stitched by friends of the bride. No two patterns seem exactly alike, just as none of the fabrics are the same, but the snowflake theme and the soft red background of the prints give the design its unity. The quilting is close diagonal lines, plus a feather pattern on the border. Appliqués were made with the fold-and-cut method illustrated on the opposite page.

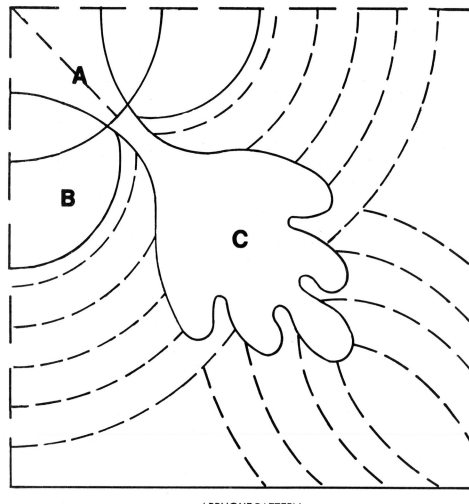

APPLIQUE PATTERN

FLOWER QUILTING PATTERN

OAK LEAF QUILT

SIZE: Approximately 80" x 100½".

EQUIPMENT: Ruler. Scissors. Thin, stiff cardboard. Tracing paper. Dressmaker's (carbon) tracing paper. Tracing wheel. Dark and light pencils. Sewing and quilting needles. Quilting frame (optional).

MATERIALS: Closely woven cotton fabric: blue print, 36" wide, 4½ yds.; white, 45" wide, 8 yds. (includes lining). White seam binding, ½" wide, 10⅛ yds. White thread. Dacron polyester or cotton batting (Taylor Bedding).

DIRECTIONS: Read General Directions on pages 6 and 7 and How to Appliqué on page 90. Quilt is constructed of 30 appliquéd blocks, set with appliquéd joining strips.

To make appliquéd block, trace actual-size pattern; complete quarter-pattern indicated by long dash lines; short dash lines indicate quilting pattern. Make separate cardboard patterns for pieces A, B, and C. Following directions in How to Appliqué, cut and prepare appliqué pieces; from blue fabric, cut 30 of piece A, 120 of B, and 120 of C.

For background of blocks, cut 30 pieces 10" square from white fabric, adding ¼" seam allowance on each side. On each white square, indicate horizontal and vertical center lines (fold and crease or mark lines with ruler and tailor's chalk). Using dressmaker's carbon and tracing wheel, transfer appliqué pattern, matching quarter-pattern to center lines. Pin, baste, and slip-stitch appliqué pieces in position on each white square.

To frame blocks, cut 120 strips 1½" wide from blue fabric, 60 10½" long and 60 12½" long (measurements include ¼" seam allowance). Sew shorter strips to opposite sides of each appliqué block, then longer strips to remaining sides. Blocks should measure 12" square, plus outside seam allowance.

For short joining strips, cut 36 pieces 3¾" x 12½" from white fabric (measurements include ¼" seam allowance). Make six horizontal rows by joining six strips and five blocks alternately for each row; place blocks so that longer blue framing strips are vertical. For long joining strips, cut seven pieces 4½" x 80" from white fabric. Join long strips and horizontal rows, with ¼" seams, to make piece 80" x 100½". To complete quilt top, cut 84 pieces 1½" x 7½" from blue fabric. Turn under all edges ¼" and press. Appliqué pieces to long white joining strips as shown, making an "X" pattern between blocks and on border.

For lining, cut two pieces from white fabric 40½" x 100½". Sew pieces together on long edges with ½" seams. *continued on page 94*

continued on page 94

***Unusually large quilt (80" x 100") was made in Vermont around 1860. Oak leaf motifs
and "garden maze" framing are appliquéd to white blocks and strips. Compare with pieced quilt on page 27.***

OAK LEAF QUILT
continued from page 92

Press seam open. Cut batting same size as quilt top and lining.

Quilting: Using dressmaker's carbon and tracing wheel, transfer quilting pattern to appliquéd blocks. Trace flower quilting pattern; complete half-pattern indicated by dash lines. Transfer flower pattern to each white section surrounding blocks. Following General Directions, pin and baste quilt top, batting and lining together. Starting at center and working around and outward, quilt on all marked lines and close to all seams, on each side.

To bind edges, place quilt between folds of seam binding; pin and baste. Slip-stitch edges of binding to top and lining of quilt.

WHIG ROSE QUILT

SIZE: About 76½" square.

EQUIPMENT: Ruler. Scissors. Pencil. Thin, stiff cardboard. Tracing paper. Dressmaker's (carbon) tracing paper. Tracing wheel. Sewing and quilting needles. Quilting frame (optional).

MATERIALS: Closely woven cotton fabric 36" wide: green*, 2¾ yds.; red, 1½ yds.; yellow, ⅛ yd.; pink print, ⅓ yd. White fabric 45" wide, 8 yds. (includes lining). White sewing thread. Dacron polyester or cotton batting (Stearns & Foster). *(In original quilt, green fabric has a small blue dot.)

DIRECTIONS: Read General Directions on pages 6 and 7 and How to Appliqué, p. 90. Quilt is made up of nine appliquéd blocks plus an appliquéd border. For appliqué pieces, trace actual-size pattern on page 97; complete quarter-pattern of center motif indicated by dash lines. Make a separate cardboard pattern for each numbered part of appliqué design. Following directions in How to Appliqué, cut and prepare appliqué pieces. From red fabric, cut nine of No. 1, 108 of No. 4, 36 of No. 9 and 36 of No. 11. From green fabric, cut 36 of No. 5, 36 of No. 6, 36 of No. 7 (for No. 6 and No. 7, add only ⅛" seam allowance), 144 of No. 8, and 72 of No. 12. From yellow fabric, cut 36 of No. 10. From pink print fabric, cut 36 of No. 2 and 108 of No. 3.

For background of each block, cut nine pieces 22" square from white fabric, adding ¼" seam allowance all around. On each white square, indicate horizontal and vertical center lines (fold and crease or mark lines with ruler and tailor's chalk). Using dressmaker's carbon and tracing wheel, transfer main outlines of complete appliqué pattern to each square by matching quarter-pattern lines to marked center lines; the center point of large leaves (No. 5) should fall on marked center lines. Piece large center flowers together, using Nos. 1, 2, 3 and 4. Pin, baste, and slip-stitch pieced center and remaining appliqué pieces in place on the squares, sewing overlapping pieces last.

Join the nine finished blocks into three rows of three blocks each, then join rows together for main body of quilt top. Piece should measure 66" square, plus outside seam allowance.

For borders, cut four 5½"-wide strips from white fabric, two 66½" long and two 76½" long (measurements include ¼" seam allowance). Using same patterns as for main body of quilt top, cut appliqué pieces for border. From green fabric, cut 48 of No. 8 and 24 of No. 12. From red fabric, cut 16 of No. 9 and 12 of No. 11. From yellow fabric, cut 16 of No. 10. To make a pattern for large green pieces of corner motifs, draw around No. 9 pattern on cardboard, then draw another line ⅝" away, following contours of first line, to make pattern about 4¼" in diameter. Using this pattern, cut four corner pieces from green fabric. Prepare pieces for appliqué. For vines, cut four ⅝"-wide bias strips from green fabric, about 80" long (piece to get this length). For stems, cut 24 bias strips ⅝" wide, but varying in length from 2" to 5", as desired. Prepare bias strips for appliqué by turning under long edges ⅛" to make strips ⅜" wide; press carefully without stretching folded edges.

Pin a large green corner piece to each end of the two longer white border strips, ⅝" from edges. Lay a long green bias strip between pieces, curving as shown in illustration; pin in place.

In same manner, pin a long bias strip on each of the two shorter white border strips, but with ends of bias strips matching ends of border strips. Pin, baste, and slip-stitch remaining appliqué pieces in place on border strips, following illustration. Then stitch the overlapping vines, stitching along inside curves of vines first, then outside curves. Sew shorter border pieces to opposite sides of quilt top, then longer border pieces to remaining sides. There will be a small gap in the vine between corner motifs and ends of shorter border strips; fill in with a bias strip. Quilt top should measure 76½" square.

For lining, cut two pieces from white fabric 38¾" x 76½". Sew together on long sides, with ½" seams. Cut batting same size as lining and quilt top.

Quilting: Trace large and small quilting patterns on page 96; complete quarter-patterns indicated by dash lines. Using dressmaker's carbon and tracing wheel, transfer wreath portion of patterns to white background of quilt top. Mark large pattern in the four areas where four quilt blocks meet, centering around the corners. Mark half of large quilting pattern (a semicircle) 20 times: mark pattern twice on each edge of main body of quilt top, centering on seam line between blocks; mark pattern midway between all blocks, centering on seam line. Mark quarter-pattern in each of four corners of main body of quilt top. Mark small quilting pattern in remaining large spaces between motifs of appliqués.

With ruler and tailor's chalk, mark triple-line pattern in center of wreaths and over all unmarked areas of white background, making all lines parallel and skipping over appliqués. Extend lines onto white background of border. On appliqués, mark center motifs and
continued on page 96

Whig Rose, made in Ohio around 1860, must have been someone's "very best" quilt. Flower appliqués, in the favorite red and green, are carefully placed to form a second pattern of overlapping circles. (For a much different approach to the same theme, see page 111.) Directions opposite; actual-size patterns on following pages.

WHIG ROSE QUILT

continued from page 94

large green leaves only with single diagonal lines ¾″ apart; follow same angle as triple lines of white background.

Pin and baste quilt top, batting, and lining together, following General Directions. Starting in center and working around and outward, quilt on all marked lines with white thread. On small leaves, buds, and small flowers, stitch ¼″ in from edge of each appliqué piece. Quilt around main outline of appliqué designs, close to seam line.

To bind edges of quilt, cut four 1″-wide strips 77″ long (piece to get lengths). Right sides together and with ¼″ seams, sew strips to front of quilt. Turn strips to back of quilt, turn in raw edges ¼″, and slip-stitch folded edge to lining. Press all edges.

QUILTING PATTERNS

APPLIQUE PATTERN

RADICAL ROSE QUILT

continued from page 110

main body of quilt top with horizontal and vertical lines ¾″ apart, skipping over appliqués. (On original quilt, grid pattern is placed on the diagonal in corners and center sides of background.) Enlarge border quilting pattern on paper ruled in 1″ squares. Using dressmaker's carbon and tracing wheel, transfer pattern, repeating it along top and bottom borders first, then sides.

Following General Directions, center quilt top, batting, and lining together; quilt top should extend ½″ beyond lining on all sides. Pin and baste layers together. Starting at center and working around and outward, quilt on all marked lines; quilt around and on each appliquéd piece, close to seam (on piece No. 5, quilt a second line indicated on pattern by short dash line); quilt on each triangle of pieced border, close to seam.

To bind edges, fold excess fabric to back of quilt, turning under raw edge ¼″; slip-stitch to lining.

COCKSCOMB CRIB QUILT

SIZE: About 42½″ square.

EQUIPMENT: Ruler. Scissors. Paper for pattern. Dark and light-colored pencils. Thin, stiff cardboard. Dressmaker's (carbon) tracing paper. Tracing wheel. Sewing and quilting needles. Quilting frame (optional).

MATERIALS: Closely woven cotton fabric 45″ wide: dark teal blue, ½ yd.; red, ⅓ yd.; white, 2½ yds. (includes lining). White sewing thread. Dacron polyester or cotton batting (Taylor Bedding).

DIRECTIONS: Read General Directions on pages 6 and 7 and How To Appliqué on page 90. Quilt is constructed of four appliquéd blocks.

Enlarge pattern for block by copying on paper ruled in 1″ squares; solid lines are appliqués and short dash lines are quilting patterns. Make a separate cardboard pattern for each lettered part of appliqué motif. Following general directions in How to Appliqué, cut and prepare pieces as follows: from red fabric cut four of A and eight of E; from blue fabric cut four of G and eight each of B, C, D, and F. For background of blocks, cut four pieces 21½″ square from white fabric (measurement includes ¼″ seam allowance). Using dressmaker's carbon and tracing wheel, transfer complete appliqué motif to each square. Following General Directions, pin, baste, and slip-stitch appliqué pieces in place on the squares.

Join the four blocks into two rows of two blocks each, then join rows of quilt top; see illustration for placement of blocks. Piece should measure 41½″ square.

For lining, cut piece 41½″ square from white fabric. Cut batting same size as lining and quilt top.

Quilting: Using dressmaker's carbon and tracing wheel, transfer quilting patterns to each block of quilt top, joining motifs carefully where they meet in center of quilt.

Following General Directions, pin and baste quilt top, batting, and lining together. Starting in center and working around and outward, quilt on all marked lines; quilt on and around appliqués, close to seams.

To bind edges, cut four strips from red fabric, 1″ x 43″. Right sides facing, sew strips to front of quilt along edges with ¼″ seams. Fold strips to back of quilt; turn in raw edges ¼″, and slip-stitch to lining. Press edges.

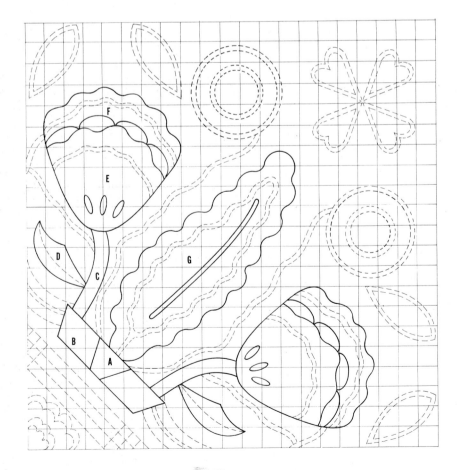

Cockscomb crib quilt is an easy one to make with only a few large appliqué pieces. The interesting quilting pattern is an important part of the overall design. Made in the late 1870's in New York State.

COCKSCOMB QUILT

BORDER APPLIQUE

FLOWER APPLIQUE

An imaginative placement of the appliqués gives this quilt an unusually sensuous appeal. Background is closely quilted in a somewhat free-form fashion with leaves and straight-line patterns. From Massachusetts; 1840-1850. Cockscomb Quilt, page 126.

LOTUS QUILT

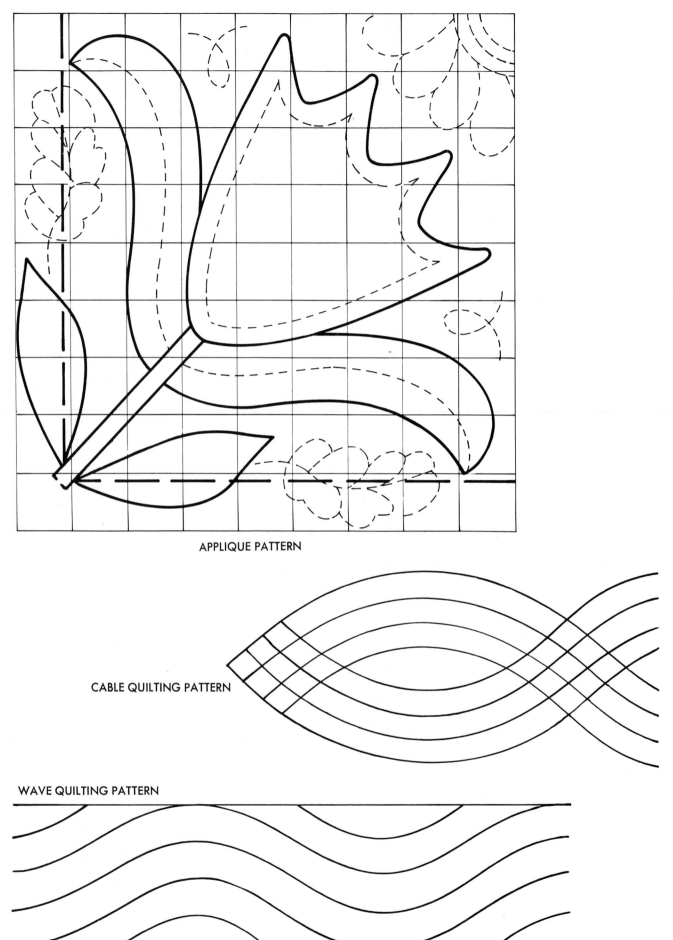

APPLIQUE PATTERN

CABLE QUILTING PATTERN

WAVE QUILTING PATTERN

The lovely lotus motif, multiplied, creates a striking overall pattern. Decorative wave and cable quilting adorns the strips joining and bordering appliquéd blocks. Made in Pennsylvania, around 1865. See opposite page for appliqué and quilting patterns; directions for Lotus Quilt are on page 107.

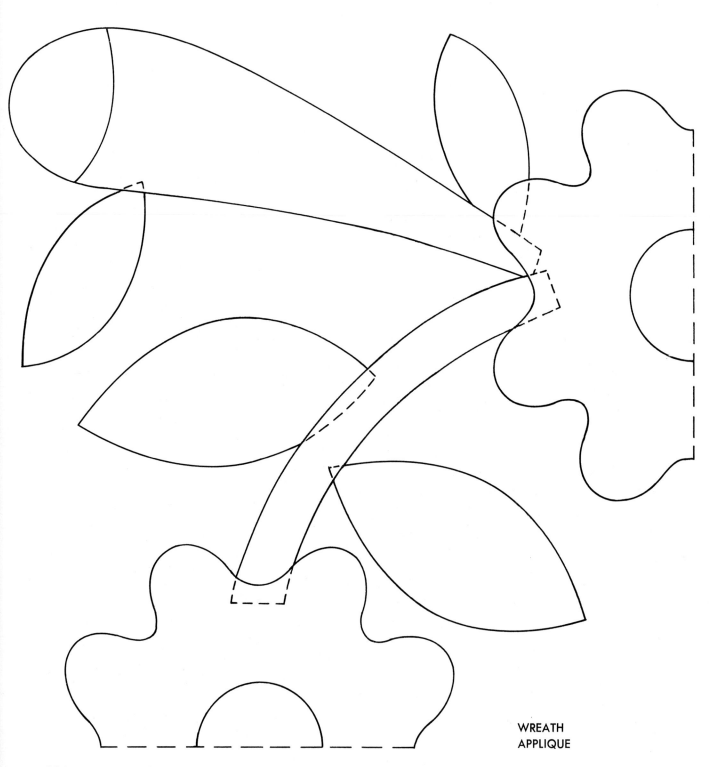

WREATH
APPLIQUE

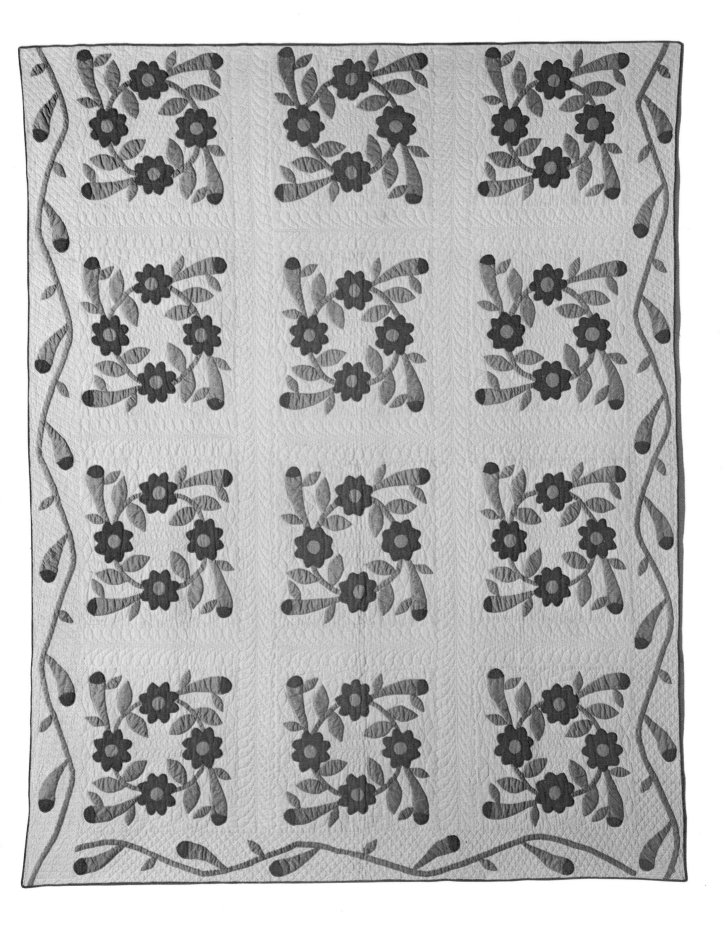

KENTUCKY ROSE QUILT
shown on page 105

SIZE: About 67½" x 83".

EQUIPMENT: Scissors. Ruler. Thin, stiff cardboard. Tailor's chalk. Straight pins. Dressmaker's (carbon) tracing paper. Tracing wheel. Sewing and quilting needles. Pencil.

MATERIALS: Closely woven cotton fabric 44"-45" wide: white, 8 yds. (includes lining); gold, ¼ yd.; red, 2¼ yds.; tan, 2½ yds. White sewing thread. Cotton or dacron polyester batting (Taylor Bedding).

DIRECTIONS: Read General Directions on pages 6 and 7 and How to Appliqué on page 90· Quilt consists of 12 identical appliquéd square blocks, set with joining strips and border.

To make square block, trace actual-size pattern on page 104 for wreath appliqué; complete quarter-pattern indicated by long dash lines; short dash lines indicate overlapped areas. Make a separate cardboard pattern for complete flower, flower center, large leaf, small leaf, bud, bud pod, and curved strip. Following directions in How to Appliqué, cut and prepare appliqué pieces: from red fabric, cut 48 complete flowers and 48 buds; from gold fabric, cut 48 flower centers; from tan fabric, cut 96 large leaves, 96 small leaves, 48 pods, and 48 curved strips.

For background, cut 12 pieces 16" square from white fabric, adding ¼" seam allowance all around. Using dressmaker's carbon and tracing wheel, transfer wreath appliqué design to center of each square. Pin, baste, and slip-stitch appliqué pieces in position on each white square, overlapping as indicated on pattern.

For the joining strips, cut 11 4½"-wide strips from white fabric: nine 16" long and two 77½" long, adding ¼" seam allowance all around. Sew appliquéd blocks into three vertical rows of four blocks each, with a 16"-long joining strip between blocks. Join rows, with a 77½"-long joining strip between rows, for center of quilt top. Piece should measure 57" x 77½", plus outside seam allowance.

For borders, cut three pieces from white fabric 5½" wide: one 57½" long and two 83" long (measurements include ¼" seam allowance all around). Using patterns for wreath appliqué, cut 20 red buds, 20 tan pods, and 19 small tan leaves. Prepare pieces for appliqué. For vines, cut three 1"-wide bias strips from tan fabric, one about 65" long and two about 100" long (piece to get lengths). Prepare bias strips for appliqué by turning under long edges ¼" to make ½"-wide strips; press carefully without stretching folded edges. Lay bias strips down center of border pieces, curving as shown in illustration; pin in place. Pin, baste, and slip-stitch buds and leaves in place on both sides of bias strips, as shown in illustration. Then stitch the overlapping vines, stitching along inside curves of vine first, then outside curves. Sew shorter border piece across bottom of quilt top. Sew longer border pieces to sides. There is no border across top. Quilt top should measure 67½" x 83".

For lining, cut two pieces from white fabric, 42" x 67½". Sew together on long sides with ½" seams; press seam open. Cut batting same size.

Quilting: Trace actual-size quilting patterns below. Using dressmaker's carbon and tracing wheel, transfer smaller quilting pattern to white background inside each appliquéd wreath in a horizontal row from flower to opposite flower. Fill in white space within wreath above and below marked pattern by repeating three loops from each respective half of the design. Make a diamond pattern about 1" wide, 2" long. Fill in white space outside appliquéd wreaths but within blocks by transferring diamond shape, singly or in clusters of two or three diamonds, as desired (in original quilt, diamond shape is used to make random patterns). Transfer larger quilting pattern to white joining strips, repeating for the length of each strip; mark pattern on the two long vertical strips first, then on the nine short horizontal strips. For borders of quilt, mark straight diagonal lines ⅝" apart in both directions, skipping over appliqués; use ruler and tailor's chalk.

Pin and baste lining, batting, and quilt top together, following General Directions. Starting in center and working around and outward, quilt on all marked lines; quilt around main outlines of appliquéd wreaths and vines.

To bind edges of quilt, cut four 1"-wide strips from red fabric, two 68" long and two 83½" long. Sew strips to front of quilt, right sides together and with ¼" seams. Turn strips to back and slip-stitch to lining, turning in edges of strips ¼". Press all edges.

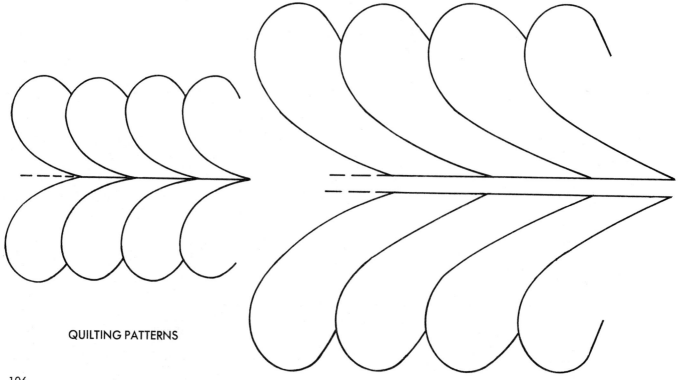

QUILTING PATTERNS

BLAZING STAR QUILT

continued from page 60

half-star blocks with extended edges of squares. Piece should measure about 66⅝″ square, plus outside seam allowance.

To make pattern for sawtooth border, draw a 1-3/16″ square on cardboard; draw a diagonal line between two opposite corners; cut on marked lines for triangle pattern. Marking pattern on wrong side of fabric and adding ¼″ seam allowance all around, cut 228 triangles each from plain red and yellow fabrics. Sew red and yellow triangles together on their long sides to make 228 patches 1-3″16/ square, plus outside seam allowance. Sew square patches into four long strips of 55 squares each, keeping red triangles on upper edge of strip and yellow triangles on lower edge (there will be four patches remaining); make two strips with right angles of yellow triangles on the left and two strips with right angles

of yellow triangles on the right. Sew strips to main body of quilt top, with red triangles inward; place strips made in same manner on sides opposite to each other. To finish sawtooth border, fill in corners with remaining four squares, placing them as shown in illustration. Piece should measure about 70¼″ square, plus outside seam allowance.

For plain border, cut four strips from dark green fabric 8″ wide, two 70¾″ long and two 85¾″ long (measurements include ¼″ seam allowance). Sew shorter strips to sides of quilt, then longer strips to top and bottom. Quilt top should measure about 85¾″ square.

For lining, cut two pieces 43⅜″ x 85¾″. Right sides together, join pieces on long sides with ½″ seams; press seam open. Cut batting same size as lining and quilt top.

Quilting: With ruler and tailor's chalk, mark quilting lines ¾″ apart in both directions over green background

squares and triangles; on squares, mark lines diagonally, starting with corner-to-corner center lines; on triangles, mark lines parallel to the two shorter sides. Using dressmaker's carbon and tracing wheel, transfer border quilting pattern to green border, starting in corners and repeating curve pattern to cover length of each side; mark pattern flush with seams joining sawtooth and green borders, leaving outer ¼″ of green border unmarked.

Following General Directions, pin and baste lining, batting, and quilt top together. Starting in center and working around and outward, quilt on each diamond and triangle patch of quilt top, close to seam on each side; quilt on all marked lines of green pieces.

To bind edges of quilt, cut four strips from plain red fabric 1″ x 86¼″ (piece to get lengths). Right sides together, sew a strip to each edge of front of quilt, with ¼″ seams. Fold strips to back of quilt, turn in raw edges ¼″, and slip-stitch to lining. Press edges.

LOTUS QUILT

shown on page 103

SIZE: About 87½″ square.

EQUIPMENT: Ruler. Scissors. Dark and light-colored pencils. Paper for patterns. Tracing paper. Dressmaker's (carbon) tracing paper. Tracing wheel. Sewing and quilting needles. Quilting frame (optional).

MATERIALS: Closely woven cotton fabric 45″ wide: red, 1⅓ yds.; light orange, 2⅛ yds.; green, 2½ yds.; white, 9 yds. (includes lining). White sewing thread. Dacron polyester or cotton batting.

DIRECTIONS: Real General Directions on pages 6 and 7 and How to Appliqué on page 90. Quilt is constructed of 16 appliquéd blocks and a three-color border.

To make appliquéd block, enlarge flower pattern on page 102 on paper ruled in 1″ squares; complete half-pattern for stem indicated by dash lines (long dash lines of pattern indicate quarter-block; short dash lines indicate quilting patterns). Make a separate cardboard pattern for flower, outer petals (one piece, overlapped by stem), stem, and a leaf. Following directions in How to Appliqué, cut and prepare pieces as follows. Cut 64 flowers from red fabric, 64 petals from orange fabric, 64 leaves and 32 stems from green fabric. For background of blocks, cut 16 pieces 16″ square from white fabric, adding ¼″ seam allowance all around. On each white square, indicate

horizontal and vertical center lines (fold and crease or mark with ruler and tailor's chalk). Using dressmaker's carbon and tracing wheel, transfer flower pattern to each quarter of white background, matching long dash lines to center lines and with stem pieces meeting in center of block; leaves will be transferred only twice. Pin, baste, and slip-stitch appliqués in place, overlapping one stem with the other.

To frame blocks, cut 12 strips 2″ x 16½″ from green fabric (measurements include ¼″ seam allowance). Sew blocks into four horizontal rows of four blocks alternating with three green strips in each row. Cut five strips 2″ x 69″ from green fabric. Sew strips between rows of blocks and to top and bottom of piece made. Cut two strips 2″ x 72″ from green fabric and sew to sides of piece made. Piece should measure 71½″ square, plus outside seam allowance.

For first border, cut four strips 3″ x 77″ from white fabric (measurements include ¼″ seam allowance). Sew strips to main body of quilt top, centering strips on each side so that an equal amount extends at each end. To miter corners of strips, lay piece flat, right side down. At corners, hold adjacent ends together with right sides facing. Keeping border flat, lift up inner corners and pin together diagonally from inner corners to outer corners; baste, then stitch on basting line. Cut off excess fabric, leaving ¼″ seam; press seam open.

For second border, cut four strips 2″ x 80″ from orange fabric. Sew on in same manner as first border, mitering corners. For third border, cut four strips 3″ x 85″ from white fabric and sew on in same manner. For fourth border, cut four strips 1¾″ x 87½″ from green fabric and sew on. Quilt top should measure 87½″ square.

For lining, cut two pieces 44¾″ x 88½″ from white fabric. Sew together on long sides with ½″ seams to make lining 88½″ square; press seam open. Cut batting same size as quilt top.

Quilting: Using dressmaker's carbon and tracing wheel, transfer quilting lines from appliqué pattern to each block. Trace actual-size wave and cable quilting patterns on page 102. Transfer wave pattern to each green framing strip and to orange and green border strips, starting in corners where strips meet and repeating waves for length of strips. Transfer cable quilting pattern to each white border strip, starting in corners.

Following General Directions, pin and baste lining, batting, and quilt top together, centering layers so that lining extends ½″ all around beyond batting and quilt top. Starting in center and working around and outward, quilt on all marked lines and around main outlines of appliqué design in each block, close to seams.

To bind edges, fold excess lining to front of quilt; turn in raw edge ¼″ and slip-stitch folded edge to quilt top. Press edges of quilt.

ROSE CROSS QUILT

SIZE: 40″ square.

EQUIPMENT: Scissors. Tailor's chalk. Ruler. Dressmaker's (carbon) tracing paper. Tracing wheel. Thin, stiff cardboard. Light and dark-colored sharp pencils. Sewing and quilting needles. Straight pins.

MATERIALS: Quilt top: Closely woven cotton fabric in small-figured prints, 36″ wide: 1⅛ yds. dark green, ¾ yd. medium green, ⅞ yd. rust, ⅛ yd. yellow, ¼ yd. red. Small amounts of solid red, solid gold, and navy print. Lining: 1⅛ yds. of 45″-wide fabric. Dacron polyester or cotton batting. Sewing thread in black and to match fabrics.

DIRECTIONS: Read General Directions on pages 6 and 7 and How To Appliqué on page 90. Enlarge flower section of Patchwork-Appliqué Pattern by copying on paper ruled in 1″ squares; complete quarter-pattern indicated by dash lines. Cut 24″-square piece from medium-green fabric, adding ¼″ all around for seam allowance. With ruler and tailor's chalk, divide green square piece into four equal sections. Transfer main outline of flower design to each section, using dressmaker's carbon and tracing wheel. For patch pieces, make a separate cardboard pattern for each part of flower design, making one for each number. Cut patch pieces as follows, marking on wrong side of fabric (light pencil on dark fabrics and dark on light) and adding ¼″ seam allowance: From red print fabric, cut four of No. 8, 16 of No. 2, 48 of No. 3; from yellow print fabric, cut 48 of No. 4; from gold, cut 32 of No. 5; from navy, 16 of No. 6; from solid red, 16 of No. 7; from dark green, 4 of No. 1 (including part overlapped by No. 8). Following General Directions, piece together four roses and 16 buds. For each rose, use one No. 1, one No. 8, four No. 2's, 12 No. 3's, and 12 No. 4's; appliqué No. 8 to center of No. 1. For each bud, use 2 No. 5's and one each of No. 6 and No. 7. Appliqué four buds and a rose to each quarter section of green background, overlapping rose over base of buds.

For border, cut four 2½″-wide strips from rust fabric, two 24½″ long and two 28½″ long. Sew shorter strips to two opposite sides of quilt top, right sides together and with ¼″ seam allowances. Sew longer strips to remaining sides in same manner, sewing sides of longer strips to ends of shorter strips. Transfer zigzag border lines of Patchwork-Appliqué Pattern to rust border, using carbon and tracing wheel. Cut 56 strips from medium green fabric, 1″ x 2½″. Appliqué strips to border, with ¼″ seam allowance. Cut four 6¼″-wide strips from dark green fabric, two 28½″ long and two 40″ long. Sew to quilt top in same manner as rust strips. Cut batting and lining the same size as quilt top.

Quilting: With ruler and tailor's chalk, mark medium-green center background of quilt top with intersecting diagonal lines, skipping over appliqué motifs; mark lines in both directions, ¾″ apart. Enlarge Border Quilting Pattern on 1″ squares and transfer to dark green border of quilt, ¾″ from edge of quilt top and repeating all around border; pattern does not join at corners.

Following General Directions, pin and baste lining, batting, and quilt top together. With black thread, quilt on marked lines, around all patch and appliqué pieces (including zigzags), and around both sides of rust border stripe.

For edging, cut four 1½″-wide strips from rust fabric, 40½″ long (piece fabric to get this length). Sew a strip to lining on each side of quilt, ½″ from edge, right sides together and making ¼″ seam allowance; turn in ends of strips. Fold strips to right side of quilt and slip-stitch to top, turning in raw edge ¼″. Press all edges lightly.

BORDER QUILTING PATTERN

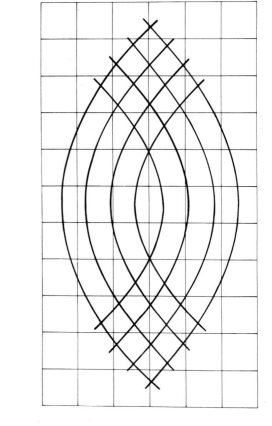

PATCHWORK-APPLIQUE PATTERN

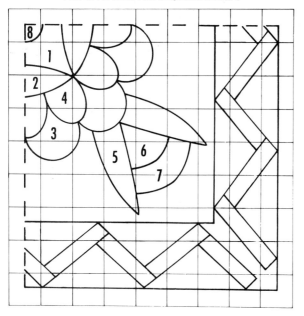

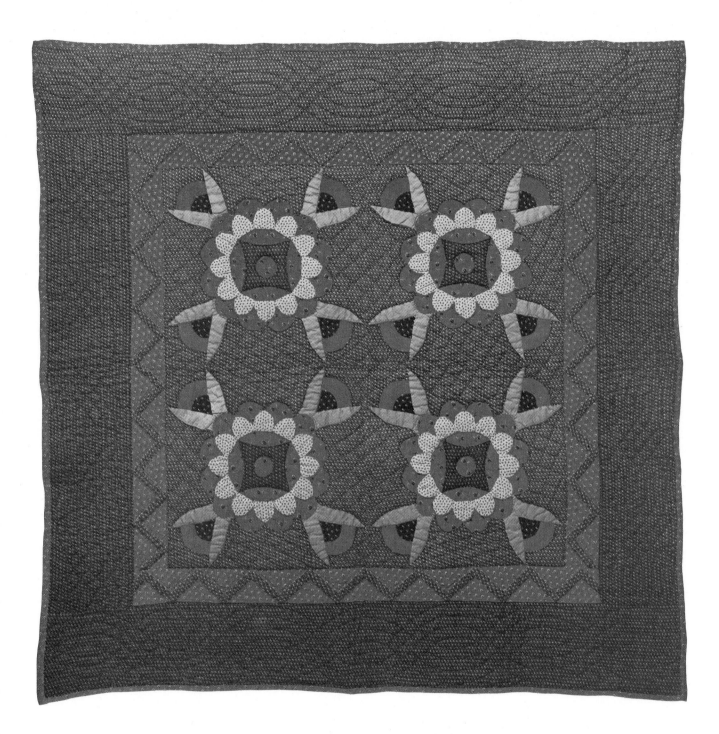

*Rose Cross Quilt was made square, in the old-fashioned
style of crib quilts. Although the entire coverlet was pieced,
we have simplified our directions to include appliquéing
patchwork roses to the background. Pennsylvania; about 1890.*

COLLECTION OF TONY ELLIS AND BILL GALLICK

RADICAL ROSE QUILT

SIZE: Approximately 83″ square.

EQUIPMENT: Ruler. Scissors. Pencil. Thin, stiff cardboard. Tracing paper. Dressmaker's (carbon) tracing paper. Tracing wheel. Tailor's chalk. Sewing and quilting needles. Quilting frame (optional).

MATERIALS: Closely woven cotton fabric 45″ wide: yellow, 4½ yds.; brown, 2½ yds.; dark blue, 1 yd.; red in a small print, ¾ yd.; lining, 4⅝ yds. Matching sewing thread. Dacron polyester or cotton batting (Stearns & Foster).

DIRECTIONS: Read General Directions on pages 6 and 7 and How to Appliqué on page 90. Quilt is made up of four appliquéd blocks plus pieced and plain borders; an extra flower is appliquéd to center joining of blocks. For appliqué pieces, enlarge pattern on paper ruled in 1″ squares; complete quarter-pattern of center flower and half-pattern of large buds indicated by long dash lines. (Short dash lines on No. 5 show quilting pattern.) Make a separate cardboard pattern for each numbered part of appliqué design. Following directions in How to Appliqué, cut and prepare appliqué pieces. From brown fabric, cut five of No. 1, five of No. 4, 32 of No. 11, 32 of No. 8, and 16 of No. 13. From yellow fabric, cut five of No. 2 and 32 of No. 10. From red fabric cut five of No. 3 and 32 of No. 9. From blue fabric cut 16 of No. 5, 32 of No. 6, 16 of No. 12, 16 of No. 7 and 16 of No. 14.

For main background of each block, cut four pieces 32″ square from yellow fabric, adding ¼″ seam allowance all around. On each yellow square, indicate horizontal and vertical center lines (fold and crease or mark lines with ruler and tailor's chalk). Using dressmaker's carbon and tracing wheel, transfer main outlines of complete appliqué pattern to each square by matching quarter-pattern lines to marked center lines; the center line of buds should fall on marked center lines. Make five large and 32 small flower appliqués, centering each piece on the next larger piece and pinning, basting, and slip-stitching in place. Pin, baste, and slip-stitch flowers and remaining appliqué pieces in place on the squares, sewing overlapping pieces last. There will be one large flower remaining.

Join the four finished blocks into two rows of two blocks each, then join rows together for main body of quilt top. Appliqué remaining large flower to center of piece. Piece should measure 64″ square, plus outside seam allowance.

For pieced border, draw a 2″ square on cardboard, draw a line connecting two opposite corners, and cut along marked lines for triangle pattern. Make several pattern pieces and replace pattern when edges begin to fray. Marking pattern on wrong side of fabric and adding ¼″ seam allowance all around, cut 132 triangles from yellow fabric and 132 from brown. Make 132 square patches by sewing brown and yellow triangles together along long edges. Sew square patches into four strips of 33 patches each, with right sides facing and keeping brown triangles all pointed in same direction. Sew strips to main body of quilt top with all yellow triangles on inside edge, one end of strip flush and other end extending one square beyond edge of quilt top. Piece should measure 68″ square plus outside seam allowance.

For plain border, cut four strips 8¼″ wide, two 68½″ long and two 84″ long; measurements include ¼″ seam allowance. Sew shorter strips to main body of quilt top on opposite sides, keeping right sides together and sewing on long edges. Sew longer strips to top and bottom. Piece should measure 84″ square.

For lining, cut two pieces 42″ x 83″. Right sides facing, sew pieces together on long edges with ½″ seams, to make piece 83″ square. Press seam open. Cut batting same size as lining.

Quilting: With ruler and tailor's chalk, mark yellow background of

continued on page 98

APPLIQUE PATTERN

BORDER QUILTING PATTERN

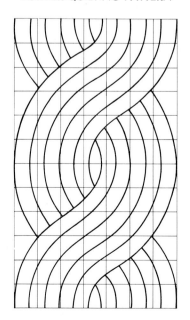

The bright colors and large, splashy pattern in the quilt above are typical of Pennsylvania. The bold appliqué design is framed by sawtooth edging and a wide, cable-quilted border. Radical Rose, made around 1900, has several other names; see Whig Rose on page 95.

THOMAS K. WOODARD AMERICAN ANTIQUES AND QUILTS

PLUME QUILT

SIZE: 85″ square.

EQUIPMENT: Tracing paper. Pencil. Stiff cardboard. Scissors. Sewing needle. Quilting needle. Tape measure. Straight pins.

MATERIALS: Closely woven cotton fabric, 36″ wide: Dark blue, 6 yards; small plaid (for lining), 6 yards; orange, 2 yards; red, 2½ yards. Sewing thread to match fabrics. Cotton batting.

DIRECTIONS: Read General Directions on pages 6 and 7 and Appliqué on page 90. Enlarge patterns for appliqués on 1″ squares **Note:** Enlarge only one diamond piece of Border Flower; complete half and quarter-patterns indicated by long dash lines.

From cardboard, cut out each pattern.

Following directions for Appliqué, cut and prepare appliqué pieces. From orange fabric, cut 16 plumes, 10 scallops, 32 diamonds, and piece 1 of center flower. From red fabric, cut 10 scallops, 16 plumes, 4 stars, piece 2 of center flower, 40 diamonds, 16 stems, and piece 1 of border flower.

For background of quilt top, cut four pieces of blue fabric each 35″ square; cut two pieces 9″ wide and 86″ long; cut two pieces 9″ wide and 69″ long.

Pin a red star at center of each blue fabric square. Place plumes around star, radiating out from center and alternating red and orange fabric. Space evenly and pin in place. Baste ap-

pliqués to blue fabric. With matching thread, slip-stitch each appliqué in place.

Stitch the four blue squares together with right sides facing, taking ½″ seams. Over center joining of the four squares, appliqué the orange and red flower pieces as shown. Along opposite sides of the joined squares, stitch a 69″ long piece with ½″ seams, for borders. Along remaining opposite sides, stitch the 86″ border pieces with equal ends extending. Stitch ends of shorter border pieces to side edges of longer border ends. Place five orange and red scallop pieces along the edge of the four sides of border, alternating colors and spacing evenly; pin in place. For bor-

continued on page 114

Pennsylvania quilt of the 1860's might have been created on the fourth of July! Four squares of blue, each appliquéd with a plume-and-star motif, are joined for center of quilt; flower medallion and swag-and-tulip border complete design. Quilting follows contours of the appliqués.

PLUME QUILT

continued from page 112

der flowers, sew together four diamonds as shown on pattern, with ⅛" seams, placing red diamonds on outside and orange in middle. Sew two red diamonds together along one side for each corner of border.

Between each border scallop, pin a stem and flower as shown. Pin two joined red diamonds between tops of corner scallops. Baste all in place; slip-stitch appliqués to background.

For quilt lining, cut two pieces of plaid fabric 36" x 86" and one piece 16" x 86". Stitch the long edges of the 36" pieces along each long edge of 16" piece, taking ½" seams. Press seams open.

Quilting: Following General Directions, pin and baste quilt top, batting, and lining together. Make quilting lines ⅛" inside each appliqué piece, following outline, then about ½" apart along length of scallops and plumes and within center flower; on stars; quilt star shapes following border flower diamond pattern. On quilt background, make lines of quilting around appliqué pieces ½" away and then ½" apart to fill areas. **(Note: If desired, quilting lines may be marked with pencil or chalk before basting the three layers together.)**

After quilting is completed, remove the basting stitches. Turn margin of plaid lining over edges of quilt to front for edging. Turn in about ¼" of margin and slip-stitch plaid edging to front of quilt for a neat finish.

EAGLE QUILT

SIZE: About 75½" square.
EQUIPMENT: Scissors. Ruler. Thin, stiff cardboard. Tailor's chalk. Pins. Paper for patterns. Tracing paper. Pencil. Dressmaker's (carbon) tracing paper. Tracing wheel. Sewing and quilting needles. Quilting frame (optional).
MATERIALS: Closely woven cotton fabric 44"-45" wide: yellow, 3½ yds.; red, 2 yds.; gray-green, 1¼ yds.; orange, ¼ yd. Lining, 4¼ yds. Cotton or dacron polyester batting. White sewing thread.
DIRECTIONS: Read General Directions on pages 6 and 7 and How to Appliqué, page 90. Enlarge appliqué patterns on pages 116, 117 on paper ruled in squares (eagle on 2" squares, center and corner appliqués on 1" squares); complete half and quarter-patterns indicated by dash lines. Make a separate cardboard pattern for each part of each appliqué motif. Following directions in How to Appliqué, cut and prepare appliqué pieces. From red fabric, cut four eagle's heads (two facing left and, reversing pattern, two facing right), four tails, four olives, eight feet, one inner piece of center appliqué, and four bases of corner appliqués. Cut out a small circle in each eagle's head for eye. From gray-green fabric, cut eight eagle's wings (four pointing left and, reversing pattern, four pointing right); one outer piece of center appliqué; and four leaves of corner appliqués. From orange fabric, cut four eagle's bodies.

For center background of quilt, cut four pieces 28" square from yellow fabric, adding ¼" seam allowance all around. To aid in placing eagle appliqués, indicate diagonal center of each yellow square by marking a line from one corner to diagonally opposite corner (fold and crease to make line or mark with ruler and tailor's chalk). Lay squares together to make one large square, with diagonal lines converging in center of large square. Lay eagle appliqués in place on each square, centering on diagonal line, with tails 11" from outer corners; see illustration for placement of heads. Pin, baste, and slip-stitch appliqués, starting with wings, feet, and tail, then head (with beak overlapping olive branch), and, finally, the orange body. Pin and stitch corner appliqués in place, matching seam allowances of red piece and yellow background, and overlapping green leaf with red piece.

Stitch the four yellow squares together, right sides facing and with ¼" seams. Pin and stitch the red center appliqué to center of background, then the green center appliqué around it. Quilt center should measure 56" square, plus outside seam allowance.

To make pattern for pieced first border, draw a 1¾" square on cardboard; draw a diagonal line from corner to corner and cut out triangle. Marking pattern on wrong side of fabric and adding ¼" seam allowance all around, cut 136 triangles from red fabric and 136 triangles from yellow fabric. Sew yellow triangles to red triangles on long sides to make 136 pieced squares. Join squares into four strips of 34 squares each, making sure triangles are all pointing in the same direction. Sew strips to quilt center, with red triangles on inside; strip will be flush with quilt center at one end and extend one square beyond quilt center at other end.

For red second border, cut four pieces 4¼" x 67½"; measurements include ¼" seam allowance all around. Sew a piece to each side of quilt center, centering piece so that an equal amount extends at each corner. To miter corners of border, lay piece flat, right side down. Hold adjacent ends at corners together with right sides facing. Keeping border flat, lift up inner corners and pin together diagonally from inner corners to outer corners; baste, then stitch on basting line. Cut off excess fabric, leaving ¼" seam; press seam open. For yellow third border, cut four pieces 4½" x 75½". Sew on in same manner as for red border, mitering corners. Quilt top should measure 75½" square.

For lining, cut two pieces 38¼" x 75½". Join pieces on long sides, right sides together and with ½" seams. Press seam open. Cut batting same size as lining and quilt top.

Quilting: With ruler and tailor's chalk, mark straight diagonal lines in both directions, 1¼" apart, over center of quilt top. Trace border quilting pattern on page 116. Using dressmaker's carbon and tracing wheel, transfer pattern to centers of both yellow and red borders, repeating the length of each strip. Pin and baste quilt top, batting, and lining together, following General Directions. Starting in center and working around and outward, quilt on all marked lines; quilt ⅛" away, around all appliqués and along both sides of seam lines.

To bind edges, cut four strips from red fabric 1½" x 76" (piece to get lengths). Right sides together, sew a strip to each edge on front of quilt, ½" from edge of quilt and with ¼" seam allowance. Turn strips to back of quilt, turning in raw edge ¼", and slip-stitch to back. Press all edges.

Four wide-winged eagles are impressive on a field of bright yellow. The eagle motif, popular since the Revolution, became bolder and more stylized in the 19th century. Eagle quilts were also known as Union quilts. Ours was made in Pennsylvania, around 1890.

COLLECTION OF GEORGE SCHOELLKOPF

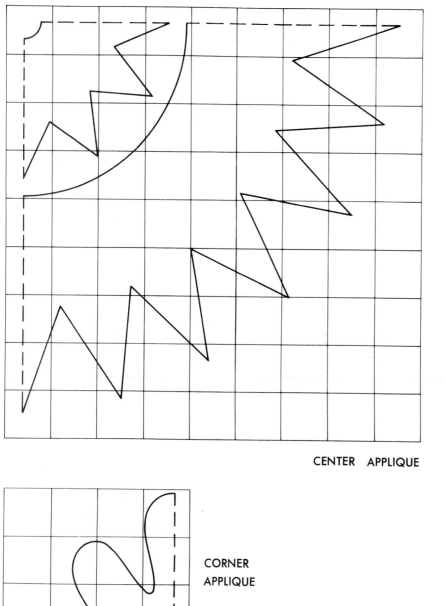

CENTER APPLIQUE

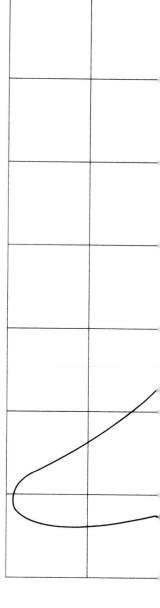

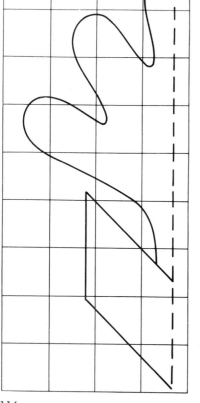

CORNER
APPLIQUE

BORDER QUILTING PATTERN

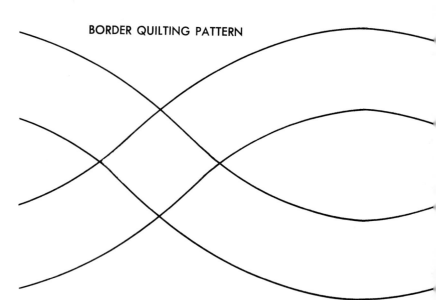

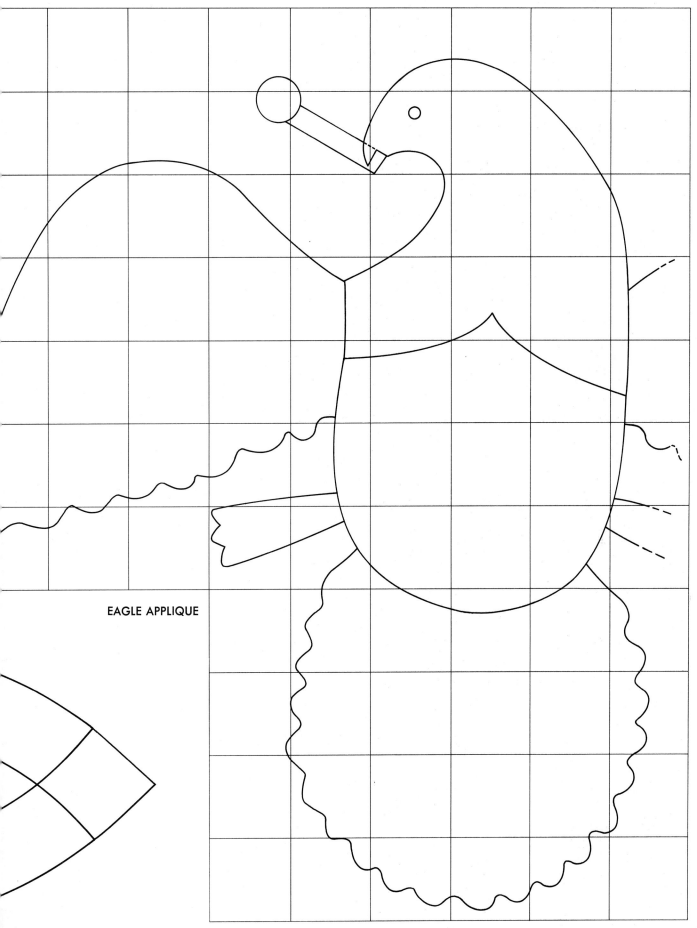

EAGLE APPLIQUE

117

COOKIE CUTTER QUILT

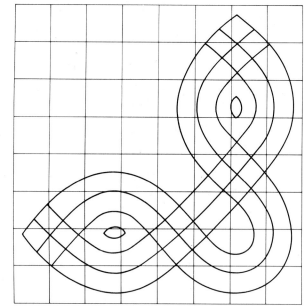

BORDER
QUILTING PATTERN

APPLIQUE PATTERNS

COOKIE CUTTER QUILT

shown on page 119

SIZE: About 71" x 81".

EQUIPMENT: Scissors. Ruler. Thin, stiff cardboard. Dressmaker's (carbon) tracing paper. Tracing wheel. Paper for patterns. Tailor's chalk. Sewing and quilting needles. Pencil. Quilting frame (optional).

MATERIALS: Closely woven cotton fabric 36" wide: green small print, 2¼ yds.; red print, 2⅛ yds.; blue print, 2 yds.; plain red, 1½ yds.; plain gray-green, 1½ yds.; lining, 4½ yds., scraps of other small print fabrics (plus a few plain, if desired) in red, blue, green, yellow, and gold. Matching sewing thread. Dacron polyester or cotton batting (Taylor Bedding).

DIRECTIONS: Read General Directions on pages 6 and 7 and How to Appliqué on page 90. Quilt is constructed of 30 appliquéd square blocks, plus a three-color border. For blocks, cut 30 10" squares, 15 from plain gray-green fabric and 15 from plain red fabric, adding ¼" seam allowance all around. For borders, cut 12 4"-wide strips: from blue print fabric, cut two 50½" long and two 67½" long; from red print fabric, cut two 57½" long and two 74½" long; from green print fabric, cut two 64½" long and two 81" long (measurements include ¼" seam allowance).

Enlarge appliqué patterns on page 118 by copying on paper ruled in 1" squares; complete half and quarter-patterns indicated by dash lines. In center of group of patterns, a small cross is superimposed on a larger cross (half-patterns); make a separate pattern for each. For hand appliqué, trace around your own hand. Make a cardboard pattern for each appliqué; make separate patterns for each part of each motif, where necessary. Place patterns for large appliqués in one group and patterns for smaller appliqués in another group.

Following directions in How to Appliqué, cut and prepare appliqués, using scraps left over from cutting borders and blocks, as well as other printed and plain fabrics. Cut 30 large appliqués, 15 from red print fabrics and 15 from green print fabrics; cut 20 small crosses and about 240 other small appliqués from random fabrics. Pin a large appliqué to center of each square block, red appliqués on green blocks and green appliqués on red blocks. Setting small crosses aside, pin remaining small appliqués on blocks, grouping about eight around large appliqué on each block. Baste and slip-stitch appliqués in place.

To assemble quilt top, sew blocks into six horizontal rows of five blocks each, alternating red and green blocks. Sew rows together to make piece 50" x 60", again alternating blocks. Pin, baste, and slip-stitch a small cross to each four-block intersection. Sew on border strips as follows, making ¼" seams: sew shorter blue strips to top and bottom of quilt top, then longer blue strips to sides; sew on red strips in same manner, then green strips. Quilt top should measure 71" x 81".

For lining, cut two pieces 36" x 81". Sew together on long edges with ½" seams to make piece 71" x 81"; press seam open. (To make striped lining as shown in illustration, cut 13 strips 61" x 81"; sew together on long edges with ½" seams.) Cut batting same size as lining and quilt top.

Quilting: With ruler and tailor's chalk, mark diagonal lines 1" apart in both directions on blue and green borders. Enlarge border quilting pattern on page 118 on paper ruled in 1" squares. Using dressmaker's carbon and tracing wheel, transfer pattern to red borders of quilt top, starting in corners and repeating cable pattern to cover length of each red border.

Pin and baste lining, batting, and quilt top together, following General Directions. Starting in center and work-around and outward, quilt around each appliqué, close to seam line; quilt close to seam lines that join blocks, on both sides of seams. Quilt borders on all marked lines.

To bind edges of quilt, cut four 2"-wide strips from blue print fabric, two 81½" long and two 71½" long, piecing to get lengths. Right sides together, sew a strip to each edge on front of quilt, ½" from edge of quilt and ¼" from edge of strip. Fold strips to back of quilt, turning in raw edge of strip ¼", and slip-stitch to lining. Press all edges of quilt.

ROSE OF SHARON QUILT

shown on opposite page

SIZE: About 84½" square.

EQUIPMENT: Ruler. Scissors. Thin, stiff cardboard. Tailor's chalk. Dressmaker's (carbon) tracing paper. Tracing wheel. Sewing and quilting needles. Straight pins. Pencil. Quilting frame (optional).

MATERIALS: Quilt top: Closely woven cotton fabric 36" wide: bright pink print, 6½ yds.; yellow print, 2 yds.; plain red, ⅔ yd.; plain dark green, 1½ yds. Lining: Cotton fabric 44"-45" wide, 4⅔ yds. Matching sewing thread. Dacron polyester or cotton batting (Stearns & Foster).

DIRECTIONS: Read General Directions on pages 6 and 7 and How to Appliqué on page 90. Quilt is made up of nine appliquéd square blocks, plus wide and narrow borders. Trace appliqué pattern on pages 122, 123; complete quarter-pattern indicated by long dash lines (short dash lines indicate quilting patterns). Make a separate cardboard pattern for each numbered part of appliqué. Following directions in How to Appliqué, cut and prepare appliqué pieces. From yellow print fabric, cut 72 of piece 2 and nine of piece 7; from red fabric, cut 81 of piece 1 and nine of piece 6; from dark green fabric, cut 72 of piece 3, 72 of piece 4, and 36 of piece 5.

For background of blocks, cut nine pieces 21" square from pink print fabric, adding ¼" seam allowance all around. On each pink square, indicate horizontal and vertical center lines (fold and crease or mark lines with ruler and tailor's chalk). Using dressmaker's carbon and tracing wheel, transfer appliqué pattern to each square, centering carefully so there is an equal margin all around; center point of large leaves (piece 5) should fall on the center lines. Pin, baste, and slip-stitch appliqué pieces in place on squares, starting with leaves, then the overlapping stems and flower pieces.

Join the nine finished blocks in three rows of three blocks each, then sew rows together for center of quilt top. Piece should measure 63" square, plus outside seam allowance.

For narrow borders, cut 12 strips 1¼" wide: from yellow print fabric, cut two strips 63½" long, two 65" long, two 66½" long, and two 68" long; from pink print fabric, cut two strips 65" long and two 66½" long (measurements include ¼" seam allowance all around). Sew 63½" yellow strips to top and bottom of quilt top, right sides together and with ¼" seams. Sew 65" yellow strips to sides of quilt top. Sew pink strips on in same manner, then remaining yellow strips. For wide border, cut four strips 9¼" wide from pink fabric, two 68" long and two 85½" long. Sew shorter strips to top and bottom of quilt top and longer strips to sides. Quilt top should measure 85" square.

For lining, cut two pieces 42¾" x 84½". Sew together on long sides with ½" seams to make piece 84½" square. Lining will be ½" smaller all around than quilt top. Cut batting same size as lining.

Quilting: With ruler and tailor's

continued on page 122

*This pretty quilt shows one version of the
"rose of Sharon" pattern, popular since the 18th century.
The bright, cheerful color scheme suggests it was made
in Pennsylvania. Directions on the opposite page.*

QUILT FROM NONESUCH LTD.

ROSE OF SHARON QUILT

chalk, mark diagonal lines 1″ apart in both directions over pink background of quilt center, skipping over appliqués. Enlarge border quilting pattern on page 54 on paper ruled in 1″ squares. Using dressmaker's carbon and tracing wheel, transfer pattern to wide pink border, repeating pattern to cover length of each strip; see illustration.

Pin and baste quilt top, batting, and lining together, following General Directions and centering layers so that quilt top extends ½″ beyond lining and batting all around. Starting in cen-ter and working around and outward, quilt on all marked lines; quilt on each appliqué, close to seam line; quilt close to seam lines joining narrow border strips, on both sides of seams.

To bind edges, turn excess fabric of quilt top to back, turning in raw edges ¼″, and slip-stitch to lining.

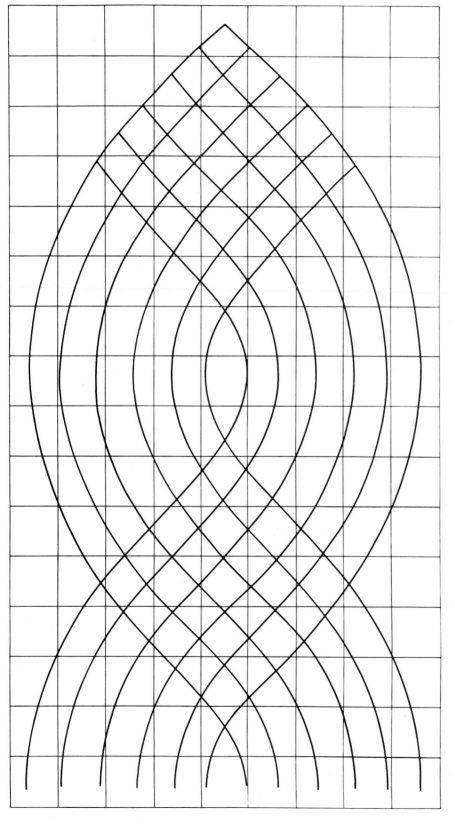

BORDER QUILTING PATTERN

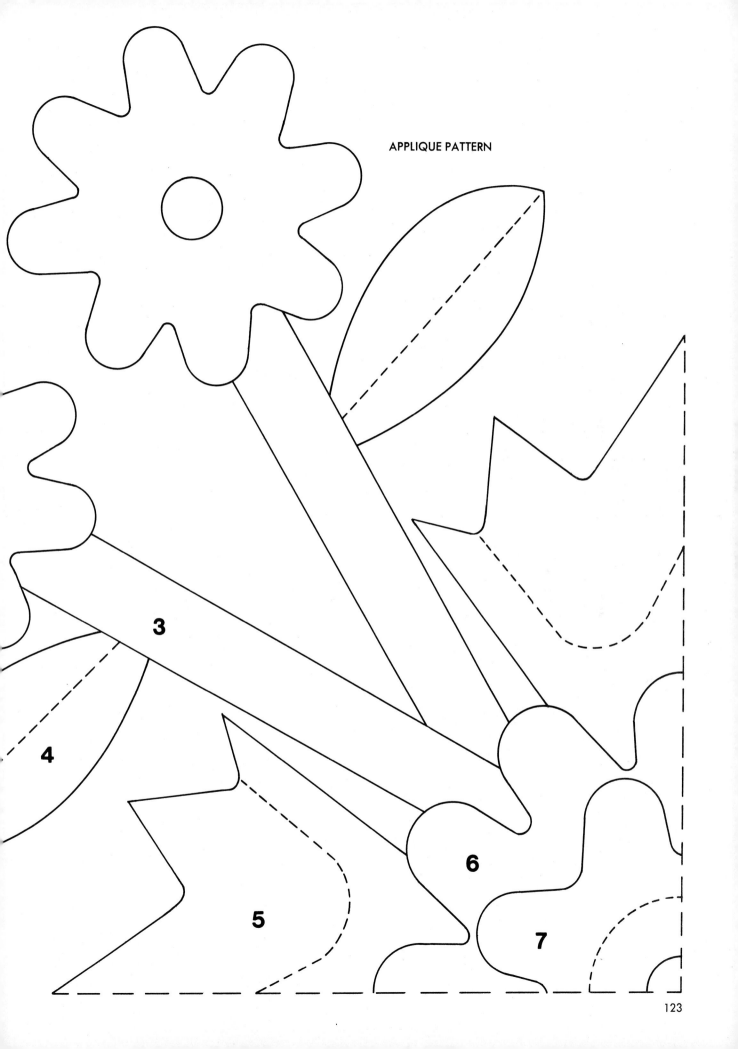

APPLIQUE PATTERN

3

4

5

6

7

123

Novelty Quilts

Puffed quilt of many-hued silks was made about 100 years ago by a 12-year old boy while convalescing. Technique is surprisingly easy: Each puff is made separately by sewing a silk square to a smaller muslin square over a piece of batting. The "biscuits" are then sewn into rows. Perfect for portable quilting!

PUFFED PATCHWORK QUILT

SIZE: 60½" x 71".

EQUIPMENT: Ruler. Yardstick. Pencil. Scissors. Silk pins. Sewing needle. Large-eyed embroidery needle.

MATERIALS: 1,080 assorted pieces of silk fabric in various colors (V), each 3" square. Pink silk (P) for outer border, 36" wide, 1¼ yards. Green silk (G) for inner border, 36" wide, 1 yard. Red silk for lining, 36" wide, 4¼ yards. Unbleached muslin, 36" wide, 8 yards. Pink embroidery floss, 10 yards. Red heavy pearl cotton for quilting. Basting thread. Sewing thread. Polyester quilt batting for full-size bed. Polyester fiber batting for stuffing puffs.

DIRECTIONS: This quilt is comprised of 1¾" (finished size) squares; it is 34 squares wide and 40 squares long. You may increase or decrease size of quilt as desired. You may also use your own color combinations, using above measurements.

Although silk was used for this quilt, any soft, lightweight fabrics may be used, such as dress cotton, corduroy, seersucker, calico, some polyesters (no knits) or rayons, etc. However, all washable fabrics, including unbleached muslin, should be preshrunk. If not, wash and press before cutting.

With yardstick and pencil, mark and cut 1,360 pieces 2¼" square from muslin. Mark and cut pieces 3" square from silk as follows: 144 from P for outer border; 136 from G for inner border; and 1,080 from V for main part of quilt. (**Note:** One yard of 36"-wide fabric will yield exactly 144 3" squares.) If there are scraps of pink and green border material left over, you may include these colors in the main body of quilt; however, these puffs should be placed away from edge.

Make each puff as follows: With wrong sides facing, pin 3" silk square to 2¼" muslin square at corners; on three sides of square, fold extra silk flat into a right-to-left pleat and pin to muslin (see diagram). Insert fiber batting through fourth side, amount depending on how full you want each puff. Pleat fourth side and pin. Baste all around, close to edge.

Sew puffs in rows of 34 (width of quilt), making ¼" seams and with right sides together. Press seams open. Puffs are now 1¾" wide.

Make two rows of 34 P puffs for each end of quilt and two rows of 1 P, 32 G, 1 P, for top and bottom inside border. Make 36 rows of 1 P, 1 G, 30 V, 1 G, 1 P for main body of quilt. With right sides together, sew rows together, beginning and ending with the two border rows. (See illustration for placement.) Press seams open. Measure quilt top.

Prepare quilt batting by using length and width measurement of quilt top and adding an additional ½" all around for border. With right side up, smooth quilt top evenly on batting. Baste all around.

Cut lining fabric in half crosswise. Trim each piece to 31½" x 73". (**Note:** Adjust this measurement to your quilt; each strip should be 1½" wider than half-finished quilt top and 2" longer.) With right sides together and making ½" seams, sew pieces together lengthwise. Press seams open. With wrong sides together and centering seam, place quilt top over lining. Be sure lining is 1" larger than quilt top all around. Pin to secure. Fold lining over ¼" (this may vary, depending on thickness of batting) and ½" again. Making sure border is ½", pin to seam line along puff edge. Miter corners. Baste. Hem all around with an invisible hemming stitch.

Using embroidery floss, embroider border along all four sides as follows: Beginning at upper left-hand corner of border, and working from left to right, work long (1") herringbone stitches (see page 148); make top of stitches ⅛" from outer edge of border and bottom of stitches ⅛" from hem edge.

On back of quilt mark out 20 evenly spaced spots for quilting, making sure each mark is on a puff seam line. With pearl cotton and embroidery needle, tack through lining, catching seam under puffs. Clip excess yarn, leaving enough to knot and tie a small bow.

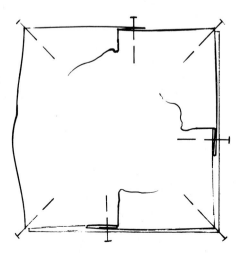

COCKSCOMB QUILT
shown on page 101

SIZE: About 80″ square.

EQUIPMENT: Scissors. Ruler. Thin, stiff cardboard. Paper for patterns. Dressmaker's (carbon) tracing paper. Tailor's chalk. Straight pins. Sewing and quilting needles. Tracing wheel. Quilting frame (optional).

MATERIALS: Closely woven cotton fabric 44″-45″ wide: white, 9 yds. (includes lining); rose, 1 yd.; light green, 2½ yds. Matching sewing thread. Dacron polyester or cotton batting.

DIRECTIONS: Read General Directions on pages 6 and 7 and How to Appliqué on page 90. Enlarge appliqué patterns on page 100 by copying on paper ruled in squares (2″ squares for the flower motif; 1″ squares for border-motif); complete half-pattern of border motif indicated by dash lines. Dotted lines indicate quilting patterns. Make a cardboard pattern for each separate part of appliqué motifs. Following directions in How to Appliqué, cut and prepare appliqués as follows: from rose fabric, cut 20 flower tops, 12 buds, and 12 bows; from green fabric, cut 20 flower bases, 12 bud bases, 12 leaves, 9 scalloped rectangles, 12 border swags, 20 flower stems, 12 leaf stems, and 12 bud stems. (**Note:** You may find it easier to substitute straight bias strips for stems cut from pattern. Cut 1″-wide strips on the bias, turn in both long edges ¼″ to make ½″ strips, and press carefully. Pin in place when appliquéing, curving to fit design.)

For background of quilt top, cut two pieces 41″ x 81″ from white fabric. Sew together on long edges with ½″ seams; press seam open. Pin appliqués in place (do not baste yet) as follows, starting with border: Pin a swag in center of each side, 1″ from edge. Pin a swag on each side of center swags, adjusting placement at corners so adjacent swags meet in one continuous curve. Pin on bows where swags meet. Pin a scalloped rectangular piece ½″ in from swags on top and bottom and middle swags of sides. Pin flower, leaf, bud, and stem pieces in place along inside edge of each rectangular piece to complete appliqué motifs around sides of quilt top. Pin remaining rectangular piece in center of quilt top; pin remaining appliqué pieces around it (see illustration for placement). At this point, examine overall design carefully and make any adjustments that seem necessary for a pleasing effect; unpin and reposition any part of side and center appliqués as desired. When design is arranged to your satisfaction, baste pieces in place and slip-stitch, starting with stems, then continuing with flower tops and buds and the overlapping green pieces.

For lining, cut two pieces 41″ x 81″ from white fabric. Sew together on long sides with ½″ seams. Press seam open. Cut batting same size as lining and quilt top.

Quilting: Using dressmaker's carbon and tracing wheel, transfer dotted-line quilting patterns to each appliqué piece. Using leaf appliqué pattern as a quilting pattern, transfer leaf design to white background where desired. (In original quilt, leaves of varying sizes and shapes were quilted at random over parts of the white background.) Remaining quilting patterns are made with double rows of lines; lines of a double row are 1/16″ apart and double rows are ¼″ apart. With tailor's chalk, mark two double rows around main outlines of appliqué pieces, including inside curves of swags. Using ruler and tailor's chalk, mark straight double rows over remaining parts of white background; make parallel lines all in on direction or vary as in original quilt (see illustration).

Pin and baste quilt top, batting, and lining together, following General Directions. Trim corners into curves, leaving at least 1½″ between points of corner bows and curves. On quilt top, mark seam allowance all around, ½″ from edge. Starting in center and working around and outward, quilt on all marked lines. Do not quilt beyond seam line marked around edge of quilt.

To finish edges, trim lining and batting to ½″ from edge of quilt top. Turn excess fabric of quilt top to back; turn in raw edge ¼″, and slip-stitch to lining. Press edges.

YO-YO QUILT

SIZE: 88″ x 90¾″.

EQUIPMENT: Ruler. Compass. Pencil. Scissors. Thin, stiff cardboard. Sewing needle. Tailor's chalk. Iron.

MATERIALS: Scraps of solid or print lightweight fabrics, in colors desired. Strong sewing thread, such as #50 or #60.

DIRECTIONS: Choose fabrics that are all of the same general type, such as all silk or all cotton. For patterns, cut several 2¾″ circles from the cardboard; replace patterns as edges become worn from use. Use pencil to trace pattern outlines on fabric; cut circles from fabric. Mark a line on right side of each circle ¼″ from edge with tailor's chalk (a 2¼″ cardboard circle would be helpful in marking). Holding circle with right side facing you, turn ¼″ margin to back of circle and sew down, ⅛″ from fold. Using thread double in the needle, sew with small even running stitches; do not backstitch as you sew or secure the end of thread until you have pulled the edge of circle into tight gathers. After circle is gathered to form a small hole in center, secure with several small backstitches. Spread the gathers evenly around the center hole. Flatten the puff to make a round patch by covering with a damp cloth and pressing with a warm iron. Patches should measure approximately 1⅜″ diameter.

After patches are made, arrange them as desired, with gathered side up. To sew together, place two adjacent patches together, right sides facing; make tiny overcast stitches through edges of both for about ¼″. Sew patches together in rows, then sew rows together with same method.

Note: To make sure you have enough fabric for entire quilt, determine the number of patches needed for size desired. Cut out all patches before beginning to stitch them together. Our quilt, which measures 88″ x 90¾″, required 4,224 patches, sewn together in 64 rows of 66 patches each.

"Cathedral Window" is traditional name for this colorful daybed coverlet. The fascinating technique uses squares of unbleached muslin folded and refolded into smaller, mutilayered squares that are sewn together for basic coverlet. Then edges from adjacent squares are sewn over a square of print fabric, to make interlocking diamond-in-circle design.

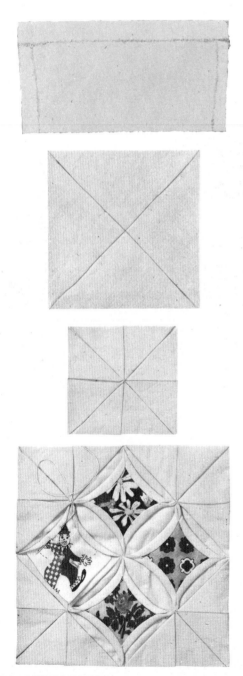

CATHEDRAL COVERLET

SIZE: 64″ x 80″.

EQUIPMENT: Ruler. Scissors. Needle. Cardboard. Straight pins. Pencil.

MATERIALS: Unbleached muslin 72″ wide, 12¼ yards. Scraps of cotton print fabrics in a variety of colors and patterns. White mercerized sewing thread.

DIRECTIONS: For this coverlet, no cotton batting is required and no actual quilting stitching is done. It is made of squares of muslin folded in such a way as to make a multithickness, and the squares are then joined together.

Wash muslin to pre-shrink, and press. For each folded square you will need a piece of muslin 7″ x 7″. To make a coverlet 64″ x 80″, you will need 616 squares. Mark edge of muslin into 7″ wide pieces. Clip the edge at each mark and tear 7″ wide strips across muslin. Mark the strips into 7″ pieces and tear each one. Cut a piece of cardboard 6″ square; use this to simplify folding ½″ seam allowances on each 7″ square of muslin.

Fold over the ½″ seams on a square of muslin and fold muslin in half with seam allowances on outside (see top detail at left). Sew edges together at sides from top open edge down 1½″ with close overcasting stitch, catching just the edges of fabric. Turn piece inside out, and refold flat so seams are at center (see second detail at left). Sew the two open edges together from center out 1½″ to each side, with slip stitch, leaving ends open; do not sew through bottom fabric. You now have a 4¼″ square. Turn square over so plain side is on top. Fold corners to center and pin. Tack corners together securely (see third detail at left). Then tack center corners through all thicknesses of square. Square is now 3″. Make three more folded squares the same. To join, hold two squares together with diagonal open seams in, and overcast one side together, taking close stitches through edges of both (this side is back of coverlet). Open out squares. Join two more squares in same manner, and sew to first two to form a block of four. Continue making blocks of four and then join blocks, overcasting edges together, to make strips of 22 squares (11 blocks). Make 14 strips in this manner. Sew the strips together in same manner, making 28″ squares on longer sides. Or, blocks of four may be added as they are made to make coverlet 22 squares by 28 squares. The squares of cathedral windows may be sewn on the blocks of four or after they are sewn into strips, or when the coverlet is completely assembled.

To make the windows, mark and cut a 2″ square of cardboard. Use this to cut pieces of print fabrics. Window patches are placed over the diamond shapes formed by two adjoining squares (see bottom detail at left). This is on the side of coverlet with unstitched folds. Trim edges of print fabric window a little smaller than diamond shape and pin in place. Fold one edge of diamond shape over on top of print window and slip-stitch across, leaving about ¼″ at ends unstitched. Repeat with next side, tacking adjacent sides together ¼″ from ends. Continue around four sides in this manner. When four windows have been put in, you will notice that the touching points form four tiny petals. Also, the sides of the windows form circles. A window patch is applied to every diamond shape of adjoining squares, blocks, and strips, except half-diamonds at edges.

When pieces have been joined as directed above, coverlet is complete; no further stitching is required.

Adaptations: The technique may be used in a number of ways to give a different effect. The squares may be made larger. For instance, start with a 9″ square of muslin; fold and sew as directed above, and the window patch will then be 3″ square.

Plain fabric in contemporary colors may be used for the windows, with a planned placement of colors. Or shades of three or four colors may be used for a rainbow effect, planning the colors in diagonal stripes. On the edges of the coverlet, the plain muslin triangular spaces may be filled by using a square of colored fabric as for windows. Sew the two sides of triangle over colored fabric in same manner as for windows. Then fold remainder of colored fabric square over edge of coverlet to back; turn in edges and slip-stitch in place. This will add an interesting border to back also.

The coverlet may be made larger or smaller by adding or subtracting squares in multiples of two.

If a window, square, or block of this coverlet becomes worn or damaged, it can be removed and replaced with a new part without disturbing the rest of the coverlet's construction.

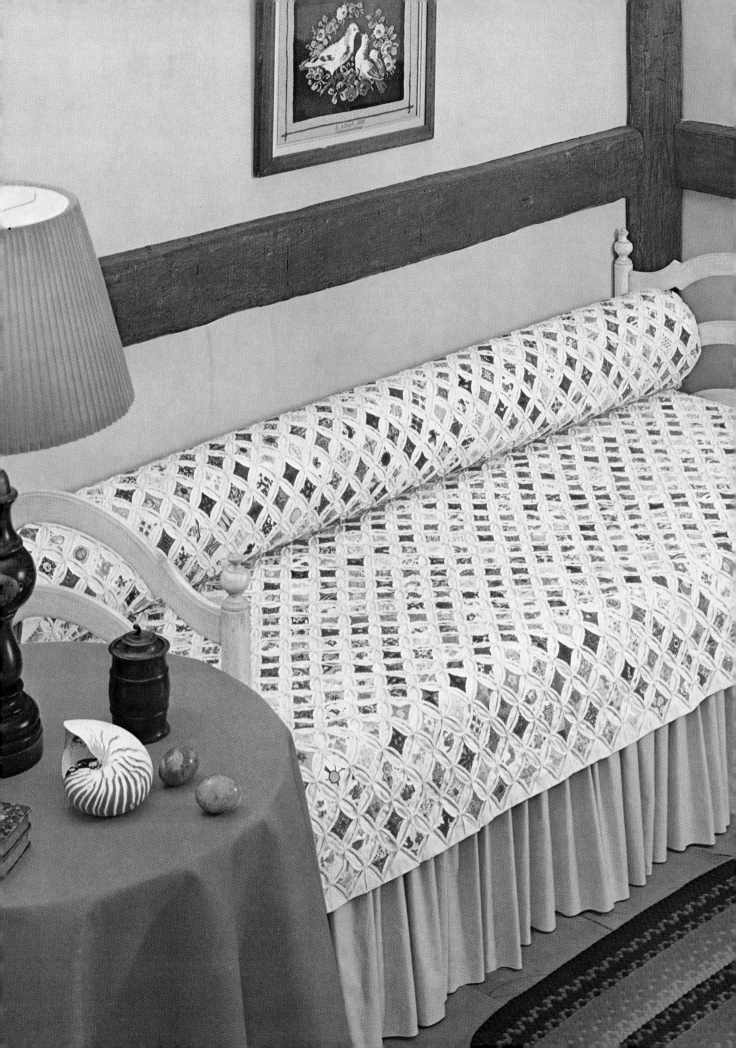

Contemporary Quilts

CLOUD COVER QUILT

SIZE: Approximately 34″ x 40″.

EQUIPMENT: Ruler. Dressmaker's carbon paper in light color. Paper for pattern. Tracing wheel, or sharp, hard pencil. Sewing needle. Knitting needle or other suitable instrument for poking stuffing into small areas. Sharp, pointed embroidery scissors.

MATERIALS: Fabric: 45″-wide off-white polyester crepe, 2 yds; dark voile or other lightweight cotton (gray, black, navy), 1 yd. Beige sewing thread. Dacron polyester or cotton batting (Taylor Bedding).

DIRECTIONS: Enlarge pattern by copying on paper ruled in 2″ squares. Using dressmaker's carbon and tracing wheel, or sharp, hard pencil, transfer pattern to one side of dark fabric. Cut two pieces of crepe, each 45″ x 36″; cut batting same size. Place dark fabric, marked side up, on wrong side of one crepe piece. Keeping raw edges even, pin and baste together. Using same color thread in bobbin and needle of machine, stitch along all outlines of design, using long machine stitch. Check bobbin and needle thread tension, as bobbin side will be right side of quilt. When stitching is completed, remove basting. Bring bobbin thread ends to wrong side of work and knot with needle thread ends close to fabric, securing beginning and end of stitching. Trim thread ends. Sew pieces together on outside line of design.

To stuff, place work with dark fabric uppermost. Make slit in dark fabric only at center of areas to be stuffed (eyelids, pupils, and mouths). Stuff these areas firmly, using knitting needle to poke small amounts of stuffing through the slits. Stuff remaining areas loosely in same manner. Check front of quilt occasionally to make sure stuffing is evenly distributed. In loosely stuffed areas and around features, a dark shadow will form when the dark fabric backing shows through. When stuffing is completed, sew slits closed.

To assemble quilt, place stuffed side of quilt right side up on flat surface. Place right side of remaining piece of crepe on top; place batting on top of these layers, making sure edges are even. Pin, baste, and stitch all layers together along seam line; leave 9″ opening at bottom of quilt for turning. Trim seam to ½″, clip curves; turn to right side. Hand stitch around main outlines of design through all layers, taking long stitch on back and short stitch on front. When sewing is completed, turn raw edges at opening to inside ½″ from edge; slip-stitch closed.

Cloud crib quilt, billowy soft, is a modern expression worked in traditional trapunto by Elsa Brown. Design is machine-stitched through two layers for a shadowy effect. Puff padding adds dimension. About 34" x 40". Directions are opposite.

ART DECO QUILT

SIZE: About 67½" x 90".

EQUIPMENT: Ruler. Scissors. Thin, stiff cardboard. Compass. Pencils. String. Paper for patterns. Dressmaker's (carbon) tracing paper. Tracing wheel. Tailor's chalk. Sewing and quilting needles. Knitting needle. Quilting frame (optional).

MATERIALS: Satin fabric 45" wide: lavender, 6½ yds. (includes lining); pink, 1 yd.; red, ½ yd.; light green, 1 yd.; dark green ½ yd.; light gold, 3⅛ yds. Sewing and button twill threads in matching colors. Dacron or cotton batting (Stearns & Foster).

DIRECTIONS: Read General Directions on pages 6 and 7 and How to Appliqué on page 90. Enlarge appliqué patterns (pp. 136-137) by copying on paper ruled in 1" squares.* Make pattern for large pink circle as follows: mark a circle 18" in diameter on paper; mark lines to divide circle into eight equal segments. Where lines touch at edge of circle, mark three points ¾" away, two on circle and one on line; draw lines to connect point, making eight indentations around edge of circle. Cut out pattern, rounding corners. Make pattern for smaller red circles in same manner, making circle 13½" in diameter and marking points ½" from where line touches circle.

Following directions in How to Appliqué, cut and prepare appliqué pieces for center motif as follows: cut one large circle and two roses from pink fabric; cut two smaller circles from red fabric; cut eight leaves from light green and four leaves from dark green fabrics. With dressmaker's carbon and tracing wheel, transfer inner lines of rose and circle patterns to right side of pieces; these will be quilting lines.

For background of center motif, cut piece 45" square from lavender fabric. Indicate center lines in both directions (fold and crease or mark with ruler and tailor's chalk). Mark a circle 45" in diameter on lavender square (use string and tailor's chalk for compass, if necessary). Place large pink circle in center of lavender square, matching quilting lines of circle to center lines of square; pin and baste in place along quilting lines, leaving outer edge of pink circle free. With pink button twill, stitch along quilting lines with running stitch, keeping stitches fairly large so as not to pucker the satin excessively. When quilting lines have been stitched, stuff batting into each segment of circle (use loose filler or cut wedge-shaped pieces of batting); topstitch edges of circle to lavender square as you go. Appliqué red circles to lavender square in same manner, placing quilting lines on center lines with edges of red circles touching pink circles; however, do not stuff

or appliqué the two outer segments of red circles, as these will be appliquéd later to gold background of quilt. Pin roses on other center lines of lavender square, with tops of roses touching pink circle. Begin stuffing from center out, quilting as you go; use knitting needle to stuff in batting. Topstitch inner edges of rose; leave outer edges free. Place light green leaves in pairs around edge of lavender circle, pointed ends touching each other and rounded ends touching a rose or red circle. Topstitch inner edges down, leaving outer edges free; do not stuff yet. Place dark green leaves as shown, with pointed ends touching light green leaves; stuff and topstitch all around.

For main background of quilt top, cut two pieces from gold satin 39" x 54½". Sew together on long sides with ½" seams to make piece 54½" x 77" (measurements include ¼" seam allowance all around). Press center seam open. Trim edges of lavender square to about 1" inside edges of outer appliqués. Place piece in center of gold background. Stuff light green leaves and the outer segments of roses and red circles; topstitch pieces on outer edges to gold background, with matching button twill.

For border, cut four panels from lavender fabric 8½" wide, two 41" long and two 63½" long (measurements include ¼" seam allowance, as do the following). Cut 32 strips 2¾" x 8½", eight each from red, pink, light and dark green. Sew a pink, light green, and dark green strip to each end of lavender piece, in that order. Cut four pieces 6" square from pink fabric. Sew two red strips to each pink square, mitering corners, to make 8½" pieced squares. Sew a pieced square to each end of a short border panel. Sew border panels to quilt top, longer pieces to sides and shorter pieces to top and bottom. Piece should measure 70½" x 93".

For corner appliqué design, make a cardboard pattern for each of the four curved pieces.* (You may find it easier to make your own pattern rather than to enlarge ours. Mark four concentric circles on cardboard, with diameters of 4½", 9", 13½", and 18". Divide largest circle into quarters; cut on marked lines of one quarter for four patterns.) Marking patterns on wrong side of fabric and adding ¼" seam allowance all around, cut four of each piece; cut smallest piece from pink fabric, next size from red fabric, next size from dark green fabric, and largest size from light green fabric. Sew pieces together on curved sides to make four corner pieces. Prepare corner pieces for appliqué and cut four wedge-shaped pieces of batting same size. Appliqué pieces to gold corners of quilt top over batting, topstitching around edge in matching colors of button twill.

For lining, cut two pieces from lavender fabric 33¾" x 89". Sew together on long sides with ½" seams to make piece 66½" x 89"; press seam open. Cut batting 67½" x 90".

QUILTING: With ruler, compass, and tailor's chalk, mark a line all around quilt top, 3¼" from edge of gold background, keeping curve at corners. Mark four more lines at top and bottom of gold background, 3¼" apart and curving to line at sides; see illustration.

Following General Directions, pin and baste quilt top, batting, and lining together, centering layers. Quilt top should extend 1½" all around beyond batting, and batting should extend ½" beyond lining.

Using matching color button twist, quilt around main outlines of center motif on lavender and gold backgrounds. Quilt on marked lines and around edge of gold background.

For border, fold excess fabric of quilt top over batting in back; fold edge of lining under ½" and pin folded edge in place over raw edge of quilt top, overlapping ½"; pin and baste in place. Stitch on lavender panels through all layers, 1¼" from edge of quilt; stitch across ends of panels, close to pink strips. Turn quilt over so lining faces up. Stitch corners of lining to turnover of quilt top, going through batting but not through front of quilt. From lining side, tuft quilt at center motif, tacking at centers of three circles and four times around sides of large circle; tack where three leaves join.

A resplendent quilt in shimmering, luscious satin—the ultimate luxury! Quilter Gail Diven, drawing inspiration from art deco design, made the appliqués big and bold, puffed them with extra padding.

A faraway land to dream on—in color! Trees, cloud are appliquéd to pieced landscape. Machine-sewn, with yarn ties for patchwork border. Quilt, 43″ x 56″, is scaled to child's own bed. By Linda Dale Brock. Landscape Quilt, page 137.

A child's spring: a fantasia of giant blooms and butterflies! Choose a fabric printed in clear, bold outlines. Hand-stitch around motifs with pearl cotton; quilt background in free-form fashion. Directions for Butterfly Quilt, page 136.

STAR OF BETHLEHEM QUILT
continued from page 78

angles, make lines parallel to short sides of pieces. Mark a line down centers of pink border strips.

Enlarge the two quilting patterns on paper ruled in 1″ squares, completing medallion quarter-pattern indicated by dash lines. Using dressmaker's carbon and tracing wheel, transfer patterns to blue border. Place a medallion in each corner and repeat cable motif around border, joining corners; place cable design against pink border strips, leaving outer edges of blue border strips unmarked.

Pin and baste quilt top, batting, and lining together, following General Directions. Starting in center and working around and outward, quilt inside of each diamond patch and along edges of pink border, close to seams; quilt on all marked lines.

When quilting is completed, trim edges of batting and lining almost to edge of cable quilting. Turn excess fabric of quilt top to back of quilt; turn in edges ¼″ and slip-stitch to lining. Press edges of quilt.

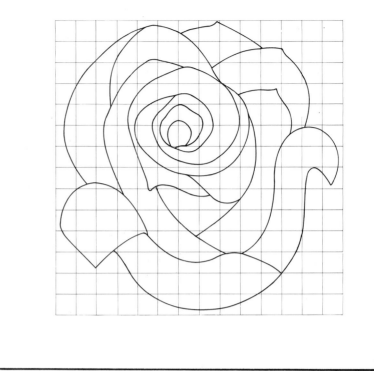

BUTTERFLY QUILT
shown on page 135

SIZE: 56″ x 84″.

EQUIPMENT. Scissors. Tape measure. Tailor's chalk. Straight pins. Sewing needle. Large-eyed embroidery needle. Quilting frame. Singer Sewing Machine. Zipper foot.

MATERIALS: Cotton fabric printed in a bold pattern, 54″ wide, about 2¼ yds. (Yardage required may depend on placement of motifs. Heavy cotton fabric for outside piping in three colors to match print fabric, 44″ wide: ½ yd. each of two inner border colors, 1½ yds. of outside border color. Dacron quilt batting from Taylor Bedding Co. Lightweight fabric, 45″ wide, 4⅔ yds. for quilt backing. Heavy cotton fabric in coordinating color for lining, 44″ wide, 4⅔ yds. Conso piping cord, ¾″ diameter, 23⅓ yds. Sewing threads to match all border colors and lining color. Black (or contrasting color) D.M.C. pearl cotton, size 5, four 49-yd. balls.

DIRECTIONS: Preshrink fabrics; press. Lay print fabric on smooth, hard surface. Mark background with lines for quilting stitches, using tailor's chalk. Make concentric free-form designs, using outlines of printed motifs as guide. Try to keep lines 1″-1½″ apart. Work over all areas and out to edges.

Cut backing fabric in half crosswise. Right sides facing, seam halves together lengthwise; trim width to 54″.

Cut quilt batting the same size as print fabric. The quilt illustrated has one layer of batting; however, if you want more bulk or warmth, use two layers. Following General Directions on pages 6 and 7, pin and baste quilt top, batting and backing together. Trim lining to same size as top. If necessary, touch up chalk lines.

Following General Directions, secure quilt in frame. Using embroidery needle threaded with comfortable working length of pearl cotton, quilt around printed motifs and along chalk lines with ¼″-long running stitches through all thicknesses. Knot ends on underside.

To make piping, cut enough 2″-wide bias strips from each ½ yd. of border fabrics to make length of 280″. Cut enough 7″-wide bias strips from 1½ yds. of outer border fabric to make length of 284″. Right sides facing, seam bias strips together to get total length needed for each color. Right sides facing and ends even, seam both 2″-wide bias strips together lengthwise with ¼″ seam allowance. Right sides facing and ends even at beginning, seam center color of two-color strip to 7″ bias strip using ¼″ seam allowance. For outer line of piping, place cord close to lengthwise seamline on wrong side of 7″ bias strip. Fold this piping fabric over cord to back; about 1¼″ of this bias strip should fit sungly over cord with seamline lying against wrong side of same strip (three colors will show on

top). Baste top to back near seamline on large strip keeping fabric snug over cord; stitch, using zipper foot. For center line of piping, insert cord between back and top along length of second bias strip. Baste and sew near seamline between the two 2″ bias strips. For inner line of piping, insert cord along length of third bias strip. Baste and sew, keeping fabric snug over cord.

Attach piping to quilt, starting at center of one shorter end. Right sides facing, pin piping around quilt, raw edges out, with last seam of piping 1″ from quilt edges. Ease piping around corners, making them slightly rounded rather than squared. Where piping ends, trim ends to overlap 1″. To fit ends together, cut ½″ off ends of three cords on one side; turn raw edges of piping under ¼″. Clip ¼″ in piping between three cords of other end and insert into trimmed ends. Using zipper foot, seam piping and quilt together with 1″ seam allowance on quilt; trim quilt corners. Trim piping allowance to 1″; clip at corners.

For quilt lining, cut fabric in half crosswise; seam halves together lengthwise with right sides facing. Trim edges to size of quilt top plus 1″ seam allowance. Place lining right side up on top of quilt backing. Turn raw edges under and pin around, leaving three rows of piping uncovered. Baste. Whipstitch around edges, catching lining and piping in seam allowance.

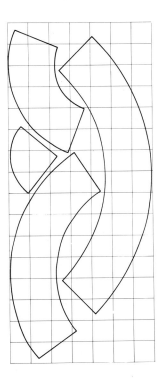

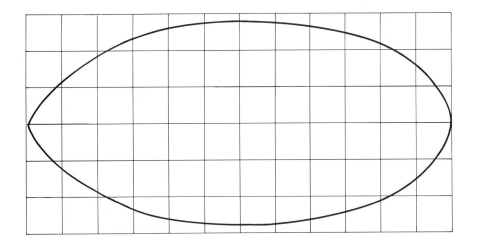

LANDSCAPE QUILT
shown on page 134

SIZE: About 43" x 56".

EQUIPMENT: Paper for patterns. Pencil. Scissors. Ruler. Straight pins. Singer sewing machine. Large-eyed needle for tufting. Dressmaker's tracing (carbon) paper. Tracing wheel. Thin, stiff cardboard.

MATERIALS: Washable lightweight fabric in prints and solids, such as cotton, polyester, or a blend: For center panel (see Patchwork-Appliqué pattern): ½ yd. color A; ⅓ yd. color B; ⅓ yd. color C; ⅔ yd. color D; scraps of colors E, F, G, and H. For border: Scraps of several different patterns, each about 5" square (or 1¼ yd. fabric in a patchwork design). For quilt lining: fabric in a solid color, 45" wide, 1⅔ yd. Taylor Bedding dacron batting. Sewing thread to match fabrics. Rickrack, about 4 yds. Knitting worsted.

DIRECTIONS: Read General Directions on pages 6 and 7 and How To Appliqué on page 90. Enlarge Patchwork-Appliqué pattern by copying on paper ruled in 2" squares. Dash lines indicate quilting lines. Using carbon paper and tracing wheel, transfer the outlines of pattern patch pieces A, B (2), C (2), and D to wrong side of proper color fabric. Cut out, adding ¼" seam allowance all around. Sew patches together on seam lines, right sides facing. This forms center panel, which should measure 26" x 38¾".

To right side of panel, mark position of appliqué pieces E, F, G and H. Following appliqué directions, cut out and prepare appliqué pieces from fabric. Transfer quilting lines to cloud. Slip-stitch appliqués to panel, adding a layer of batting underneath cloud. Transfer remaining quilting lines to center panel.

For patchwork border, cut several 4¼" patches from thin cardboard. Following General Directions, cut 76 square patches from fabric scraps, marking on wrong side of fabric and adding ¼" seam allowance. Sew square patches into four borders: two borders of two rows of 10 squares each (20 squares each strip) and two borders of two rows of nine squares each (18 squares each strip). Right sides facing, sew an 18-square strip to each long side of center panel. Then sew a 20-square strip to top and bottom of center panel and to ends of 18-square strips.

Following General Directions, assemble quilt top, two layers of batting, and lining, making lining 1" larger all around than quilt top. Stitch along quilting lines on machine, using contrasting color of thread where desired. Sew rickrack all around edges of center panel. With single strand of yarn in needle, make tufting at corners of border squares, except on outer edges. Tack through all thicknesses with yarn ends on front of quilt; clip excess yarn, leaving enough to tie double knot; trim ends to ½". Topstitch all around through all layers of quilt, ¼" from edges. Fold and press ¼" of quilt lining to front. Fold ¾" to front, encasing quilt top and batting edges; topstitch close to folded inside edge.

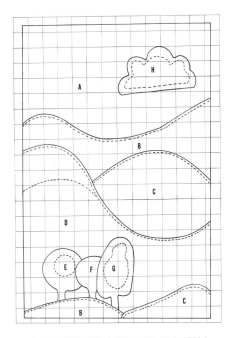

PATCHWORK-APPLIQUE PATTERN

BORDER BED SET

QUILT SIZE: 82″ x 125½″.

EQUIPMENT: Paper for pattern. Pencil. Ruler. Straight pins. Sewing needle. Singer sewing machine. For headboard: Hammer. Saw. Staple gun. Tailor's chalk.

MATERIALS: Fabric with small or medium-size regular print, 36″ wide: 7 yds. for quilt, 2½ yds. for headboard. Border fabric at least 8″ wide, with large print in colors coordinated with other print, 9¼ yds. for quilt, 2⅔ yds. for headboard, 4¼ yds. for pillow. Stearns & Foster Mountain Mist quilt backing in white (81″ x 96″ packages): 2 packages for quilt, 1 package for headboard. Stearns & Foster dacron batting (90″ x 108″ packages): 2 packages for quilt, 1 package for headboard. Dacron fiberfill for pillow. Muslin for inner pillow, ⅔ yd. White piping for pillow, 2 yds. For piping on headboard, ⅜″ cording, 90″. Sewing thread to match colors. For headboard: 2″ x 2″ lumber, 13 ft.; plywood ¼″ thick, two pieces 25″ x 40″. Finishing nails, 2½″ and 1″ long.

DIRECTIONS: Read General Directions on pages 6 and 7. Because machine-quilting a large piece is cumbersome, the center small-print area is quilted in three sections, which are then sewn together. Cut one piece 36″ x 123″ and two pieces 18″ x 123″ each from small-print fabric, batting, and backing. On small-print fabric, mark diagonal lines 3½″ apart between every four rows of flower motifs, marking in both directions to form diamonds (or adjust measurement to your own fabric). Make sure that motifs and quilting lines will match up when sewing the three sections together. Baste the three components of each section together and machine-quilt along marked lines. Sew the three sections together to make one piece, long sides together and wider section in center, making ½″ seams and with right sides together. Trim corners at one end (bottom) of quilt, making a curved edge.

Border: If necessary, trim border fabric to overall width of 8″. Pin border fabric around sides and bottom end of quilt, making a dart at each curved corner to fit. Unpin border, and sew darts. Using border as a pattern, cut backing in three pieces — two long strips that include curved corners of border and a straight strip between corners; sew together. Sew backing to border around outside edges, with right sides facing and making ½″ seams. Cut batting to fit inside this strip; insert between two layers and baste. Quilt as desired, letting the design of the fabric dictate the quilting design (we used a wavy line through center of garland all the way around border). Sew quilted border around quilt, right sides together and with ½″ seam. Make 1″ hem at top (straight) edge of quilt.

Headboard: Size: 40″ x 41″ high. Make frame as follows: Cut 2″ x 2″ lumber into two 41″ long pieces (uprights) and two 36½″ long pieces (crosspieces). Using longer nails, nail one crosspiece between the two uprights, top edges even; this forms an inverted "U." Nail the second crosspiece between the "U" with the bottom of the crosspiece 25″ below the top of the "U." Using shorter nails, nail plywood pieces to front and back of frame, to the uprights and crosspieces.

Frame is finished with a "slipcover." Slipcover front: Cut one 20″ x 28½″ piece each from small-print fabric, batting, and backing. For quilting lines, mark diagonal lines in both directions as for quilt. Baste small-print fabric, batting, and backing together, and quilt along the marked lines. Sew border-print fabric around top and sides of quilted piece, mitering corners.

Boxing: From small-print fabric, piece together 2¾″-wide strips to make one strip 92″ long. For piping, piece together 1¾″-wide bias strips to make one strip 92″ long. Place cording along inside center of bias strip; fold strip in half lengthwise and stitch close to cording. (**Note:** You will have 1″ of empty piping at each end; this is to reduce bulk when turning under hem later.) Pin and baste piping to right side of slip-cover front, raw edges out; baste boxing over it. Sew all around through all three layers. For slipcover back: Cut piece 26½″ x 41″ from small-print fabric; sew to boxing strip. Make 1″ hem all around bottom edge of slipcover. Cut batting 26¾″ x 43½″; cut 1¾″ squares out of top corners. Place on front of headboard, folding edges over frame; staple along top and sides. Place slipcover carefully over padded headboard.

Pillow: Size: 14″ x 20½″. Enlarge pattern by copying on paper ruled in 2″ squares; complete half-pattern indicated by dash lines. For front of pillow, cut the four pieces from border-print fabric, adding ½″ seam allowance; place patterns so that longest sides are all on the same edge of border fabric and opposite sides will match when they meet in center of pillow. Sew pieces, right sides together. Repeat for back of pillow. Pin and baste piping all around right side of pillow back, raw edges out; stitch all around. Right sides facing, stitch pillow front and back together, making ½″ seams and being careful to stitch over piping seam-line; leave opening for turning. Turn right side out. For inner pillow, cut two pieces of muslin, each 15½″ x 22″. Stitch together all around, making ½″ seams; leave opening for turning. Turn right side out, stuff fully, and slip-stitch opening closed. Insert inner pillow in outer pillow; slip-stitch closed.

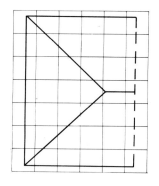

Hand-blocked prints from Provence harmonize for an ensemble fresh with country charm. The small even print offers a ready-made quilting guide; border fabric has a single waving line quilted through center of garland. All machine sewn. Directions include making headboard.

PRINT FABRICS COURTESY OF
LA PROVENCE DE PIERRE DEUX, N.Y.
• SINGER SEWING MACHINE

COLOR WHEELS QUILT

SIZE: 74″ x 94″.

EQUIPMENT: Paper for pattern. Tracing paper. Pencil. Ruler. Compass. Scissors. Thin, stiff cardboard. Straight pins. Sewing and quilting needles.

MATERIALS: Cotton fabric such as poplin, 44″ wide, 6 yds. white; ½ yd. each of bright blue, purple, dark green, bright yellow, orange, and red; ¼ yd. black. Muslin for lining, 44″ wide, 5½ yds. White quilting thread. Sewing thread to match fabric colors. Dacron batting, 81″ x 96″.

DIRECTIONS: Read General Directions on pages 6 and 7 and How To Appliqué on page 90. Enlarge Wedge Pattern on 1″ squares. The quilt is made up of twelve 18½″-square blocks of white cotton fabric that are appliquéd with colored wedges, then sewn together; the border is then sewn on and the whole piece is quilted.

To make each block, cut a 19″ square of white fabric (this allows for ¼″ seams). Trace wedge pattern onto cardboard; cut out. Cut wedges as indicated in General Directions, marking on wrong side of fabric and adding ¼″ seam allowance; make sure that the lengthwise center of each piece is placed on the straight of fabric. For each block, cut a wedge of red, orange, yellow, blue, green, and purple. Using compass and light-colored pencil, mark a 2¾″-diameter circle on wrong side of black fabric. Cut out circle, adding

¼″ all around. Clip all curves and press ¼″ under on all edges.

Lightly mark a 17″-diameter circle on center of white square. Having outer edges flush with marked circle, arrange and pin colored wedges evenly spaced around circle, leaving equal wedge-shaped area of white fabric between each colored wedge (see illustration and quilting pattern). Pin the black circle in center, overlapping ends of wedges and with a small amount of batting under circle to pad lightly. Slip-stitch each piece in place. Make eleven more blocks in same manner, keeping the color sequence the same, but moving the colored wedges clockwise into a different position each time.

With right sides facing and making ¼″ seams, sew the twelve blocks together in four rows of three across, then sew the rows together to make center of quilt.

For borders, cut four 11″-wide strips of fabric, two 75″ long, two 95″ long. With right sides facing, sew a long strip to each side of quilt and a short strip to each end, having equal lengths extending at corners. To miter corners, hold adjacent ends at corners together with right sides facing. Keeping border flat, lift up inner corners and pin together diagonally from inner corner to outer corner; baste. Stitch on basting line. Cut off excess fabric to make ½″ seam. Round off each corner (see illustration). Press all seams to one side.

Quilting: Following Center Quilting Diagram, lightly mark quilting lines

on quilt top for each color wheel square. Around each 17″-diameter circle, make 17 concentric circles ¼″ apart. Outer circles will meet the curved lines from outer circles of adjacent squares (you need not mark if you can work evenly freehand, following circular contour).

For border quilting design, mark a line all around border ½″ beyond seam line. On each corner, center cardboard wedge pattern, with narrow end at line just marked for quilting; lightly mark around outline of cardboard. Mark another wedge on each side of corner with narrow ends touching (see illustration). Continue marking wedge shapes along border approximately 6½″ apart at narrow ends. For swag part of quilted border design, make a cardboard pattern for each curve. Mark each curve on quilt border between each border wedge.

Cut two pieces of lining fabric, each one-half the width of quilt plus 1″ for seam allowances and the length of quilt plus 1″ for seam allowances. Making ½″ seam, sew the two halves together along long edges. Trim corners of lining edges to match shape of quilt top. Cut batting ½″ smaller all around than lining. Pin and baste quilt top, batting, and lining together, and quilt along marked lines and around each 17″ wheel as instructed in General Directions, quilting the center first. When quilting is completed, turn edges of fabric in ½″; slip-stitch together all around. Remove basting.

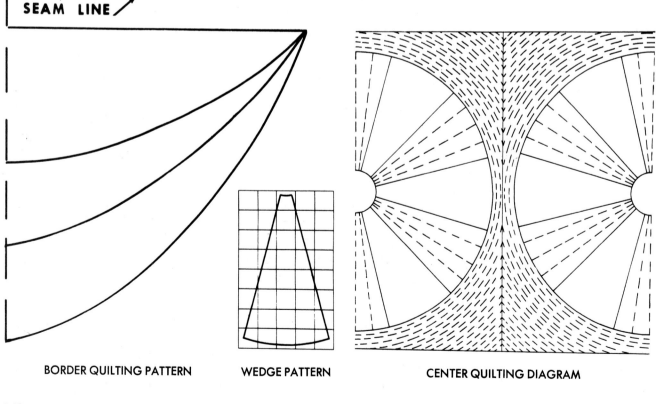

BORDER QUILTING PATTERN   WEDGE PATTERN   CENTER QUILTING DIAGRAM

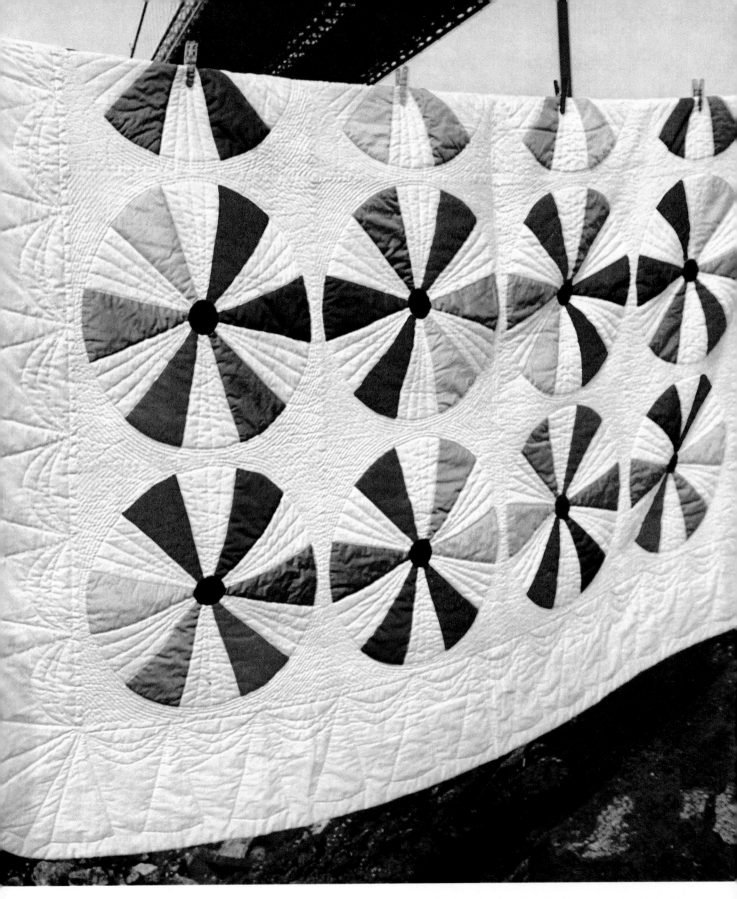

Color wheels spin a brilliant pattern in big, bold appliqué. All wheels have the same colored spokes in the same order, but each is slightly turned until all colors come around full circle. Center quilting follows wheel and spoke motifs; border is stitched with elegant swags and darts. Designed by Mary Borkowski.

Charming quilt in two calicoes—same pattern, different colors—is pieced in an extended windmill pattern. The quilt blocks and strips are stitched together by machine; quilting stitches are done by hand. Unbleached muslin was used for backing. Size: About 70″ x 90″.

WINDMILL QUILT

SIZE: Fits twin bed.

EQUIPMENT: Paper. Lightweight cardboard. Pencil. Ruler. Scissors. Straight pins. Quilting needle. White tailor's chalk. Quilting frame (optional). Sewing machine (optional).

MATERIALS: Unbleached muslin, 2½ yards, 72″ wide. Calico-like flower print cotton: red 3 yards; yellow 4¾ yards. White sewing thread. Cotton batting.

DIRECTIONS: Read General Directions on pages 6 and 7. Quilt blocks and strips are stitched together by machine; quilting stitches are done by hand. Quilt is made of 8″ square windmill blocks with strips of 2″ squares for "windmill extensions" in between. Windmill blocks are made of four 4″ squares; 4″ squares are made of two triangles.

To make triangle pattern: Draw a 4″ square on paper. Draw a diagonal line from one corner to opposite corner, forming two triangles. Cut either of cardboard.

There are 192 triangles of each color print fabric. Mark outlines of cardboard pattern on wrong side of fabric, leaving at least ½″ between triangles. Cut out triangles, adding ¼″ on all edges for seam allowance. Use marked lines for stitching lines. With right sides facing, pin one red and one yellow triangle together along long edge to form a square. Stitch on stitching line. Square measures 4½″ x 4½″. Make 192 squares of this size. Leave 52 squares for later.

Make 35 windmill blocks as follows: Pin four squares together, right sides facing, to form an 8½″ square, so yellow alternates with red, giving a windmill effect. Stitch the four blocks to each other.

Join windmill blocks in strips as follows: Cut a 2″ square out of cardboard. Using this as pattern, cut two red and two yellow squares, adding ¼″ to edges as for triangles. Stitch squares together to form a 2½″ x 8½″ strip in the following sequence: 1 yellow, 2 red, 1 yellow. Make eight strips. With right sides facing, pin and stitch a strip between top and bottom of each of seven windmill blocks, beginning and ending with a 2½″ strip. Make five vertical strips of seven windmills each. Stitch two of the 4½″ squares (made from two triangles) to top and bottom of each strip; make sure left square has red triangle in upper right corner and right square has red triangle in lower right corner, in keeping with the windmill pattern. Strips should measure 80½″ x 8½″.

Windmill strips are joined with strips of squares. Each strip is made of 16 red and 24 yellow 2½″ squares. Cut squares out as above. Stitch together in following sequence: 1 red, 3 yellow, 1 red. Repeat sequence eight times for each strip. Strip should measure 80½″ x 2½″. Make six strips. With right sides facing, pin and stitch windmill strips and strips of squares together, beginning and ending with a strip of squares. Make two more strips as follows: Cut a yellow and a red 2½″ square, using cardboard pattern as before. With right sides facing, pin and stitch squares together along one edge, making a short strip measuring 4½″ x 2½″. With right sides facing, pin and stitch 4½″ long edge of strip to one of remaining 4½″ squares; with right sides facing, pin and stitch remaining 4½″ long edge of strip to a second 4½″ square (make sure lower square has red triangle in lower right corner, red square of strip is at left, and that second square has red triangle in lower left corner, in keeping with pattern of rest of quilt). Repeat seven times. Make second strip the same. With right sides facing, pin and stitch on to each side edge of large center piece. Entire

continued on page 151

NIGHT AND NOON QUILT

SIZE: Approximately 88″ x 100″.

EQUIPMENT: Ruler. Scissors. Thin, stiff cardboard. Dark and light-colored pencils. Candlewick or large-eyed needle. Sewing needles.

MATERIALS: Closely woven cotton fabrics 36″ wide in a large variety of prints: dark prints, totaling about 1½ yds.; medium prints, about ¼ yd.; and light prints, about 2¾ yds. For border, blue print fabric 45″ wide, 2⅓ yds. White or off-white fabric (such as unbleached muslin) 45″ wide, 7⅔ yds. (includes lining). White sewing thread. Yellow pearl cotton. Dacron polyester or cotton batting (Stearns & Foster).

DIRECTIONS: Read General Directions on pages 6 and 7. Quilt is constructed of 34 pieced blocks set with a wide border.

To make patterns for patch pieces, see Piecing Diagram, which is one block. Cut patterns from cardboard as follows. For pattern A, cut a 5⅝″ square. For pattern B, mark a 4″ square; draw diagonal lines in both directions between opposite corners to divide square into four right-angle triangles; cut on marked lines for triangle. For patterns C and D, mark a 4″ square; draw a diagonal line between two opposite corners; mark a point 2⅛″ from a third corner on both sides; draw a line connecting the two points; cut on marked lines for smaller triangle (D) and strip (C).

Marking patterns on wrong side of fabric and adding ¼″ seam allowance all around, cut patch pieces as follows: use a different print for each one of the colored pieces: from dark prints, cut 34 of A and 136 of D; from medium prints, cut 136 of D; from light prints, cut 272 of B and 136 of C; from white fabric, cut 136 of B and 136 of C.

To make one block, join 29 pieces, following diagram; start by making the four corner squares, then add adjacent light B triangles to two of the squares and sew to opposite sides of A square; sew white and remaining light B triangles into larger triangles and sew to remaining corner squares; sew corner pieces to remaining sides of A square. Block should measure 12″ square plus outside seam allowance. Make 33 more blocks in same manner. To assemble main body of quilt top, sew 30 blocks into six horizontal rows of five blocks each; sew rows together. Piece should measure 60″ x 72″, plus outside seam allowance.

For borders, cut four strips 13″ wide from blue print fabric, two 60½″ long and two 72½″ long (measurements include ¼″ seam allowance). Sew a block to one end of each strip. Sew strips to main body of quilt top, longer strips to sides and shorter strips to top and bottom; in each strip block will extend beyond edge of quilt top while other end is flush. Quilt top should measure 85″ x 97″, plus outside seam allowance.

For lining, cut three pieces 35½″ x 91½″. Sew pieces together on long sides with ½″ seams, to make lining 91½″ x 103½″; press seam open. Cut batting 88″ x 100″.

Quilting: Following General Directions, pin and baste lining, batting, and quilt top together, centering layers carefully. Batting will extend 1½″ beyond quilt top on all sides and lining will extend 1¾″ beyond batting.

Following General Directions on page 7, tuft blocks at corners of each C-D square and in center of each A square; use a single strand of yellow pearl cotton knotted on front of quilt; trim strands to ¾″. Continue tufting pattern on blue border of quilt, making three rows of tufting 4″ apart.

To bind edges, fold excess lining to front of quilt over margin of batting, turning under raw edges ¼″. Slip-stitch folded edge of lining on long sides to quilt top. Slip-stitch top and bottom edges of lining to quilt top, making a right-angle fold at ends, for a mitered effect. Press edges of quilt.

PIECING DIAGRAM   DARK   LIGHT   MEDIUM   WHITE

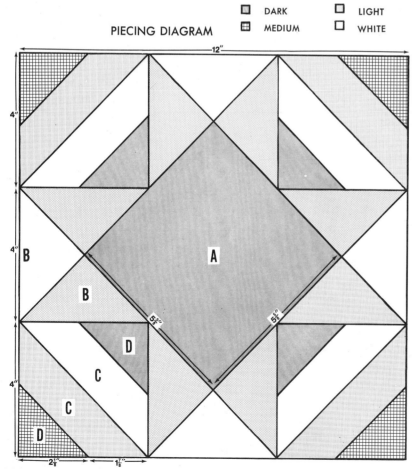

*The patchwork pattern called Night and Noon makes
a very pretty quilt in modern fabrics. Print patches in
light, medium, and dark shades are pieced into blocks
that create an overall prismatic effect when joined. Four extra
blocks are added to borders at corners. Quilting is
simple tufting. By Robyn Lamb of Patience Corner Patchwork.*

145

CARD TRICK CRIB QUILT

SIZE: Approximately 52″ square.

EQUIPMENT: Ruler. Scissors. Thin, stiff cardboard. Dark and light-colored pencils. Tailor's chalk. Sewing and quilting needles. Quilting frame (optional).

MATERIALS: Closely woven cotton print fabric 36″ wide, ½ yd. each of the following colors or combinations of colors:* blue/green in a large print (A), blue/green in a small print (B), rose in a large print or stripe (C), rose in a small print (D), brown (E), blue/red in a large print (F), blue/red in a small print (G), lavender in a large print (H), lavender in a small print (I), yellow/blue in a large print (J), yellow/blue in a small print (K), yellow (L), and purple (M). Fabric for lining, 36″ wide, 3 yds. White sewing thread. Dacron polyester or cotton batting.

DIRECTIONS: Read General Directions on pages 6 and 7. Quilt is constructed of nine pieced blocks and a pieced border. See Piecing Diagram for one block. A block is made up of nine square patches, pieced from large and small right-angle triangles. Make patterns for triangles as follows. For large triangles, mark a 4″ square on cardboard, draw a diagonal line connecting two opposite corners, and cut on marked lines for pattern. For small triangle, make same pattern as large triangle, then cut in half.

Marking patterns on wrong side of fabric and adding ¼″ seam allowance all around, cut nine large triangles and nine small triangles from colors A, B, C, E, F, G, I, and M. Cut nine large triangles from colors D, H, J, and K. Cut 36 small triangles from color L.

Piece large and small triangles together to make the nine square patches of one block, following diagram and color key; large triangles are joined on their long sides and short triangles on their short sides. Join the nine patches into three rows of three patches each, then sew rows together to complete block. Make eight more blocks in same manner.

Join six blocks into two rows of three blocks each, positioning blocks with large A triangle at upper right; these will be rows 1 and 3. Make row 2 in same manner, but positioning middle block with A triangle at lower left. Sew the three rows together for main body of quilt top. Piece should measure 36″ square, plus outside seam allowance.

For border, cut 36 pieces 4½″ x 8¾″ (measurements include ¼″ seam allowance): six each from colors M, E, A, and C and 12 from color L. Sew pieces together on long sides to make four border strips of nine pieces each; see illustration for order of colors, which corresponds to colors all around edge of main body of quilt top.

Cut four pieces 8¾″ square, one each from colors A, C, E, and M. Sew a square to each strip, matching colors. Sew strips to main body of quilt top, again matching colors. Quilt top should measure 53″ square. Trim corners to a rounded shape; see illustration.

For lining, cut two pieces 27″ x 53″. Sew together on long edges with ½″ seams; press seam open. Cut batting 52″ square.

Quilting: Using ruler and tailor's chalk, mark lines over quilt top, following Quilting Diagram; the line all around outside of quilt is 2″ from edge.

Following General Directions, pin and baste quilt top, batting, and lining together, centering layers. Starting in center and working around and outward, quilt on all marked lines. Trim corners of lining to match quilt top; trim corners of batting ½″ smaller.

To finish edges of quilt, fold edge of quilt top under ½″ to cover batting; pin and baste. Fold edge of lining in ½″; pin and baste. Slip-stitch edge of quilt top to lining.

QUILTING DIAGRAM

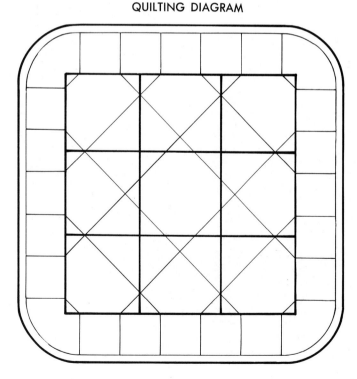

PIECING DIAGRAM

A—BLUE/GREEN (LARGE PRINT)
B—BLUE/GREEN (SMALL PRINT)
C—ROSE (LARGE PRINT)
D—ROSE (SMALL PRINT)
E—BROWN
F—BLUE/RED (LARGE PRINT)
G—BLUE/RED (SMALL PRINT)

H—LAVENDER (LARGE PRINT)
I—LAVENDER (SMALL PRINT)
J—YELLOW/BLUE (LARGE PRINT)
K—YELLOW/BLUE (SMALL PRINT)
L—YELLOW
M—PURPLE

A careful balancing of colors gives an unusually subtle harmony to the patchwork in this crib quilt. Nine blocks, pieced in a pattern called Card Trick, make up the main part of the quilt, with the colors around the edge extending onto borders. Quilt is by Beth and Jeffrey Gutcheon.

Decorating with Quilting

GALAXY WALL HANGING

SIZE: 58" x 65".

EQUIPMENT: Paper for patterns. Brown wrapping paper. Thin, stiff cardboard. Pencil. Ruler. Scissors. Dressmaker's tracing (carbon) paper. Tracing wheel. Embroidery and sewing needles. Zigzag sewing machine. Compass.

MATERIALS: Closely woven cotton fabric, 45" wide: For quilt top: solid purple, 3 yds.; scraps of batik-printed fabric in bright colors. For lining, border, and hanging loops: batik-printed fabric in deep pink and purple, 3¼ yds. (see Note below). Sewing thread in bright colors for zigzag stitching and in purple for straight-stitch quilting. For embroidery: Crewel wool or six-strand embroidery floss in bright colors. Cotton or dacron quilt batting.

Note: Hand-batiked fabrics were used for quilt. Batik-printed fabric may be purchased in some areas. If unavailable, use subtle "watery" prints or solids.

DIRECTIONS: Read General Directions on pages 6 and 7. Piece fabric for quilt top to measure 58" x 65". Piece brown wrapping paper to same size for quilting pattern. Following Quilting Diagram for a general outline, draw waving lines on brown paper, horizontally and vertically. Using carbon paper and tracing wheel, transfer horizontal lines to quilt top.

Enlarge patterns for half-moon and the various stars by copying on paper ruled in 1" squares. Cut cardboard patterns for each; also cut several circle patterns with diameters ranging from 1" to 4". Referring to illustration for color ideas, cut stars, half-moons, and circles from fabric scraps. Vary the shapes as much as desired. Arrange appliqués within the three wide horizontal areas (see illustration and diagram). Place stars on larger circles; place small circles on large circles and on larger stars; insert a layer of batting under some pieces. For large "sun," place large star on a 9" circle with batting underneath. Cut out long triangles for "rays," and arrange as shown in illustration. Pin and baste appliqués in place. Using zigzag stitch in various widths, stitch around appliqué edges, using thread in bright colors. Add extra rows of zigzag stitching around circles, using contrasting colors. Zigzag-stitch along six of the marked horizontal lines, using deep pink thread; omit bottom line. Embroider herringbone stitch around some appliqués, lengthening and shortening the stitches as shown in illustration. Work French knots at points of some stars. See stitch details.

Piece lining to measure 63" x 70".

Quilting: Transfer vertical lines of brown wrapping-paper pattern to quilt top, using dressmaker's carbon and tracing wheel. Following General Directions, assemble quilt top, batting, and lining, leaving 2½" quilt lining margin all around. Using purple thread and straight stitch, quilt through all three layers along vertical lines; quilt along zigzag-stitched horizontal lines and on bottom horizontal line. Straight-stitch all around sides of quilt, ½" in from quilt-top edges. Trim batting even with quilt top. Turn lining edges ¼" to front all around; press. Fold margins over quilt top 2¼"; topstitch close to inner fold, folding under neatly at corners. Embroider all around inner fold with red yarn in herringbone stitch.

Loops: Cut seven 5½" x 8" strips. Fold in half lengthwise, right sides together, and stitch long sides, making ¼" seam. Turn right side out. Press, with seam running down center back. Turn raw edges in ¼"; press. Stitch loops to back of quilt along top, spacing evenly and with 1" overlapping edge.

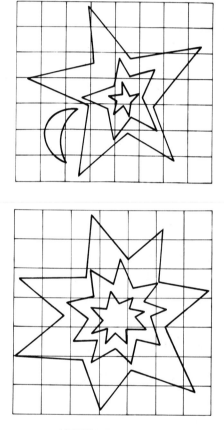

APPLIQUE PATTERNS

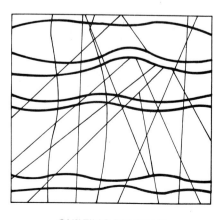

QUILTING DIAGRAM

FRENCH KNOTS

HERRINGBONE STITCH

A galaxy of heavenly bodies makes a dazzling display on a brilliant wall hanging by Ann Ammons Bryant. Star, circle, and half-moon appliqués are cut from batik prints free-hand (or use our patterns) and embellished with hand and machine embroidery. A random design is machine-quilted on the deep purple background.

WATER LILY PICTURE

SIZE: 26" x 32".

EQUIPMENT: Brown wrapping paper for pattern. Pencil. Ruler. Dressmaker's tracing (carbon) paper. Tracing wheel. Straight pins. Sewing needle. Zigzag sewing machine. Staple gun.

MATERIALS: Closely woven medium-weight fabrics such as shantung, a brocade, velveteen, satin or sateen in the following amounts and colors: off-white, ⅔ yd.; olive green, ½ yd.; dark aqua, ⅔ yd.; pale yellow-green, ⅓ yd.; light aqua, ½ yd.; navy blue, ⅓ yd.; dark turquoise, ½ yd. (for border); scraps of periwinkle, medium yellow-green, medium blue, pink, and pale pink. For backing, lightweight fabric, two pieces each about 23" x 30". Dacron batting, one piece about 23" x 30". Lining fabric, one piece 26½" x 32½". Cotton sewing thread in navy blue, aqua, olive green, and pale pink. Artists' canvas stretchers, one pair 26" long and one pair 32" long.

DIRECTIONS: Enlarge appliqué pattern by copying on paper ruled in 2" squares. Transfer pattern to one backing piece, using dressmaker's carbon and tracing wheel. Transfer outline of each appliqué piece to proper color fabric (see color key), marking on right side of fabric with carbon paper and tracing wheel. Cut pieces from fabric, ¼" outside marked outline. Cut tree as one piece; dash lines indicate overlapping of pieces underneath. Cut olive green area as one piece; medium olive-green pieces overlap. Cut light aqua area as one piece; lily pads overlap.

Baste the two backing pieces together, with batting in between; make basting lines along vertical and horizontal center, diagonally from corner to corner, and around sides, ½" in from edges. One at a time, pin and baste appliqués on prepared foundation. Sew appliqués to foundation in same order in which they appear in color key, except for lily pads, which go on last. After basting in place, straight-stitch each appliqué by machine along marked outline. Then trim excess fabric of appliqué ⅛" from

stitching. When all pieces have been stitched and trimmed, set machine on fine-stitch length and #3 stitch width. Satin-stitch all around appliqués, concealing straight stitching and raw edges. Use navy thread for tree, olive green thread for off-white and olive and medium green appliqués, pale pink thread for lily appliqués, and aqua thread for remainder.

Trim outer edges of piece to measure 29¾" x 22¾". Cut two strips of border fabric, each 3⅛" x 22¾". Right sides facing, stitch one to each side of appliquéd top, making ¼" seams; press seams open. Cut two strips of border fabric 3⅝" x 35" and sew to top and bottom as for sides.

Assemble stretchers to form a frame 26" x 32". Place appliquéd piece face down on flat surface and center frame on top. Fold fabric margins to back and tape in place temporarily. Check front to see that borders are even all around. Using staple gun, secure margins to frame back, folding edges neatly at corners. Fold edges of lining fabric under ¼"; staple to frame.

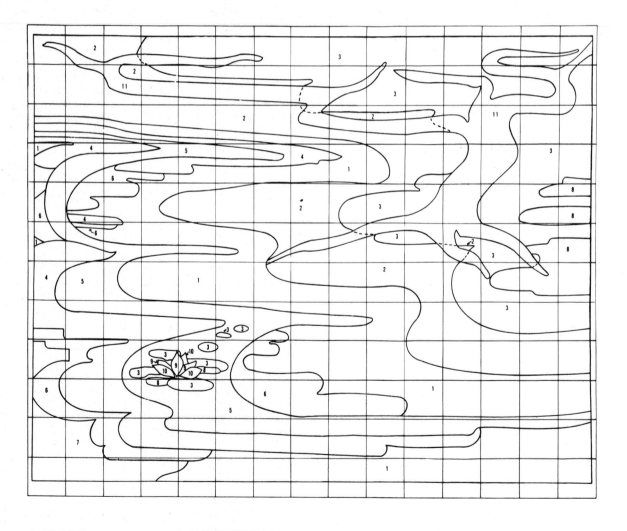

1—DK. AQUA	4—PALE YELLOW-GREEN	7—MED. BLUE	10—PINK
2—OFF-WHITE	5—LIGHT AQUA	8—MED. YELLOW-GREEN	11—NAVY BLUE
3—OLIVE GREEN	6—PERIWINKLE	9—PALE PINK	

A quiet scene suggesting pond and shore — romantic in silks, brocade, and velvet. Each curving segment of picture is a separate appliqué, machine-stitched over padding; the quilting adds dimension to design. By Laura Crow.

FROM DOMINO PATCHWORKS

WINDMILL QUILT

continued from page 143

piece: 80½" x 60½".

Around all sides of center piece are yellow borders. Cut 5" wide strips; stitch together to make two 60½" x 5" strips and two 89½" x 5" strips. With right sides facing, pin and stitch long edge of each 60½" long strip to each 60½" long edge of center piece. With right sides together, pin and stitch long edge of remaining strips to remaining edges of center piece.

Press both seam allowances together to one side. Cut unbleached muslin lining the same size as quilt top.

Quilting: Use ruler and tailor's chalk to mark quilting lines on quilt top: Mark smaller triangles ¼" in from seams for triangle pieces; mark smaller squares ¼" in from seams for squares. Mark lines on yellow borders ½", 1¾", 3", and 4½" from inside seams.

Pin and baste quilt top and quilt lining together, with batting in between, as directed in General Directions. Quilt with quilting needle and white thread; work borders last.

When quilting is completed, finish edges with yellow binding, made by stitching together 1" wide strips of yellow print fabric, as for border. Make four binding strips long enough to cover each edge. Turn under ¼" along both long edges of each strip; steam-press. Fold strips in half lengthwise, wrong sides together. Insert raw edges of quilt between folded edges of binding strip and baste. Stitch close to turned under edge, using small running stitches as for quilting. Overlap ends of binding at corners; turn in ¼" and whipstitch to finish edging.

BOWL OF FRUIT QUILT

SIZE: About 106½″ x 127½″.

EQUIPMENT: Ruler. Scissors. Thin, stiff cardboard. Dark and light-colored pencils. Paper for patterns. Sewing needles. Sewing machine.

MATERIALS: Closely woven sturdy cotton fabrics 36″ wide, in a variety of prints (plus a few solids) in each color: light blue (A), 1½ yds.; dark blue (B), ⅝ yd.; green and blue-green (C), 4¼ yds.; ¼ yd. each of yellow-green (D), bronze green (E), gold (G); ½ yd. each of yellow (F), orange (H), peach and pink (N); red (I), ⅓ yd.; ¼ each of red-brown (J), purple (K), lavender (L), magenta (M); black and white (O), 1⅞ yds.; beige and tan (Q), 1⅝ yds. Cotton fabrics 45″ wide in solid colors: black (P), ⅛ yd.; white, ½ yd.; navy, 2 yds.; medium blue (for lining), 9 yds.; fabric for inner lining, about 7 yds. Navy sewing thread. Dacron polyester or cotton batting.

DIRECTIONS: Read General Directions on pages 6 and 7. Bowl of fruit design is pieced entirely with square patches; corners are appliquéd.

To make pieced design, see Piecing Diagram on page 154. Each square on chart represents one square patch of design. To make patterns for patches, cut several pieces 1¾″ square from cardboard; replace when edges begin to fray. Marking pattern on wrong side of fabric and adding ¼″ seam allowance all around, cut patch pieces as follows: from light blue fabrics (A), cut 457 patches; from dark blue (B), 142; green and blue-green (C), 837; yellow-green (D), 46; bronze green (E), 59; yellow (F), 120; gold (G), 49; orange (H), 127; red (I), 149; red-brown (J), 34; purple (K), 43; lavender (L), 28; magenta (M), 26; peach and pink (N), 99; black and white (O), 480; black (P), 23 (or cut one strip 23 squares long); beige and tan (Q), 401.

Quilt is pieced and quilted in sections, starting in the center and working outward. Begin with the bunch of grapes, left of center. Following Piecing Diagram, stitch I, J, K, L, and M patches into rows, then rows into a section indicated by heavy outline. Turn under outside seam allowance of section and press. Cut batting and inner lining a little larger than grape section. Following General Directions, pin and baste lining, batting, and pieced section together. Set sewing machine for wide, close zigzag stitch. Machine-stitch over seams dividing color areas, indicated on diagram by light lines; use navy thread. Trim batting and lining to match folded edge of grape section, then trim away about ⅛″ more from batting all around. Make second pieced section that includes the H, N, I, and E

areas, but do not turn under outside seam allowance. Quilt on seams indicated by heavy lines dividing the color areas, in same manner as for grapes. To join the two sections made, place edge of first section on second section, overlapping edge ¼″; baste, using navy thread. Zigzag the pieces together, then snip away basting thread. Make a section of the D and N areas at left of grapes and quilt on seam dividing color areas. Join section to left side of grapes. (As you join sections, overlap edges as for first and second sections.) Make bowl section (do not quilt on seam joining P and O areas) and join to fruit section. Make a section of sun, window at right, bananas. apple stem and leaf; quilt on dividing lines (do not quilt inside sun). Join section to I, E, and O sections of bowl of fruit. Make wall (C) section at right and join, then a section of table (Q) and small wall area (C) at left. Make window section at left, then join to upper wall section (C); join combined sections to piece. Trim lining and batting around edge of quilt top to outside seam allowance.

For first border, cut four strips from white fabric 2¼″ wide, two 88″ long and two 112½″ long (measurements include ¼″ seam allowance all around). Using straight stitch, sew strips to main body of quilt top, through all layers; sew shorter strips to sides, then longer strips to top and bottom. For second border, cut four strips from navy fabric 8¼″ wide, two 91½″ long and two 112½″ long. For corners, cut four pieces 8¼″ square from a print fabric. For appliqués, enlarge patterns below on paper ruled in 1″ squares. Make a cardboard pattern for each separate part of each design. Marking patterns on wrong side of fabric and adding ¼″ seam allowance all around, cut appliqué pieces from print or plain fabrics in appropriate colors. Prepare pieces for appliqué (see page 90), then pin and baste to center

of print squares. Stitch appliqués in place, using zigzag stitch. Sew a square to each end of the two longer navy strips; sew shorter navy strips to sides of quilt top, then longer strips to top and bottom, using straight stitch for all. Piece should measure 106½″ x 127½″, plus outside seam allowance. Turn ¼″ seam allowance; baste.

If using piece for a wall hanging, fruit and bowl areas of design may be given extra dimension with trapunto. If using piece as a bed covering, the trapunto is best omitted. To trapunto, turn work with inner lining side up. In center of each quilted area of fruit and bowl, slit lining only. Stuff with extra batting, then sew slits closed.

For lining, cut three pieces from medium blue fabric 107″ long, two 43½″ wide and one 43″ wide. Sew 43½″-wide pieces to 43″ wide piece on long sides with ½″ seams, to make lining 107″ x 128″. Turn under ¼″ all around edge of lining and baste in place. Cut batting 106″ x 127″.

Following General Directions, pin and baste lining, batting, and quilt top together, centering layers so that lining and quilt top extend ¼″ beyond batting. Using zigzag stitch, stitch along inner and outer seam lines of white border, around corner squares, and ¼″ in from edge of quilt.

To make loops for hanging, cut seven pieces from blue lining fabric, 5½″ x 7″. Fold each strip in half lengthwise, with right sides facing. Stitch ¼″ from long raw edges; turn strips to right side and press. Stitch along both long edges of strips, ⅛″ from edge. Fold strips in half crosswise, and fold raw ends in ½″; stitch across ends, ¼″ from fold. Place strips along top edge of quilt, matching stitched end to upper edge of lining; place a strip at both ends of top edge, ¼″ from sides, and other strips evenly placed across top. Baste strips in place; zigzag-stitch. Loops fold up to hang.

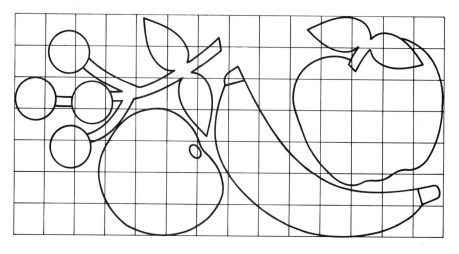

Traditional patchwork worked in a most untraditional manner creates a dramatic still life! Entire design is made with square patches, cut from bold-print fabrics. Piecing and quilting are done in sections, working from a chart. Machine quilting follows main outlines of design. King-size quilt (127" wide) is shown here as a wall hanging, with trapunto padding giving extra dimension to the fruit and bowl. By Liz Dominick of Domino Patchworks.

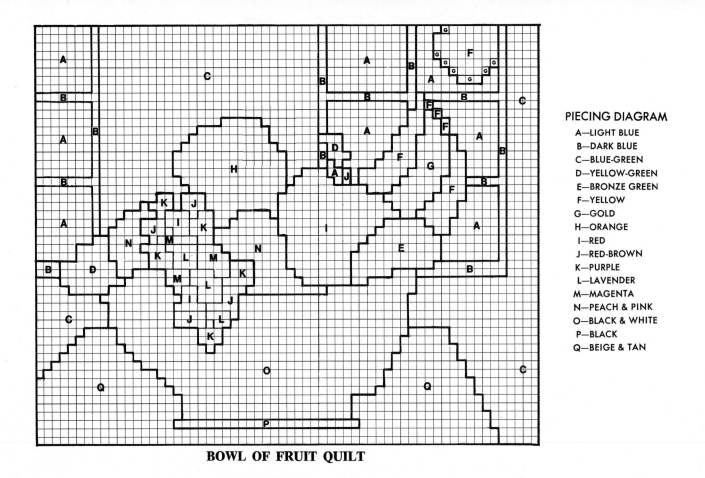

BOWL OF FRUIT QUILT

PIECING DIAGRAM

A—LIGHT BLUE
B—DARK BLUE
C—BLUE-GREEN
D—YELLOW-GREEN
E—BRONZE GREEN
F—YELLOW
G—GOLD
H—ORANGE
I—RED
J—RED-BROWN
K—PURPLE
L—LAVENDER
M—MAGENTA
N—PEACH & PINK
O—BLACK & WHITE
P—BLACK
Q—BEIGE & TAN

AUTUMN REFLECTIONS

SIZE: 18″ x 34″.

EQUIPMENT: Ruler. Pencil. Scissors. Straight pins. Staple gun. Sewing machine. Masking tape.

MATERIALS: Scraps of several fabrics printed in large, bold patterns, plus a few with smaller-figured prints. For border: solid-color fabric 36″ wide, ½ yd. For backing: lightweight cotton fabric, one piece 16″ x 32″. For lining: lightweight fabric, one piece 19″ x 35″. Dacron batting, one piece 16″ x 32″. Sewing thread to match fabrics. Artists' canvas stretchers: one pair 18″ long and one pair 34″ long.

DIRECTIONS: Picture is made with 22 strips of fabric in widths varying from ½″ to 3½″, sewn together to make a piece 15″ x 31½″. Sixteen of the strips are cut in wider widths from large-print fabrics; six are cut in narrower widths from smaller-print fabrics. Mark 15″-long strips on wrong side of fabrics, in widths that will total 31½″ when all are sewn together. Cut out strips, adding ¼″ seam allowance to long sides and ½″ seam allowance to ends. Arrange strips one under the other in various ways until pleased with design. Sew strips together, right sides facing and making ¼″ seams. When completed, piece should measure 16″ x 32″, including outside seam allowances. Press all seams open.

Place wrong side of pieced fabric on backing fabric, with batting in between. Baste together through all three layers; make basting lines along vertical and horizontal center, diagonally from corner to corner, and all around perimeter, 1″ from edges. Using contrasting thread, machine-stitch through all three layers where desired, following printed shapes and joining some shapes to others with a line of stitching.

Cut two 4″ x 32″ strips of the border fabric. Right sides facing, stitch to sides of quilted piece, making ½″ seams. Press seams open. In same manner, cut two 4″ x 22″ strips of border fabric and stitch to remaining sides of piece. Press seams open. Place quilted piece face down on a flat surface. Assemble stretcher pieces to form 18″ x 34″ frame. Position frame over wrong side of quilted piece. Fold margins of border to wrong side of frame and tape in place temporarily. Check front to see that borders are equal all around. Staple top and bottom margins to frame, folding fabric under neatly at corners. Staple margins at sides. Fold lining fabric under ½″ all around edges; press. Position on underside of frame and staple in place, concealing margin of hanging under lining.

*Autumn Reflections: narrow strips
cut from many prints are sewn
into an abstract composition;
quilting pattern unifies design. By
Liz Dominick. Bubble Pillows:
Textured circles, appliquéd to
pillows, are padded for dimension.*

FROM DOMINO PATCHWORKS

BUBBLE PILLOWS

shown on page 155

EQUIPMENT: Thin, stiff cardboard. Pencil. Ruler. Dressmaker's (carbon) tracing paper. Tracing wheel. Scissors. Straight pins. Sewing needle. Zigzag sewing machine. Heavy sewing machine needle, such as #12. Compass.

MATERIALS: For each pillow: Heavy fabrics such as fur fabric, suede, suedecloth, velveteen, buckskin, corduroy, tweed plaid: ½ yd. of solid color for pillow; scraps for appliqués. For inner pillow, ½ yd. unbleached muslin. Sewing thread. Dacron stuffing.

DIRECTIONS: Cut two 16″ squares from pillow fabric, for pillow front and back. Draw circles about 1½″ to 5″ in diameter on cardboard for circle appliqués, using compass. (Pillow at left has 13 circles; pillow at right has 17.) Mark outlines of circle appliqués on desired fabric scrap. Cut pieces from fabric, ¼″ outside marked outline.

Lay circles on pillow front in various arrangements until satisfied with design. Pin and baste appliqués in place. Straight-stitch each appliqué by machine along marked line. Trim excess fabric of appliqués ⅛″ from stitching. Set machine on fine-stitch length and #3 stitch width. Sew all around appliqués, concealing straight stitching.

Pad the larger areas of the design as follows: Slash an opening in the pillow top under the appliqué. Stuff area firmly, using the blunt end of a large needle to push wads of batting between appliqué and pillow top. Slip-stitch the slashed opening closed.

Right sides facing, sew pillow top to back along three sides, making ½″ seams. Clip seams at corners, and turn right side out. For inner pillow, cut two 17″ squares from muslin. Stitch together around three sides, making ½″ seams. Turn right side out; stuff firmly, and slip-stitch remaining side closed. Insert in outer pillow; slip-stitch remaining side closed.

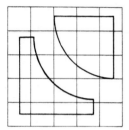

PATCH PATTERNS

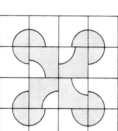 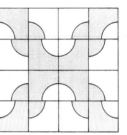 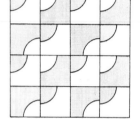

PIECING DIAGRAMS

DRUNKARD'S PATH PILLOWS

SIZE: 20″ square.

EQUIPMENT: Paper for patterns. Thin, stiff cardboard. Scissors. Pencil. Ruler. Light and dark-colored sharp pencils. Straight pins. Sewing and quilting needles.

MATERIALS: For each pillow: closely woven fabric, 36″ wide: ¾ yd. bold-print fabric and ¼ yd. white fabric. White cotton backing and lining, 44″ wide, 1¼ yds. (1⅔ yds. for two pillows). Dacron quilt batting. Polyester fiberfill, 1 lb. Matching sewing threads. White silk button hole twist, one 10-yd. spool.

Note: We used Japanese silk fabric in a large, bold print and white silk-like fabric for these large pillows. Other contrasting fabrics, print or plain, may be used to create the same general effect. Size of fabric design is related to size of pillow, i.e., if using a small-figured print, adjust directions to make smaller pillows.

DIRECTIONS: For Each Pillow: Read General Directions on pages 6 and 7. Before cutting patches from print fabric, cut one 20″ square for back and four strips 3½″ x 20″ for borders, marking on wrong side of fabric and adding ¼″ seam allowance all around.

Enlarge the two patch patterns on paper ruled in 1″ squares; make several cardboard patterns for each. Replace patterns as edges become worn. Following General Directions for cutting patches, cut eight of each shape from print fabric and eight from white fabric (total of 32 pieces); mark on wrong side of fabric and add ¼″ seam allowance all around. To make 3¼″ squares, sew a print patch of one shape to a white patch of other shape along their curved edges; stitch along pencil lines, matching them carefully and easing the curves into one another. Clip into seam at curve; press seam in one direction. Make 16 squares in this manner.

Following one of the Piecing Diagrams, stitch 16 squares together to form a block, right sides facing and making ¼″ seam allowances; shading in diagram indicates print patches. Press seams open.

Sew a border strip to each side of pieced block, right sides facing and making ¼″ seams; center block so that equal lengths of border fabric extend at corners. To miter corners, hold adjacent ends of border together at corners with right sides facing. Keeping border flat, lift up inner corners and pin together diagonally from inner corner to outer corner; baste. Stitch on basting line. Cut off excess fabric to make ½″ seam; press seams to one side.

Cut batting and white cotton piece for lining, both same size as pillow top. Place pillow top on lining with batting in between; baste through all thicknesses according to General Directions. Using buttonhole twist and ⅛″-long running stitches, quilt around outline of design created by print patches, stitching on white areas close to seam lines. Quilt around patchwork block, just inside border seam line.

Stitch pillow front to pillow back around three sides, right sides together and making ¼″ seams; turn to right side. Cut two 20½″ squares from white cotton fabric for inner pillow; stitch together, making ¼″ seams and leaving 6″ opening in center of fourth side. Turn to right side and stuff evenly with filling; whipstitch closed. Insert pillow into cover, whipstitch closed.

Drunkard's Path patchwork, traditional in calicoes, becomes exotic made in vivid Japanese silks. The idea stays the same, however: corner segments seem to be transposed within light and dark squares. Arrangement of squares determines final design; here are just three of the many patterns.

STRAWBERRY PILLOWS

SIZE: Approximately 11″ x 14″.

EQUIPMENT: Paper for patterns. Tracing paper. Pencil. Ruler. Scissors. Dressmaker's tracing (carbon) paper in a light color. Tracing wheel. Sewing needle. Tailor's chalk.

MATERIALS: Chintz fabric: For each pillow top, one piece with strawberry or other motif (background plain), approx. 6½″ x 9½″. Celery green or complementary color for borders and backs, 1½ yds. For quilting backing: soft fabric, 1 yd. white. Unbleached muslin, 1½ yds. Interfill batting, two layers for each pillow. Cut-N-Stuff polyester stuffing. Cotton thread to match all colors. Century Quality Ribbon: **For Left Pillow:** ¼″ Jerilyn (velvet), poppy red, 8 ft., ½″ Picot, moss green, 4 ft.; **For Center Pillow:** ¼″ Jerilyn (velvet), moss green, 9 ft.; **For Right Pillow:** ¼″ Jerilyn (velvet), moss green, 4½ ft., poppy red, 3¼ ft.

DIRECTIONS: Read General Directions on pages 6 and 7. For each pillow choose one motif on chintz fabric; mark off rectangle 7½″ x 10½″, with motif in center. Cut out rectangle, allowing ½″ seam allowance all around.

Enlarge border quilting patterns by copying on paper ruled in 1″ squares. These are quarter patterns; long dash lines indicate repeat lines. Short dash lines indicate quilting, and fine solid lines indicate ribbon placement.

Complete each pattern on tracing paper. With length of pattern following grain of fabric, transfer all markings onto plain chintz for border. Cut out, adding ½″ seam allowance on inside edge of border and ½″ plus 2″ extra on outside edges of border. On inside edge, clip to corners as indicated and press under seam allowance to inside. Place border fabric on motif fabric, aligning seam lines; baste all around close to inside border edge. Topstitch all around. For background area of motif fabric on right pillow, mark vertical quilting lines ½″ apart, making sure not to mark over motif itself; use ruler and tailor's chalk. Backgrounds of other two pillows are unquilted.

Quilting: Pin and baste pillow top, two layers of batting, and backing fabric together. Using sewing thread to match areas to be quilted, begin quilting around outlines of motif for left and center pillows. For right pillow, quilt vertical background lines only. Quilt borders of right and center pillows as indicated on pattern.

Ribbon Trimming: Pillow top will be slightly smaller after it has been quilted. Replace tracing-paper pattern on pillow top and re-mark outer edge of border. Apply ribbons by slip-stitching both edges alternately as you go along; miter corners. The outermost ribbon for all pillows should be sewn just inside seam line. Inner seam lines are also ribbon placement lines for right and center pillow. **For left pillow:** Place poppy red velvet on fine inner line of pattern, moss green picot on fine outer line and poppy red velvet near outer seam line. **For center pillow:** Cut ribbons, allowing ends to extend into seam allowances. Using moss green velvet, begin with inner ribbons, then outer ribbons, interweaving at corners. **For right pillow:** Use poppy red velvet on inner seam line and moss green velvet near outer seam line.

For each pillow, baste all around along outer seam line; cut out ½″ beyond basting for seam allowance.

For each pillow back, cut rectangle 12″ x 15″ from plain chintz. With right sides together, pin and baste pillow front and back together along seam line. Machine-stitch, leaving a 7″ opening in bottom end of pillow; clip corners and trim seams to ¼″. Turn to right side.

For each inner pillow, cut two rectangles 12″ x 15″ of unbleached muslin. Construct in same manner as pillows. Turn right side out and insert inner pillow into pillow with open ends at same end. Stuff inner pillow with batting, being sure corners are well stuffed. Whipstitch inner pillow closed. Slip-stitch outer pillow closed.

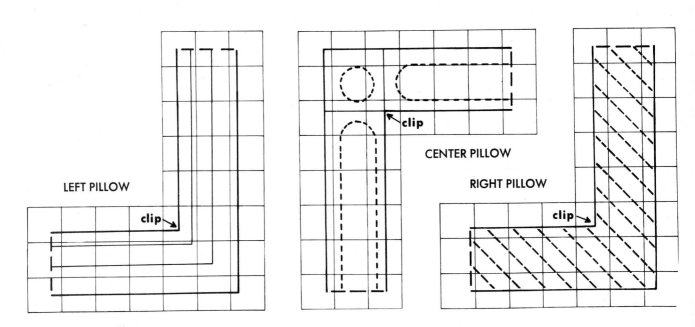

LEFT PILLOW

clip→

CENTER PILLOW

←clip

RIGHT PILLOW

clip→

Luscious strawberries — a tempting subject to quilt into pillows! For an attractive grouping, choose any fabric printed in a series of related designs (fruit, flowers, birds, etc.) and stitch around the motifs. On one pillow, for contrast, quilt background only. Vary border treatment as well, combining ribbon trims with quilting.

Index

[Page numbers printed in **boldface** type refer to illustrations.]